A Reader on Net Neutrality and Restoring Internet Freedom

Randolph J. May

Seth L. Cooper

The Free State Foundation

A Reader on Net Neutrality and Restoring Internet Freedom
by Randolph J. May and Seth L. Cooper

Published by The Free State Foundation, Inc., Potomac, MD

Copyright © 2018 by Randolph J. May and Seth L. Cooper

Author services provided by Pedernales Publishing, LLC
www.pedernalespublishing.com

Library of Congress Control Number: 2018948391

ISBN-13: 978-0-9993608-3-5   Digital edition
          978-0-9993608-1-1   Paperback edition

For my grandchildren Samantha, Ciaran, Benjamin, Francis, and Zachary, with the hope that sometime before they have children of their own, the "net neutrality" controversy will be ancient history, or at least history.

Randolph May

In memory of my grandmother, Ruth Vera Dunlap (1918-2017).

Seth Cooper

CONTENTS

INTRODUCTION: RESTORING INTERNET FREEDOM

On December 14, 2017, the Federal Communications Commission adopted its *Restoring Internet Freedom Order* (*RIF Order*), repealing the public utility-like regulations applied to broadband Internet service providers in 2015 by the Obama Administration's FCC.[1] The *RIF Order*'s return to a light-touch federal broadband Internet policy that makes free market competition its touchstone is very important to the Internet's future. By undoing the FCC's imposition of public utility-like regulation, the December 2017 order will enhance consumer welfare and reinvigorate economic investment and technological innovation in the broadband services market. Significantly, the *RIF Order* also provides a framework that ensures consumers are protected from anticompetitive conduct as well as from unfair and deceptive trade practices.

In the context of providing what we believe is a convincing defense of the FCC's *Restoring Internet Freedom Order*, *A Reader on Net Neutrality and Restoring Internet Freedom* provides key insights into the long-running debate surrounding "net neutrality" regulation. The selected writings that comprise this *Reader* explore both legal and policy rationales that support the Commission's December 2017 action. They explain why, in our view, the agency's pro-investment, pro-innovation, and pro-consumer approach to broadband Internet services regulation adopted in the *RIF Order* should be preserved.

At the outset, we readily acknowledge that there are those with very different views than the views contained in this *Reader*, and we do not question the good faith of those who espouse views differing from ours. Those opposing views are readily available to the interested reader. But the purpose of this *Reader* is to present a collection of materials that defends Internet freedom – including the approach taken by the FCC in its December 2017 action.

The Source, Texts, and Context of this *Reader*

The contents of *A Reader on Net Neutrality and Restoring Internet Freedom* were authored by Free State Foundation scholars, including those affiliated with FSF by virtue of their membership on its distinguished Board of Academic Advisors. The Free State Foundation is a non-profit, nonpartisan think tank whose purpose is to promote, through research and educational activities, understanding of free market, limited government, and rule of law principles, especially those applicable to the communications and other high-tech industries.

Over the past dozen years, Free State Foundation scholars have been a leading voice for reform of federal communications law and policy. Free State Foundation scholars consistently have advocated a less regulatory and more competition-focused framework for broadband Internet services to match the dynamic technological advances and market realities of the Digital Age.

Most of the individual writings selected for *A Reader on Net Neutrality and Restoring Internet Freedom* were originally published as part of the Free State Foundation's *Perspectives from FSF Scholars* series. A few originally were published in established media venues or on the Free State Foundation blog. They are all reproduced here in their original form, save for only a few minor non-substantive edits. The *Reader's* contents are divided into sections that correspond to different phases of FCC activity regarding the regulation of broadband Internet services, ranging between late 2013 and early 2018. Because the "net neutrality" issue has been active at least since 2005, it would have been possible to include many pre-2013 Free State Foundation materials. But this would have increased the length of the *Reader* without a commensurate benefit.

The individual writings in each part generally are arranged chronologically based on their original publication dates. In order to place the *Reader's* contents in context amidst shifting phases of FCC policy, a brief overview follows of the most relevant provisions of federal communications law and of FCC regulatory actions and court decisions regarding broadband Internet access services.

A Free Market Unfettered by Regulation: Inauguration of the Light-Touch Regulatory Approach to Broadband Internet Services

The Telecommunications Act of 1996 – the first major revision of the Communications Act since 1934 – established the policy of the United States "to preserve the vibrant and competitive free market that presently exists for the Internet . . . unfettered by Federal or State regulation."[2] Passage of the 1996 Act presaged a light-touch national regulatory policy for the Internet. The bipartisan nature of that light-touch policy was epitomized by the Clinton Administration FCC's resistance to pleas in the late 1990s to regulate then-emerging cable broadband services on the same basis as telephone common carriers. As FCC Chairman William Kennard declared in 1999:

> So, if we have the hope of facilitating a market-
> based solution here, we should do it, because the
> alternative is to go to the telephone world, a world
> that we are trying to deregulate and just pick
> up this whole morass of regulation and dump it

wholesale on the cable pipe. That is not good for America.[3]

The bipartisan light-touch regulatory policy for the Internet generally prevailed from the time of the Clinton Administration until the latter half of the Obama Administration – when it was sharply reversed in 2015 by what is generally referred to as the *Title II Order*.[4] Under the prior light-touch policy, and pursuant to a series of FCC orders issued between 2002 and 2007, "broadband Internet access services" were classified as unregulated, or minimally regulated, "information services" under Title I of the Communications Act.

Title I of the Act defines "information services" as "the offering of a capability for generating, acquiring, storing, transforming, processing, retrieving, utilizing, or making available information via telecommunications."[5] FCC regulations define "broadband Internet access services" as mass marketed wireline and wireless services that provide data transmission capabilities to and from all, or nearly all, Internet endpoints.[6]

Beginning with its 2002 *Cable Modem Order*, the FCC recognized that broadband Internet access services provide all the functional capabilities delineated in the Act's definition for information services.[7] The FCC's 2002 classification determination was upheld by the Supreme Court in 2005 in *NCTA v. Brand X Services*.[8] Subsequently, the FCC's *Wireline Broadband Order* and *Wireless Broadband Order* similarly classified broadband Internet access services offered by providers over those respective platforms as Title I lightly regulated information services.[9] Significantly, and simultaneous with the adoption of its *Wireline Broadband Order* in 2005, the FCC unanimously adopted an *Internet Policy Statement* endorsing four "Internet freedoms": the right to access lawful content; to use applications; to attach personal devices to the network; and to obtain service plan information.[10]

Subjecting the Internet to Regulation: The FCC's Incremental Increase in Regulatory Restrictions on Broadband Internet Services

A shift to a more pro-regulatory policy was attempted when the FCC, under then-Chairman Kevin Martin, issued its *Comcast/BitTorrent Order* in 2008.[11] In that order, the FCC attempted to turn the four Internet freedoms contained in the Commission's *Internet Policy Statement* into enforceable government mandates. However, in *Comcast v. FCC*, the U.S. Court of Appeals for the D.C. Circuit ruled that the Commission failed to justify its order as an exercise of whatever ancillary authority the agency possesses under Title I for the Communications Act.[12]

Following the D.C. Circuit's ruling, under the leadership of then-Chairman Julius Genachowski, the FCC imposed no-blocking, no-unreasonable discrimination, and other rules on broadband Internet access providers. This 2010 *Open Internet Order* staked the Commission's authority for such regulation on Section 706 of the Telecommunications Act of 1996.[13] This reversed agency precedent that had regarded Section 706 as a hortatory declaration of policy rather than as an affirmative source of regulatory power.[14] Nonetheless, the 2010 Order retained Title I classification status for wireline and mobile wireless broadband services.

Yet the D.C. Circuit also vacated the 2010 Order. In *Verizon v. FCC* (2014), the court concluded that the Commission's rules, in effect, imposed common carrier regulation on the Internet service providers and that the agency lacked authority to do so because broadband Internet access services remained classified as "information services" under Title I of the Communications Act, not "telecommunications services" under Title II's common carrier provisions.[15]

Thinking the Unthinkable: The FCC's Imposition of Public Utility-Like Regulation on Internet Service Providers

Despite two judicial rebukes to its attempts to impose net neutrality restrictions on Internet service providers, the FCC refused seriously to reconsider whether the need for such regulation was even warranted. The FCC similarly refused to pursue a more modest regulatory approach to ensuring Internet openness under Title I, which the decision in *Verizon v. FCC* appeared to leave available to the agency.[16] Instead, in February 2015, under then-Chairman Tom Wheeler, the FCC followed President Barack Obama's urging – delivered publicly in a highly unusual YouTube video released in November 2014 and accompanied by a presidential statement[17] – that the agency reclassify broadband Internet access services as Title II telecommunications service. In doing so, the Commission subjected those services to public utility-like regulation.

The writings contained in Part I of the *Reader* were published over a span of time ranging from shortly before to after the Obama Administration FCC announced plans to subject broadband Internet access to public utility-like regulation. Collectively, the writings contained in Part I describe the benefits of Internet freedom with regard to market investment, technological innovation, and consumer welfare. Equally important, they provide warnings against the detrimental effects of public utility-like restrictions on broadband Internet services. More particularly, they call attention to the tendencies of such restrictions to insulate major online content or edge providers such as Google or Netflix from competition by new entrants or from pricing arrangements that could potentially reduce retail prices for consumers.

In the name of establishing stringent "net neutrality" protections, the Obama Administration's FCC imposed significantly stricter controls over broadband Internet service providers in February 2015.[18] The order claimed authority for those controls based on Title II of the Communications Act as well as Section

706 of the Telecommunications Act of 1996.[19] Hence, the February 2015 order became known as the *Title II Order*.

The *Title II Order*'s reclassification of broadband Internet access services as telecommunications services under Title II reversed several prior Commission determinations that regarded broadband Internet access services as lightly or non-regulated Title I information services.[20] Also, the *Title II Order* redefined the Commission's regulatory definition of the public switched telephone network in order to bring mobile broadband Internet access services under the Title II public utility model.[21] The FCC refused to conduct a cost-benefit analysis of the potential impact of its proposed restrictions. Nor did the *Title II Order* cite any new or contemporary instances of genuine harm taking place in the broadband services market. Instead, the *Title II Order* simply recounted a few minor incidents that pre-dated the *Comcast/ BitTorrent Order* and which were all quickly resolved without significant regulatory intervention.[22]

The FCC rejected any need to tie its regulatory intrusive regime to actual findings of market power and anticompetitive conduct. Indeed, the *Title II Order* explicitly stated that the Commission "need not conclude that any specific market power exists in the hands of one or more broadband providers in order to create and enforce these rules."[23] And with respect to its imposition of public utility regulation on broadband Internet access services, the order similarly stated: "[T]hese rules do not address, and are not designed to deal with, the acquisition or maintenance of market power or its abuse, real or potential."[24]

The Title II regulation for broadband Internet established in the *Title II Order* included so-called "bright line rules" that prohibited broadband Internet access service providers from blocking, throttling, or degrading subscribers' access to legal content of their choice.[25] The *Title II Order* also included a vague "general conduct" standard by which the Commission empowered itself to sanction any ISP conduct that it deemed to "unreasonably interfere with or unreasonably disadvantage" users or edge providers.[26] In a moment of candor, the Commission conceded that this was a "catch-all standard" that it would apply based on the "totality of the circumstances" and according to seven equally vague factors from an acknowledged "non-exhaustive" list that the Commission retained discretion to create and apply however and whenever it saw fit.[27]

Additionally, one of the *Title II Order*'s bright line rules banned so-called "paid prioritization" arrangements.[28] These are arrangements whereby broadband Internet service providers offer specialized services with quality-of-service guarantees for dedicated purposes requiring a high level of end-to-end reliability that reduces or eliminates undesirable data traffic congestion or transmission delays. The order's ban disregarded the fact that paid prioritization arrangements are commonplace in other sectors of the economy and that evidence in other markets shows that such arrangements generally lead to increased capital investment and consumer welfare.[29]

Furthermore, the Federal Trade Commission's (FTC) jurisdiction to protect the privacy of broadband consumers was stripped as a result of Title II reclassification of broadband Internet services.[30] This resulted in an anomalous privacy enforcement vacuum with regard to broadband Internet services and also with respect to the jurisdictional authority of the FTC. Despite its status as the federal government's traditional enforcer of privacy protections, and a history of over 150 privacy and data security enforcement actions, the *Title II Order* precluded the FTC from protecting consumer privacy in personal information collected by broadband service providers.

Part II of this reader addresses some of the highly dubious aspects of the FCC imposition of public utility-like regulation on broadband Internet access services through its *Title II Order*. A necessary consequence of the FCC's Title II reclassification decision and its ban on paid prioritization arrangements between broadband Internet access providers and edge content providers is the agency's assumption of power to control rates for broadband services. Indeed, the FCC's assumption of rate control authority increasingly belied an interest in protecting major online edge providers.

For example, the focus on protecting edge providers seemingly caused the Commission to lose sight of consumers' interests in benefitting from "free data" or sponsored data mobile plans or from paid prioritization arrangements that could support innovative online offerings to consumers. Indeed, after the *Title II Order* was issued, the FCC's Wireless Bureau conducted an investigation of free data plans that lasted over a year. In early 2017, with the approval of then-Chairman Wheeler, the Wireless Bureau issued a report purporting to find that free data programs offered by AT&T and Verizon Wireless potentially were harmful to consumers and, therefore, might be proscribed by the "general conduct" standard. In other words, the report warned that consumers potentially are harmed by being offered mobile service plans that enable access to popular content without additional data charges.[31]

Additionally, the *Title II Order*'s claims that its restrictions partly were justified by mobile wireless broadband service providers enjoying gatekeeper power due to high switching costs was contradicted by evidence of contemporary market trends favoring "no contract" plans as well equipment subsidies to induce subscribers to switch providers.[32] Also, as described, the *Title II Order*'s "general conduct" or "catch-all" provision suffered from serious vagueness problems that made it difficult to predict what types of broadband service provider practices would be permitted given the agency's seemingly unfettered regulatory power over ISPs' conduct.[33]

Part III focuses primarily on economic perspectives that describe the harms resulting from the FCC's imposition of public utility-like regulation on broadband Internet services. Each of the contributing authors to Part III are Ph.D. economists who bring their technical expertise and knowledge of the relevant economic literature to bear in critiquing the *Title II Order*'s analytical pretensions and its departures from academic findings. Economic analysis is particularly important for the light it sheds on the pro-investment and pro-consumer benefits of many paid prioritization arrangements, which were categorically banned by the *Title II Order*.

Laying the Groundwork for a Restored Light-Touch Regulatory Approach to Broadband Internet Services

The D.C. Circuit's decision in *US Telecom v. FCC* (2016) upheld the *Title II Order* by applying a standard of review that was highly deferential to the agency's interpretations and policy judgments.[34] Just a few months later, the Obama Administration's FCC followed up the *Title II Order*'s removal of FTC authority over broadband consumer privacy by adopting stringent new "opt-in" rules as well as bans on "financial inducement practices," such as offering discounts for use of personal information.[35] Problematically, the effect of the FCC's *Broadband Privacy Order* (2016) was that more stringent mandates were applied to broadband Internet service providers than those that applied to online edge providers like Google or Facebook under FTC jurisdiction. Had these more stringent privacy requirements been implemented by the FCC, they would have discouraged broadband service providers from offering consumer welfare-enhancing targeted marketing deals, selling ads to personalize consumer experiences, or offering sponsored data as well as free data or zero-rated plans, even though the edge provider web giants like Facebook and Google acquire and retain more personal data than the ISPs.

However, the change of administrations at the FCC that was brought about by the 2016 Presidential election made possible a reversal of the harmful effects of the *Title II Order*. With the approval of new FCC Chairman Ajit Pai, the Wireless Bureau promptly rescinded the anti-free data report issued during the final days of the prior administration.[36] On April 3, 2017, President Donald Trump signed a Congressional Review Act resolution repealing the rules adopted in the *Broadband Privacy Order*.[37] And on May 18, 2017, under the leadership of Chairman Pai, the FCC adopted a notice of proposed rulemaking to return to a light-touch policy by once more reclassifying broadband Internet access services as information services under Title I.[38] The effect of such reclassification would be to repeal the public utility-like regime and prescriptive rules imposed on ISPs by the *Title II Order* and to restore the FTC's authority to enforce a uniform privacy regulatory regime on both ISPs and edge providers.

The writings comprising Part IV of this reader were published during the lead-up to and aftermath of the FCC's proposal to repeal the *Title II Order*'s public utility-like regime. The contents of Part IV describe policy alternatives for protecting Internet openness and freedom, consistent with a restored light-touch regulatory approach to broadband Internet access services. From a policy standpoint, protecting Internet openness and freedom is not a binary choice between public utility regulation and no regulation at all. Rather, antitrust enforcement by the Department of Justice and the Federal Trade Commission as well as FTC enforcement against unfair and deceptive trade practices are preferable means of protecting consumers from actual or likely anticompetitive harms, while at the same time preserving market freedom to innovate and generate new sources of value for consumers.

Whereas the *Title II Order* imposed a regime of prescriptive *ex ante* anticipatory prescriptive restrictions on broadband service provider conduct, antitrust and FTC Act authorities are premised on *ex post* remedial action informed by microeconomic analysis that takes into account competitive market conditions and consumer harm. Thus, under these alternative regulatory regimes, intrusion into market freedom is called for only where demonstrable market power concerns exist and there is evidence of harm to consumer welfare.

The *Restoring Internet Freedom Order*: Returning to the Light-Touch Regulatory Approach to Broadband Internet Services

As described at the outset, on December 14, 2017, the FCC adopted the *Restoring Internet Freedom Order* (*RIF Order*) by a 3-2 vote.[39] Following the Commission's May 2017 proposal, the *RIF Order* repealed public utility-like regulation and reestablished light-touch regulation as federal broadband Internet policy. Part V of this reader contains defenses of important aspects to the *Restoring Internet Freedom Order*, including its legal basis, the transparency of the administrative process that preceded its adoption, as well as the policy merits of the order.

In short, the *RIF Order* is a welcome initiative that will benefit American consumers and the overall economy in the years to come. The FCC majority determined, correctly, that the text and structure of the Communications Act, strongly supports an interpretation that broadband Internet access services are information services under Title I rather than telecommunications services under Title II.[40] Further, the underlying logic of the order's reclassification of broadband services as Title I information services, based on straightforward statutory interpretation, was affirmed by the Supreme Court's 2005 decision in *NCTA v. Brand X Services*.

Correctly, the *Restoring Internet Freedom Order* also recognized that Congress never granted the FCC authority to impose public utility-like regulation on broadband Internet service providers. Rather, the *Title II Order*'s reclassification of broadband services under Title II involved a major question of "economic and political significance."[41] To justify the shattering of the long-standing bipartisan light-touch consensus by imposing Title II regulation on an Internet service, a clear statement by Congress conferring such authority on the agency was required. But Congress nowhere provided a clear statement of that kind, which the Supreme Court's "major questions" doctrine requires.

Moreover, the *Restoring Internet Freedom Order*'s preemption of conflicting state regulations of broadband Internet access services is backed by Congress's delegation of authority to the Commission to oversee nationwide advanced communications services.[42] Federal preemption of state-level net neutrality regulation is consistent with the 1996 Act's policy directive that the competitive free market for Internet services should remain "unfettered by Federal or State regulation."[43] The order also properly concluded that Section 706 of the 1996 Act, which directs the FCC to promote the timely deployment of advanced telecommunications services to all Americans, is best understood as hortatory and not as a separate source of regulatory power.[44]

The competitive conditions of today's dynamic broadband Internet services market make it ideally suited for the light-touch regulatory approach that was re-established by the *Restoring Internet Freedom Order*. The broadband market's competitiveness is reflected in the choices that consumers enjoy across a range of competing platforms. Today, these services are offered to end user subscribers by major providers such as AT&T, CenturyLink, Charter Communications, Comcast, Cox Communications, Frontier Communications, and Verizon Communications, as well as by regional and local providers across the country. Additionally, broadband Internet access services are widely offered by major mobile wireless providers such as AT&T, Sprint, T-Mobile, and Verizon Wireless, as well as by regional and local mobile wireless providers.

Data in the FCC's *Internet Access Services Report* indicates that at the end of 2016, 82% of census blocks with housing units were served by three or more broadband Internet service providers offering speeds of 10 Mbps or higher, and 98% of census blocks were served by two or more providers offering speeds of

10 Mbps or higher.[45] Consumers also have access to competing mobile wireless broadband Internet service providers. According to the FCC's *Twentieth Wireless Competition Report* (2017), as of December 2016, 99% of the U.S. population had access to two or more 4G LTE providers and 96.6% had access to three of more 4G LTE providers.[46]

Also, a report by Ookla indicates average LTE download speed increased to 22.69 Mbps in the first half of 2017, up from 14.4 Mbps in the first half of 2014.[47] Increasing speeds and capacity make mobile wireless broadband platforms increasingly attractive potential substitutes for fixed broadband platforms. The availability of competitive choices for broadband Internet service spurs providers to satisfy their subscribers and to attract new ones, while also providing a valuable check against harmful practices that risk alienating subscribers and causing them to switch to competitors.

Additionally, the *RIF Order* is backed by empirical evidence that financial investment in network infrastructure by Internet service providers slowed under the public utility-like regulation that was imposed in 2015. The order, for instance, cites Hal Singer's recent study indicating investment by major ISPs dropped $3.6 billion or 5.6% between 2014 and 2016.[48] The overall thrust of those studies are in line with a May 2017 estimate by Free State Foundation Research Fellow Michael J. Horney that "foregone investment in 2015 and 2016 was about $5.6 billion, an amount providers likely would have invested in a business climate without Title II public utility regulation."[49] And with respect to mobile broadband investment, CTIA's annual survey for year-end 2016 found that wireless providers' investment declined from $32.1 billion in 2014 to $26.4 billion in 2016, a drop of $5.7 billion or 17.8%.[50] Restoring a light-touch regulatory environment will revitalize capital investment in next-generation broadband infrastructure deployments, thereby expanding and enhancing service options for consumers.

The foregone investment that resulted from the regulatory strictures imposed by the *Title II Order* squares with economic theory. The economic literature reveals that public utility regulation suppresses innovation and investment when market failure and consumer harm are absent. And the economic literature recognizes that paid prioritization arrangements are presumptively beneficial to consumers or, in the absence of market power, are at least competitively benign. The economic perspectives provided in Part III of this *Reader* corroborate the order's conclusions in these regards.

The *RIF Order*'s repeal of public utility-like regulation will help ensure that the Internet continues to develop in ways that supply consumers with new product, service, and pricing options and that enable rapid responses to changing preferences of consumers. In view of today's technologically dynamic Internet marketplace, it is consumers who ultimately suffer when broadband service providers are discouraged from investing in new facilities and offering innovative new products and services. By removing the broad looming shadow of rate regulatory authority and by repealing vague prescriptive rules of seemingly boundless scope – as described in Part II of this *Reader* – the *RIF Order* provides broadband Internet service providers with renewed freedom to innovate and to invest in robust high-speed broadband networks.

Importantly, the *RIF Order* established an alternative base of protections for consumers against claimed harmful practices by broadband service providers. The analytical underpinnings of the order's new framework for consumer protection are outlined in Part IV of this *Reader*. By operation of its repeal of the Title II common carrier classification of broadband Internet access services, the FCC restored the FTC's jurisdiction over unfair and deceptive trade practices by broadband service providers as well as the FTC's authority to protect ISPs' subscribers' privacy.

Under the new enforcement framework established by the *RIF Order*, broadband service providers that include in their terms of service representations to refrain from harmful forms of paid prioritization arrangements or promises not to block, throttle, or degrade subscriber access to lawful Internet content of their choice will be subject to FTC investigation and enforcement actions for unfair and deceptive trade practices if they do not adhere to their representations.[51] New FCC transparency rules adopted in the *RIF Order* require broadband service providers to make disclosures if they engage in practices relating to blocking, throttling, or prioritizing Internet traffic.[52] Those disclosures will further assist FTC enforcement efforts. And pursuant to a December 14, 2017, memorandum of understanding between the agencies, the FCC and FTC have pledged to coordinate and cooperate with each other with respect to monitoring and enforcement activities to protect consumers.[53]

On February 26, 2018, in *Federal Trade Commission v. AT&T Mobility*, the U.S. Court of Appeals for the Ninth Circuit, sitting *en banc*, unanimously reaffirmed the FTC's authority over the non-common carrier activities of common carriers.[54] Its decision effectively vindicated the *RIF Order*'s premise that the FTC has authority to pursue enforcement actions against broadband Internet service providers for deceptive or unfair trade practices, even though these ISPs may be part of a firm that offers other services on a common carrier basis. Antitrust law also provides a viable means for addressing potentially anticompetitive conduct in the broadband Internet market.[55] Rather than leaving the broadband Internet services market a regulatory Wild West or blindly trusting the good will of broadband service providers, the *Restoring Internet Freedom Order* provides a solid base of enforceable protections for the benefit of consumers.

An Insightful Resource for Defending Internet Freedom

The FCC's adoption of the *Restoring Internet Freedom Order* is by no means the end of the debate over net neutrality regulation and Internet freedom. In both the Senate and House, resolutions of disapproval were filed pursuant to the Congressional Review Act (CRA).[56] On May 16, 2018, the Senate passed its disapproval resolution by a 52-47 vote.[57] Should either resolution be approved by Congress and signed by the President, the *RIF Order* would be repealed and presumably the rules adopted by the *Title II Order*, at least to some extent, would be reinstated.[58]

Several states have considered or passed legislation that would seek to reimpose at the state level rules that are identical or similar to those repealed by the *RIF Order*.[59] Governors in a few states have issued executive orders purporting to restrict state contracting to broadband ISPs who pledge to adhere to the substance of the Title II rules that were repealed by the *RIF Order*.[60] Legal challenges to the order filed by advocacy groups, local governments, edge provider companies, and 22 State Attorneys General have been consolidated in a case now pending before the U.S. Court of Appeals for the D.C. Circuit.[61]

Amidst the perhaps inevitable but nevertheless regrettable overheated rhetoric regarding the *Restoring Internet Freedom Order*, careful attention to the actual terms of the order and its predecessors as well as to the underlying ideas of the legal and policy debate is needed. *A Reader on Net Neutrality and Restoring Internet Freedom* serves as a one-stop resource – admittedly one with an acknowledged deregulatory perspective – for enhancing one's understanding of the legal, economic, and other policy issues at stake as the debate moves forward. As this *Reader* is intended to show, the future of Internet freedom and American consumers' enjoyment of the choices enabled by that freedom depends upon broadband Internet access services remaining free from innovation-inhibiting and investment-suppressing harmful public utility-like regulation.

We hope that policymakers of all stripes at the federal and state level, academics and analysts, and interested citizens alike will benefit from the insights provided by Free State Foundation scholars in this *Reader*. We know that even as we put the finishing touches on this *Reader* the net neutrality saga continues to unfold. Of course, Free State Foundation scholars continue to address the latest developments. There is a natural temptation to continue adding even more recent materials to the volume in the interest of up-to-date "completeness." But we are convinced the greater imperative is to make available the *Reader* as it currently stands – so that the public can have the benefit of its contents as they now stand without further delay.

Time enough later for a sequel if need be!

. . .

Finally, we extend our appreciation to Kathee Baker, the Free State Foundation's Communications and Events Coordinator, for her editorial assistance in this *Reader's* preparation and for her continuing good cheer as she goes about the business of getting FSF's work product into the hands of the public.

Randolph J. May
Seth L. Cooper

Rockville, Maryland
May 2018

Endnotes

1   FCC, *Restoring Internet Freedom*, Declaratory Ruling, Report and Order, and Order ("*Restoring Internet Freedom Order*") WC Docket No. 17-108, (released January 4, 2018), available at: https://apps.fcc.gov/edocs_public/attachmatch/FCC-17-166A1.pdf.

2   47 U.S.C. § 230(b)(2).

3   "Consumer Choice Through Competition," Remarks by William E. Kennard, Chairman, FCC, at the National Association of Telecommunications Officers and Advisors, 19th Annual Conference, Atlanta, GA, September 17, 1999, at 5, available at: https://transition.fcc.gov/Speeches/Kennard/spwek931.html.

4   FCC, Protecting and Promoting the Open Internet, GN Docket No. 14-28, Report and Order on Remand, Declaratory Ruling, and Order ("*Open Internet Order*") (released March 12, 2015).

5   47 U.S.C. § 153(24).

6   47 C.F.R. § 8.11(a).

7   FCC, Inquiry Concerning High-Speed Access to the Internet Over Cable & Other Facilities; Internet Over Cable Declaratory Ruling; Appropriate Regulatory Treatment for Broadband Access to the Internet Over Cable Facilities, GN Docket No. 00-185, CS Docket No. 02-52, Declaratory Ruling and Notice of Proposed Rulemaking ("*Cable Modem Order*") (2002).

8   *National Cable & Telecommunications Assoc. v. Brand X Services*, 545 U.S. 967 (2005).

9   FCC, Appropriate Framework for Broadband Access to the Internet over Wireline Facilities, Report and Order and Notice of Proposed Rulemaking ("*Wireline Broadband Order*"), CC Docket 02-33, *et al.*, (released September 23, 2005), affirmed by *Time Warner Telecom, Inc. v. FCC*, 507 F.3d 205 (3d Cir. 2007); FCC, Appropriate Treatment for Broadband Access to the Internet Over Wireless Networks, WT Docket No. 07-53, Declaratory Ruling ("*Wireless Broadband Order*") (released March 23, 2007).

10   FCC, Appropriate Framework for Broadband Access to the Internet over Wireline Facilities, Policy Statement (*"Internet Policy Statement"*), CC Docket 02-33, *et al.*, (released September 23, 2005).

11   Formal Complaint of Free Press and Public Knowledge Against Comcast Corporation for Secretly Degrading Peer-to-Peer Applications; Broadband Industry Practices; Petition of Free Press et al. for Declaratory Ruling that Degrading an Internet Application Violates the FCC's Internet Policy Statement and Does Not Meet an Exception for "Reasonable Network Management, Memorandum Opinion and Order (*"Comcast/ BitTorrent Order"*), File No. EB-08-IH-1518, WC Docket No. 07-52, (released August 20, 2008).

12   *Comcast Corp. v. FCC*, 600 F.3d 642 (D.C. Cir. 2010).

13   FCC, *Preserving the Open Internet; Broadband Industry Practices*, GN Docket No. 09-191, WC Docket No. 07-52, Report and Order, ("2010 Order") (released December 23, 2010).

14   *RIF Order*, at ¶ 270 fn.994 (citing FCC, Deployment of Wireline Services Offering Advanced Telecommunications Capability, Memorandum Opinion and Order, and Notice of Proposed Rulemaking (*"Advanced Services Order"*), CC Docket 98-147, *et al.* (released August 7, 1998), at ¶¶ 69-77.

15   *Verizon v. FCC*, 740 F.3d 623 (D.C. Cir. 2014).

16   FCC, Protecting and Promoting the Open Internet, Notice of Proposed Rulemaking, GN Docket No. 14-28 (released May 15, 2014), at ¶¶ 115, 147.

17   President Barak Obama, The President's Message on Net Neutrality (November 10, 2014), at: https://obamawhitehouse.archives.gov/node/323681; President Barak Obama, Statement by the President on Net Neutrality (Nov. 10, 2014), at: https://obamawhitehouse.archives.gov/the-press-office/2014/11/10/statement-president-net-neutrality.

18   FCC, Protecting and Promoting the Open Internet, GN Docket
     No. 14-28, Report and Order on Remand, Declaratory Ruling,
     and Order ("*Title II Order*"), (released March 12, 2015).

19   *Title II Order*, at ¶¶ 275-282.

20   *Title II Order*, at ¶¶ 355-387. *See also Cable Modem Order,
     Wireline Broadband Order*, and *Wireless Broadband Order, supra.*

21   *Title II Order*, at ¶¶ 388-408.

22   *Title II Order*, at ¶ 65, fn.69 (citing FCC, Madison River
     Communications, File No. EB-05-IH-0110, Order, (Enforcement
     Bureau) (released March 3, 2005) (adopting consent decree)).

23   *Title II Order*, at ¶ 11, fn.12.

24   *Title II Order*, at ¶ 11, fn.12.

25   *Title II Order*, at ¶¶ 110-132.

26   *Title II Order*, at ¶¶ 133-137.

27   *Title II Order*, at ¶ 21; *id.* at ¶¶ 138-145 *et seq.*

28   *Title II Order*, at ¶ 18, ¶¶ 125-132.

29   *See* especially the writings contained in Section III of this *Reader.*

30   *See RIF Order*, at ¶ 183 (discussing the effect of the *Title II
     Order*'s reclassification decision in removing FTC jurisdiction).

31   FCC (Wireless Telecommunications Bureau) "Wireless
     Telecommunications Bureau Report: Policy Review of Mobile
     Broadband Operators' Sponsored Data Offerings for Zero-Rated
     Content and Services" (released January 11, 2017).

32   *See* especially Seth L. Cooper, "Wireless Report Data
     Undermines the FCC's Rationale for Regulation," reprinted in
     this *Reader. See also* Seth L. Cooper, "Wireless Report Evidence
     of Effective Competition Contradicts the FCC's Pro-Regulatory
     Agenda, *Perspectives from FSF Scholars*, Vol. 11, No. 35 (October
     20, 2016) (explaining how data about market trends favoring "no
     contract" plans and equipment subsidies cited in the *Nineteenth
     Wireless Competition Report* (2016) further contradicted the

Title II Order's claims about gatekeeper power enjoyed by mobile wireless ISPs), at: http://www.freestatefoundation.org/ images/Wireless_Report_Evidence_of_Effective_Competition_ Contradicts_the_FCC_s_Pro-Regulatory_Agenda_102016.pdf.

33   *See* especially Seth L. Cooper, "FCC's Vague 'General Conduct' Standard Deserves Closer Legal Scrutiny," reprinted in this *Reader*. *See also* Seth L. Cooper, "Response: In Defense of Vagueness," *Perspectives from FSF Scholars*, Vol. 11, No. 38 (November 8, 2016) (describing how the vagueness problem of the "no-unreasonable interference/disadvantage" standard is compounded by the pro-regulatory bias of the enforcement procedures reflected in the *Title II Order*), at: http://www. freestatefoundation.org/images/Response_-_In_Defense_of_ Vagueness_110716.pdf.

34   *United States Telecommunications Association v. FCC, 825* F.3d 674 (D.C. Cir. 2016), rehearing *en banc* denied, 855 F.3d 381 (D.C. Cir. 2017).

35   FCC, Protecting the Privacy of Customers of Broadband and Other Telecommunications Services, WC Docket No. 16-106, Report and Order ("*Broadband Privacy Order*") (released November 2, 2016).

36   FCC (Wireless Telecommunications Bureau), Wireless Telecommunications Bureau Report: Policy Review of Mobile Broadband Operators' Sponsored Data Offerings for Zero-Rated Content and Services, Order (released February 3, 2017) (rescinding report released January 11, 2018).

37   U.S. Congress. Senate. *A joint resolution providing for congressional disapproval under Chapter 8 of Title 5, United States Code, of the rule submitted by the Federal Communications Commission relating to "Protecting the Privacy of Customers of Broadband and Other Telecommunications Services,"* 115th Cong. 1st sess. S.J.R. 34, available at: https://www.congress.gov/ bill/115th-congress/senate-joint-resolution/34; The White House, Office of the Press Secretary, Press Release: "President Donald J.

Trump Signs H.J. Res. 69, H.J. Res. 83, H.R. 1228, S.J.Res. 34 into Law" (April 3, 2017), available at: https://www.whitehouse.gov/the-press-office/2017/04/03/president-donald-j-trump-signs-hjres-69-hjres-83-hr-1228-sjres-34-law.

38 FCC, Restoring Internet Freedom, WC Docket No. 17-108, Notice of Proposed Rulemaking (released May 23, 2017), available at: https://apps.fcc.gov/edocs_public/attachmatch/FCC-17-60A1.pdf.

39 *RIF Order, supra.*

40 *RIF Order*, at ¶¶ 26-64. *See also id.* at ¶¶ 65-85 (restoring the prior regulatory classification of mobile broadband Internet access services based on statutory text and structure considerations).

41 *RIF Order*, at ¶ 161 (internal citations omitted).

42 *RIF Order*, at ¶¶ 194-204.

43 *RIF Order*, at ¶ 203 (citing 47 U.S.C. § 230(b)(2)).

44 *RIF Order*, at ¶¶ 267-283.

45 FCC, *Internet Access Services Report: Status as of December 31, 2016* ("*Internet Access Services Report*") (Wireline Competition Bureau) (released February 2018) at 6.

46 FCC, Implementation of Section 6002(b) of the Omnibus Budget Reconciliation Act of 1993; Annual Report and Analysis of Competitive Market Conditions With Respect to Mobile Wireless, Including Commercial Mobile Services, WT Docket No. 17-69, Twentieth Report ("*Twentieth Wireless Competition Report*"), at 81 (Appendix III: Table III.D.iv) (released September 27, 2017).

47 Ookla, Speedtest: United States: Mobile (September 7, 2017), at: http://www.speedtest.net/reports/united-states/.

48 *RIF Order*, at ¶ 91 (citing Hal J. Singer, *2016 Broadband Capex Survey: Tracking Investment in the Title II Era* (Mar. 1, 2017), at:

https://haljsinger.wordpress.com/2017/03/01/2016-broadband-capex-survey-tracking-investment-in-the-title-ii-era/).

49   Michael J. Horney, "Broadband Investment Slowed by $5.6 Billion Since Open Internet Order," *FSF Blog* (May 5, 2017), available at: http://freestatefoundation.blogspot.com/2017/05/broadband-investment-slowed-by-56.html.

50   CTIA, Annual Year-End 2016 Top-Line Survey Results (2017), at: https://api.ctia.org/docs/default-source/default-document-library/annual-year-end-2016-top-line-survey-results-final.pdf.

51   *RIF Order*, at ¶¶ 181-184.

52   *RIF Order*, at ¶¶ 215-231.

53   FCC, FTC, FCC Outline Agreement to Coordinate Online Consumer Protection Efforts Following Adoption of the Restoring Internet Freedom Order (December 11, 2017), at: https://apps.fcc.gov/edocs_public/attachmatch/DOC-348191A1.pdf.

54   *Federal Trade Commission v. AT&T Mobility*, No. 15-16585 (9th Cir. February 26, 2018) (*en banc*). *See also* FCC Chairman Ajit Pai, Chairman Pai Statement on Ninth Circuit Decision Regarding FTC Authority to Regulate Internet Service Providers (February 26, 2018).

55   *RIF Order*, at ¶¶ 143-154.

56   U.S. Congress. Senate. *A joint resolution providing for congressional disapproval under Chapter 8 of Title 5, United States Code, of the rule submitted by the Federal Communications Commission relating to "Restoring Internet Freedom."* 115th Cong. 2nd Sess. S.J. Res 52; U.S. Congress. House. *Providing for congressional disapproval under Chapter 8 of Title 5, United States Code, of the rule submitted by the Federal Communications Commission relating to "Restoring Internet Freedom."* 115th Cong. 2nd Sess. H.J.R. 129.

57   S.J. Res 52 Rollcall Vote No. 96 Leg. Congressional Record. Vol. 164 No. 80 (May 16, 2018) p. S2698.

58   *But see* Randolph J. May, "Thinking Things Through on Net Neutrality – Maintain that Policy Line," *FSF Blog* (February 27, 2018), at: http://freestatefoundation.blogspot.com/2018/02/thinking-things-through-on-net.html; Randolph J. May, "Thinking Things Through – Maintain Privacy Protections in Place," *FSF Blog* (May 4, 2018), at: http://freestatefoundation.blogspot.com/2018/05/thinking-things-through-maintain.html.

59   *See, e.g.*, WA Legis. House. Protecting and Open Internet in Washington State. Reg. Sess. SHB 2282 (2017-2018) (signed by Governor on March 5, 2018 and with an effective date of June 7, 2018); CA Legis. Senate. *Communications: Broadband Internet Access Service* Reg. Sess. SB 460 (2017-2018) (passed CA Senate on January 29, 2018); CA Legis. Senate. *Communications: Broadband Internet Access Service* Reg. Sess. SB 822 (2017-2018). *But see* Randolph J. May, "Thinking Things Through – Maintain that National Policy Line," *FSF Blog* (March 9, 2018), at: http://freestatefoundation.blogspot.com/2018/03/thinking-things-through-maintain-that.html.

60   *See, e.g.*, N.Y. Gov. Exec. Order No. 175 (January 24, 2018); MT Gov. Exec. Order No. 3-2018 (January 22, 2018). *But see* Seth L. Cooper, "State Executive Orders Reimposing Net Neutrality Regulations Are Preempted by the Restoring Internet Freedom Order," reprinted in this *Reader*.

61   *Mozilla Corp. v. FCC*, No. 18-1088 (D.C. Cir. April 2, 2018) (Clerk's order consolidating cases involving legal challenges to the *RIF Order*).

Part I – Advanced Warnings Against Public Utility Regulation of Broadband Internet Access Services

1.
It's the Consumer, Stupid!

Randolph J. May

FSF Blog, **September 16, 2013**

"It's the consumer, stupid!"

No, I don't mean to call anyone stupid. You know me better than that. But with an obligatory nod to James Carville, I just want to grab your attention in order to emphasize a point I wish to make.

At last Monday's oral argument before the D.C. Circuit in the *Verizon v. FCC* case in which Verizon is challenging the lawfulness of the FCC's net neutrality regulations, a considerable part of the argument focused on the business relationship between Internet services providers and a so-called "edge providers." The reason for the focus on edge providers is that, in essence, the Commission's regulations, in the form of a prohibition on discrimination, prevent the development of what economists call a "two-sided" market.

In the context of the Internet marketplace environment, what this prohibition on a two-sided market means is that the FCC's net neutrality regulations don't allow an Internet services provider like Verizon to charge an edge provider like Google for the use of Verizon's Internet facilities as Verizon's customers access Google's content and applications – even though Google might willingly agree to pay Verizon for some form of premium access, say, ensured faster delivery. Of course, the same prohibition applies to any Internet services provider vis-à-vis any other content provider.

Again, a good part of last week's oral argument focused on the way the net neutrality regulations' discrimination prohibition impacts the Internet provider – edge provider commercial relationship. Most observers came away from the argument with a sense that the court is likely to hold unlawful at least the regulations' discrimination prohibition, if not all the other provisions. As I said in this post-argument media advisory:

> "[T]he court seemed to agree with Verizon -- and
> this is a point that I have also made repeatedly
> and for years -- that the FCC's rules, as a practical
> matter, amount to converting Verizon's Internet
> access service into a common carrier service and
> that this is prohibited by the Communications Act.
> Or put another way, the FCC lacks authority to
> impose a common carriage mandate on Internet
> providers."

And in an appearance on C-SPAN on this week's *The Communicators* show, along with Public Knowledge President Gigi Sohn, I explained in some detail why I believe the FCC's regulation preventing Internet providers from discriminating against edge providers will be held unlawful. [As I said on the program, the usual caveat applies: Predicting the outcome of court cases can be hazardous to your reputation as a fortuneteller!]

What I want to do now is relatively simple, but nevertheless important. With all the back-and-forth at the argument focusing – properly in the context of the legal argument – on the discrimination prohibition, the prevention of two-sided pricing, and the prohibition's impact on edge providers, it is easy to lose sight of what all of this means for the consumer.

And, after all, what should be most important is not the impact of net neutrality mandates on edge providers like Google or Netflix, *per se*, or on Internet providers like Verizon or Time Warner Cable, *per se*, but rather the impact of the rules on consumers. And despite the fact that in other contexts prohibitions against "discrimination" may be quite proper, or even necessary, in the context of a competitive market environment, such as the Internet provider marketplace, a "discrimination" prohibition can be quite harmful to consumers and long-run consumer welfare.

This is because the FCC's discrimination prohibition imposes a regulatory straightjacket on Internet providers that prevents them from experimenting with new business models or service variations that may, in fact, meet changing consumer demands. To the detriment of consumers, this regulatory straightjacket impedes the innovation that normally occurs when businesses are free to differentiate their services. In this case, Internet providers are discouraged from innovating because they know that they and their competitors are, to a meaningful extent, all "stuck in the same boat."

And consumers may be especially adversely affected by the regulations' prohibition on two-sided pricing – again, the focus of so much of the oral argument. Two-sided pricing might well prove beneficial to consumers and edge providers alike, if Internet providers possessed the freedom – which other participants in a competitive marketplace possess – to experiment with various pricing models that reflect relative cost and value considerations.

For example, it is well established that certain edge providers like Netflix and Google are responsible for generating outsized amounts of web traffic. If Internet providers were free to charge edge providers fees that, at least to some extent, reflected the outsized usage generated by them – and the associated costs imposed on Internet providers' networks – this would mean that lighter users would not be forced, in effect, to subsidize those entities that generate much heavier use of the Internet providers' facilities.

The FCC-imposed regime, which in the name of preventing "discrimination," enforces such subsidization of heavier users by lighter users, and which thereby deters investment in facilities, is by no means necessarily consumer-friendly. And it is by no means necessarily consumer-friendly for lower-income persons who may prefer to forego faster or otherwise premium services in exchange for the opportunity to choose more affordable services. If two-sided pricing were permissible, it is more likely that a broader array of innovative service choices, including more affordable pricing options, would emerge in response to variations in consumer demand.

So, amidst all the discussion concerning the net neutrality regulations' discrimination prohibition, the two-sided pricing ban, and the impact on edge providers, please don't forget whose welfare is really impacted:

"It's the consumer, stupid."

PS – Again, you can watch *The Communicators* program here.

2.

Two Sides of the Internet's Two-Sidedness: A Consumer Welfare Perspective

Justin (Gus) Hurwitz *

Perspectives from FSF Scholars, September 30, 2013, Vol. 8, No. 25

This month's Open Internet argument before the DC Circuit was exciting for many reasons – including many aside from the substantive arguments about the FCC's authority to issue the rules under review. I'd like to look closely about one of these reasons in particular: the argument that consumer broadband Internet providers are part of a so-called two-sided market, and the implications that this argument has for consumers. Whether or not this is a two-sided market (or could be, absent the FCC rules) is important to understanding how the Open Internet rules affect the development of the broadband Internet market – and ultimately how they affect consumers.

But first, what is a two-sided market? The most basic definition of a two-sided market is a market with two distinct groups of consumers for some good, where the number of consumers from each group consuming that good affects the demand of the consumers of the other group for that good. Examples should help: nightclubs are generally two-sided markets, because the number of men at a given club affects how much women will want to go to that club, and vice versa; health insurance plans are two sided markets, because the number of doctors in a plan's network affects consumers' willingness to be part of that plan, and vice versa; computer operating systems are another example, because the number of applications available for an operating system affects consumers' willingness to use that operating system, and the number of potential users affects programmers' willingness to develop applications for a given operating system.

So do broadband Internet service providers operate in a two-sided market? It seems so: all else equal, consumers are going to have greater demand for an ISP that gives them access to a wider range of content providers (such as Google and Netflix) rather than a smaller range. And content providers are going to care more about connecting to backbones and broadband ISPs (the largest of which are tier 1 and tier 2 backbone providers) with more customers rather than fewer.

But there is something missing from the discussion so far: why do we care if a market is two-sided? Because in most two-sided markets, the purveyor of the intermediary goods that the two sides are consuming – that is, the owner of the nightclub, the HMO provider, the OS developer, or the broadband ISP – sets different prices for each side of the market in order to maximize the value of the market. Why? Because doing so allows it to increase its own revenue! So nightclubs let women in for free, to attract more men; HMOs might make it easy for doctors to join in order to attract more customers; and OS developers may give away their APIs and SDKs for free, to make it easier for programmers to write the programs that will attract users.

This is part of the argument that Verizon made before the DC Circuit: the Open Internet rules, by preventing Verizon from charging firms like Google and Netflix for access to its network, prevent this market from behaving like a two-sided market. (As a brief technical aside, it is entirely possible for a "two-sided" market to have more than two sides. For example, there could well be four "sides": consumers, high-value high-bandwidth services (Netflix), high-value lower-bandwidth services (Google, Facebook), and all other services. The economic analysis of such "multi-sided" markets is more complicated than of two-sided markets, but the idea is the same.)

The poignancy of this argument is that the economic literature makes amply clear that different price structures have powerful effects on the value of a given two-sided market to consumers. A nightclub that subsidizes women's entry may well attract far more consumers (both men and women!) than one that charges men and women the same cover or than one that subsidizes men's entry. The Open Internet rules impose a given price structure on the broadband market, Verizon's argument goes, without any evidence that that price structure is, in fact, the one that maximizes the value that that market creates for consumers.

Verizon's basic argument here is almost certainly correct: figuring out the best price structure in two-sided markets is complicated, and there is little reason to believe *a priori* that the Open Internet rules' prohibition on charging content providers is optimal. To the contrary, the economic literature suggests that the Open Internet rules can have a negative effect on the value created by the Internet, and that allowing broadband ISPs to charge content providers can benefit consumers and increase infrastructure investment.

What is more, the literature also suggests that the Open Internet rules are most likely to be harmful where there is little competition between ISPs – in other words, the world in which Network Neutrality advocates are generally eager to remind us we live in, where most consumers have access to only a few ISPs, is the world in which the Open Internet rules are most likely to be harmful.

The takeaway is that today's broadband Internet market is

precisely the sort of market in which the FCC's "prophylactic" approach is inappropriate. It is, instead, one in which we should seek out opportunities to experiment with multisided price structure – and even reward firms for taking the risk of experimenting – in order to maximize the value of the Internet to consumers.

But wait! There's more! Many strands of the literature on two-sided markets introduce an additional requirement for a market to be two-sided: the parties on either side of the market need to be unable to bargain around the price structure. This means, to take a pointed example, that if Netflix can pass any charges that Time Warner Cable levies upon it back onto its customers, then Netflix is not party to a two-sided market.

This example offers another motivation for content providers – at least, those able to pass costs back on to their customers – to favor Open Internet rules. If a content provider's services stress an ISP's network, that ISP faces two options: either allow the quality of its network to fall or invest in upgrades. If it incurs the cost of upgrading the network, those costs will be passed on to its customers. In either case, the ultimate cost is borne by consumers.

This allocation of costs – spread as it is across all of the ISP's customers – makes little sense. Far preferable, at least for consumers and ISPs, would be a price structure that initially allocates the cost of network upgrades to those whose use of specific services requires those upgrades be made. Otherwise the least resource-consuming users are subsidizing the most resource-consuming users. And this creates an incentive for all users to consume more resources (the low-use users because they're paying for it, and the high-use users because their use is being subsidized). (Query, for readers interested in game theory: where's the stable equilibrium?)

Of course, this system isn't bad for everyone: the content providers prefer the Open Internet model. Under this model, they are shielded from needing to increase their prices – that consumer-angering move is passed on to the ISPs. They also benefit from the subsidy from low-use users to high-use users, because this effectively subsidizes use of the content providers' services. What's more, they benefit yet again from the incentive that this system creates for users to consume more resources – to consume, that is, more of the content providers' services.

It should be noted that this is exactly the sort of feedback loop that we expect to see in a two-sided market – indeed it is the mechanism that causes these markets to create value for consumers. But this is entirely consistent with Verizon's and other ISPs' presumed desire to experiment with two-sided price structures. It could well be the case that the value of this market is maximized by ISPs, instead of content providers, passing infrastructure costs on to the consumers (query how they would be apportioned, evenly across all consumers or by usage). But if that is, indeed, the value maximizing outcome, it could obtain by agreements between ISPs and content providers, whereby they split the increased revenue that results from increased consumer demand.

Either way you have it – whether or not broadband Internet service is a two-sided market – the Open Internet rules are potentially a bad deal for consumers. We can't say categorically that this is the case. But "I dunno, maybe?" isn't a good enough basis for policy. What is clear is that these rules are a subsidy to content providers.

It's a shame that broadband Internet services and content providers are the two sides of these policy debates, when the consumers are the only side that really matters.

* Justin (Gus) Hurwitz, a member of the Free State Foundation's Board of Academic Advisors, is an Assistant Professor of Law at the University of Nebraska College of Law. The Free State Foundation is an independent, nonpartisan free market-oriented think tank located in Rockville, Maryland.

3.
Net Neutrality v. Consumers

Randolph J. May *

Perspectives from FSF Scholars, **August 26, 2014, Vol. 9, No. 29**

Rep. Anna Eshoo says she wants to re-brand "net neutrality." According to the National Journal report, Rep. Eshoo thinks the terminology surrounding the debate has left the American people "with a muddled understanding of what to support."

I don't pretend to be a marketing expert. In any event, Rep. Eshoo has launched some type of contest on Reddit to pick a new "brand" for what I'm going to continue, in the meantime, to call "net neutrality." So I'll leave the re-branding to those who think that merely changing the name of a highly problematic endeavor somehow will resolve the endeavor's problems.

Wasn't it Abraham Lincoln who said: "You can fool some of the people some of the time, and some of the people all the time, but you cannot fool all the people all of the time."

Re-branding of the net neutrality campaign is not what the American consumer needs. What consumers need is better informed continuing education concerning the real-world implications of the net neutrality regime the advocates seek to impose.

In the cause of furthering such consumer understanding,

let's begin by reviewing excerpts from recent *Wall Street Journal* stories about new wireless pricing plans offered by Sprint and T-Mobile.

- "For about $12, Sprint Corp. will soon let subscribers buy a wireless plan that only connects to Facebook. For that same price, they could choose instead to connect only with Twitter, Instagram or Pinterest—or for $10 more, enjoy unlimited use of all four. Another $5 gets them unlimited streaming of a music app of their choice." "Sprint Tries a Facebook-Only Plan," *Wall Street Journal*, July 30, 2014.

- "T-Mobile US Inc. will let customers listen to several popular music services without counting it toward their data use, giving up a potential revenue source to bolster its subscriber base. The country's fourth-largest wireless carrier said it is going to waive data charges when subscribers use services like Spotify, Pandora and Rhapsody." "T-Mobile Will Waive Data Fees For Music Services," *Wall Street Journal*, June 18, 2014.

Each of the plans announced by Sprint and T-Mobile would appear to be attractive to consumers. In one way or another, they all offer subscribers additional choices for accessing services the subscribers wish to enjoy at a price lower than otherwise would be available or, alternatively, without incurring data usage charges that otherwise would be incurred. In the latter instance, such as the T-Mobile's "Music Freedom" plan, this feature has become known as "zero-rating" because data usage charges do not apply when subscribers access sites covered by the plans.

I do not know whether these new wireless plans ultimately will prove successful in the marketplace, which continues to evolve at a rapid pace. But I have not heard of any meaningful consumer discontent with the plans. To the contrary, I surmise that consumers welcome the additional options, especially low-income or budget-conscious consumers who either are unable or unwilling to pay for wireless plans that are not limited in some fashion.

America's consumers may welcome these new plans – but not Washington's self-designated consumer advocates who purport to speak in their name. In each instance, these consumer advocates have expressed opposition to the new plans on the basis that they violate the net neutrality non-discrimination principle. This is because, in their view, all applications and content must be treated exactly in the same way – that is to say, with perfect "neutrality." In this view, it is a violation of net neutrality principles for Sprint to offer a low-budget plan that allows subscribers to connect only to Facebook and not to Myspace, or for T-Mobile to offer a plan that "zero-rates" data usage for certain popular music services but not for other music sites, or, say, popular poetry sites – or you name your favorite site.

Thus, in response to Sprint's announcement, Free Press' Matt Wood said: "That helps lock in the existing choices and not let the new ones grow more organically. That's just not the way the Internet has worked."

Shortly after T-Mobile's plan was revealed, Public Knowledge's Michael Weinberg said this: "T-Mobile's announcement that they will exempt a handful of music streaming services from their data cap is but the latest example of ISPs using data caps to undermine net neutrality….This type of gatekeeping interference by ISPs is exactly what net neutrality rules should be designed to prevent."

Matt Wood told *Ars Technica* that, "even if all music apps are on equal footing, they are advantaged against other kinds of apps. That kind of favoritism skews innovation because it favors certain content, business models and technologies over others."

About all the wireless plans, Jason Abbruzzese said this in a post on Mashable: "Mobile carriers have begun to give the world a picture of what a net neutrality-free Internet could look like. Wireless companies have slowly but surely begun to roll out plans that favor certain content providers or entirely limit access to particular sites and apps."

Now, with the features of the new plans in mind, along with the opposition of the consumer advocates, let's be clear: These wireless plans, and variations of these plans with similar parameters, do, as Mr. Abbruzzese asserts, "favor certain content providers or entirely limit access to particular sites and apps." And, if a net neutrality non-discrimination prohibition were applicable to wireless providers – which presently it is not – then their lawfulness certainly would be called into question, at least under the stringent version of net neutrality advocated by Free Press and Public Knowledge. Recall, according to Mr. Weinberg, "this type of gatekeeping interference by ISPs is exactly what net neutrality rules should be designed to prevent."

To be fair, by far the most common rationale offered for the consumer advocates' opposition to plans like those described is this: If the service provider is allowed to "pick winners and losers," then the "next Google" or "next Facebook" may not be able to emerge from the garage because it will be disadvantaged. I do not question the good faith or motivations of the consumer advocates advancing this claim, including the ones quoted above.

I am willing to grant that, under certain market conditions, particular practices of Internet service providers, including wireless broadband providers, *possibly* might present competitive concerns that *could* harm consumers. But in the context of the current competitive marketplace, such concerns are much more hypothetical than real. In the present environment, if the next Google or next Facebook has an application or content site that is truly attractive to consumers, that entity most likely will be able to secure the financing and other backing that will allow it to compete. Indeed, the reality is that in order for the "next Google" or the "next Facebook" to compete against those well-entrenched giants, the putative new entrant might well be looking to negotiate some arrangement with a service provider that will give it a fighting chance of competing with the entrenched giants by differentiating itself.

But, here, for present purposes, I want to assume the legitimacy of the concern that some practices involving "discrimination," or what I prefer to consider differentiation of services, possibly might raise competitive concerns. The question then becomes: What is the preferred approach for addressing such concerns. In my view, taking into account the absence of any apparent present market failure and consumer harm, the preferred approach would be for the FCC to forbear from adopting any new net neutrality mandates at all, leaving it to the antitrust authorities to investigate and address any anticompetitive concerns that arise. Failing that, and assuming a majority of the FCC commissioners moves forward to adopt some form of new net neutrality regulation, the preferred approach then would be adoption of the "commercial reasonableness" approach articulated initially by FCC Chairman Tom Wheeler and incorporated into the Commission's Open Internet rulemaking notice. For this approach to be acceptable, there must be enough flexibility built into the "commercial reasonableness" regime so that Internet service providers are allowed to differentiate their offerings in ways that are responsive to consumers' needs.

Consumers' needs. This brings me back to the main point: It is unlikely that a version of net neutrality – or, I might say, a vision of net neutrality – that is sufficiently rigid that it leads its advocates inexorably to oppose the wireless plans described above is in consumers' interest. Such an inflexible version of net neutrality, espoused most fervently by those who insist Internet providers must be classified as common carriers under "Title II" of the Communications Act, is, I maintain, at odds with consumers' interests.

Indeed, I maintain that the vast majority of consumers, if

asked the question in a fair way, would say they are pleased with the additional choices they now have available under the Sprint and T-Mobile plans. I suspect they would say they are not aware that self-designated consumer representatives have opposed these very plans in their name.

In sum, I don't believe re-branding of net neutrality is what is needed. What is needed is more consumer education concerning why a strictly neutral Internet – neutral in the sense of prohibiting all product differentiation and innovation along the lines of the Sprint and T-Mobile wireless plans – would be detrimental to consumers' own interests.

* Randolph J. May is President of the Free State Foundation, an independent, nonpartisan free market-oriented think tank located in Rockville, Maryland.

4.
Thinking the Unthinkable:
Imposing the "Utility Model" on Internet Providers

Randolph J. May *

Perspectives from FSF Scholars, September 29, 2014,
Vol. 9, No. 32

Back in 1997, then-FCC Chairman Reed Hundt titled a speech, "Thinking About Why Some Communications Mergers Are Unthinkable." In his address, Mr. Hundt explained why, in his view, it was "unthinkable" to contemplate a merger between AT&T and one of the Bell Operating Companies. A principal reason had to do with what Mr. Hundt claimed would be the "resulting concentration" of "the long distance market."

Well, this thinking about the unthinkable was not very prescient regarding the development of what, even then, was a rapidly changing marketplace. There is no longer any meaningful "long distance market." Long distance is long gone.

But the regulatory immodesty that leads FCC commissioners, even well-meaning ones, to think that they can predict – and then manage for the benefit of consumers – increasingly fast-paced technological and marketplace changes is not, like long distance, long gone. Indeed, I fear that, right now, such immodesty is at a dangerously high point.

So much so that in recent days I have found myself "thinking the unthinkable." It now looks possible that FCC Chairman Tom Wheeler and his two Democrat colleagues, Mignon Clyburn and Jessica Rosenworcel, might actually vote to classify broadband Internet service providers (ISPs) as common carriers under Title II of the Communications Act. This means regulating Internet providers under a public utility-type regime that was applied in the last century to the monopolistic Ma Bell – even though the Internet service provider market is now effectively competitive.

It means regulating Internet providers under a regime like the one applied to electric utilities. Susan Crawford, one of the leading advocates of Title II regulation, explicitly equates the provision of electricity service and Internet service and advocates regulating them the same way. On page 265 of her book, *Captive Audience*, she concludes that "America needs a utility model" for Internet providers. Professor Crawford's thinking is fully in line with that of other Title II advocates.

Well, I think it is unthinkable that Chairman Wheeler and his two Democrat colleagues might adopt a utility model for broadband. Sure, I understand that there are various theories going around that, after imposing Title II regulation, the Commission could then decide to forbear from actually applying some of the Title II common carrier requirements, such as requiring advance agency permission before ISPs construct new networks, or imposing agency-prescribed regulatory accounting requirements and equipment depreciation schedules on ISPs, or prescribing the value of the providers' property. But the Commission is not even proposing at this time to exercise such forbearance authority. And, in any event, it has exercised forbearance authority only sparingly, and then only very slowly, since the Telecommunications Act of 1996 granted the agency such authority. And through its precedents the Commission has established high hurdles to granting forbearance.

More to the point, while a few of the Title II advocates suggest the FCC could forbear from applying all but Title II's Section 202 nondiscrimination prohibition, this is a distinct minority view. Most do not advocate forbearing from Section 201's rate regulation provision. After all, the "utility model" advocated by Professor Crawford and others has rate regulation at its very core. Many of the complaints of these Title II advocates concerning Internet provider practices, including wireless Internet providers, concern what they claim are "unreasonable" data tiers or limits, and they routinely seek to have the FCC compel the production of information concerning demand and usage levels, service provider costs, and service revenues. This is the very type of information central to traditional utility rate cases.

In a recent letter to Verizon Wireless concerning the way Verizon administers its unlimited data plan, FCC Chairman Wheeler questioned whether the provider was trying to "enhance its revenue streams." Frankly, I don't believe America's Internet providers could have invested over $1.3 trillion since 1996 – and $75 billion just in 2013 –if they didn't have an eye on their revenue streams. But what is most important to appreciate is that FCC inquiries regarding Internet provider revenue streams, usage levels, data tier modeling, and cost of providing service presage rate regulation under Title II.

To me, it is unthinkable that the FCC would now consider going backwards by imposing Title II common carrier regulation on broadband Internet providers. In 2002, the Commission declared "broadband services should exist in a minimal regulatory environment that promotes investment and innovation in a competitive market." In classifying cable broadband, and then wireline broadband, as information services rather than services subject to Title II regulation, the Commission emphasized it wanted to create a rational framework "for the competing services that are provided via different technologies and network architectures." It recognized, in 2002, that Internet access already was "evolving over multiple electronic platforms, including wireline, cable, terrestrial wireless and satellite."

Of course, since the FCC adopted a "minimal regulatory environment" for broadband in 2002 – and then successfully defended its decision all the way to the Supreme Court in the *Brand X* decision – the broadband Internet market, in fact, has become increasingly competitive, with facilities-based competition evolving over multiple platforms as the Commission envisioned. Now, I understand that Professor Crawford wrote an entire book, *Captive Audience*, in an attempt to demonstrate that cable operators have a "monopoly" in the provision of Internet service because, in her view, only they can provide the speed of 100 Mbps that she claims qualifies as high-speed (or "high-enough" speed) broadband.

Recently, Chairman Wheeler gave a speech in somewhat the same vein. He acknowledged that 80% of American households have access to a broadband connection that delivers a speed of 25 Mbps or better, and that a majority of households have access to a speed of 100 Mbps. Then, remarkably, he suggested it is "unacceptable" that 40% presently do not have access to 100 Mbps.

Of course, we all want to see deliverable speeds continue to improve as they steadily have improved over the past decade. But it is wrong – and it leads to the wrong policy prescriptions – to suggest that the "market" is uncompetitive by defining market parameters in a Crawford-like way that necessarily excludes alternative service providers that satisfy consumer demand at prices consumers are willing to pay. In his speech, Chairman Wheeler did something like this by concluding that wireless is just not a "full substitute" for fixed broadband – this despite accumulating evidence to the contrary. Indeed, three of the four major wireless providers in the U.S. already offer average actual speeds of over 30 Mbps, and 91.6% of the U.S. population has access to three or more wireless Internet providers. But if "full substitute" is taken to mean that, in every case and at all times, wireless will satisfy the demands of all consumers, then this is just a mistaken attempt at unsupportable market definition narrowing.

It is wrong to ignore the remarkable progress in broadband that American consumers have enjoyed since 2002 when the Commission adopted the minimal regulatory broadband regime, which has, for the most part, prevailed since then. It is wrong to suggest market definitions that do not comport with the way consumers see the available choices for services they demand.

Indeed, perhaps recognizing, at least *sub silentio*, that claims that the broadband market is uncompetitive are wrong, the FCC is proposing to impose new net neutrality regulations without requiring any showing of market failure or consumer harm resulting from existing Internet provider practices.

Even though I once thought the notion of imposing the Title II "utility model" on Internet providers was unthinkable, most unfortunately, it is now thinkable. And, even though Chairman Wheeler and his two Democrat colleagues will say they are acting in the name of consumers, and in conformance with the wishes of "consumer advocates," I am convinced such action will harm consumers and diminish overall consumer welfare.

In order to avoid the unthinkable, it will be necessary for Chairman Wheeler very shortly to begin to mount a vigorous principled defense of his proposal to adopt a "commercial reasonableness" standard for assessing the lawfulness of Internet provider practices. As I have stated here many times, in light of the lack of evidence of present market failure or consumer harm, the preferred course at this time is for the Commission not to adopt any new net neutrality regulations. (The transparency regulation remains in effect, and it is a useful consumer protection measure.) But assuming there is Commission majority for adopting additional regulatory mandates, from a consumer welfare standpoint, the "commercial reasonableness" proposal under Section 706 is superior to adoption of the Title II utility model.

As for consumer welfare, which ought to be the Commission's

lodestar, I want to end on this point, one I made in remarks during the FCC's first Open Internet Roundtable and in this Free State Foundation *Perspectives*, "Net Neutrality v. Consumers." The most vocal Title II advocates, including those in the Roundtable in which I participated, Public Knowledge's Michael Weinberg and Stanford's Professor Barbara van Schewick, insist that new so-called "zero-rating" wireless plans, such as those introduced by Sprint and T-Mobile, must be considered discriminatory and, therefore, unlawful under the net neutrality regime they advocate. Essentially, these plans, in one way or another, limit consumers' access to the entire Internet in exchange for offering a lower price for access, or they prefer some sites over others for purposes of avoiding data charges. You can read the details of the plan in my "Net Neutrality v. Consumers" piece. I agree with the Title II advocates that these plans are based on a form of "discrimination," as they use the term, because the plans do not treat all bits in a completely "neutral" fashion. So they claim such plans are inconsistent with an "Open Internet."

I maintain plans, such as those offered by T-Mobile and Sprint, are attractive to consumers, especially low income and minority consumers. Indeed, I am confident that if consumers are asked, "If an Open Internet is interpreted to mean that plans like T-Mobile's and Sprint's must be withdrawn, do you favor an Open Internet?" the vast majority of consumer would say "no." This is a much different, but much more meaningful – and much more honest – question to ask than "Do you favor an Open Internet?"

As far as I know, unlike the Title II advocates, neither Chairman Wheeler nor Commissioners Clyburn or Rosenworcel have yet taken the position that, in their view, "zero-rating" plans like T-Mobile's and Sprint's harm consumers. But as they seemingly go further down the road towards adopting the utility model for the Internet, including for wireless Internet providers, they should ask themselves, and then tell the rest of us, whether they agree that those plans, and similar ones, should be banned as discriminatory and inconsistent with an Open Internet. Because, if they do think so, then I don't think they will find themselves on the side of the majority of consumers.

So, it comes to this: At least under the multi-factored "commercial reasonableness" standard, properly implemented, there would be an opportunity to defend, in a principled way, innovative, consumer-friendly plans. But the Title II advocates will settle for nothing less than rigid interpretations that outlaw any differential treatment of data, regardless of consumer benefits.

If the unthinkable of regulating broadband under the "utility model" is not going to become the reality, it is time for Chairman Wheeler, along with all those on the side of consumers, to make clear the stakes. In 1999, FCC Chairman William Kennard firmly rejected the notion of dumping the "whole morass of regulation" of the utility model on the cable pipe. He concluded: "This is not good for America."

Given that competition in the broadband Internet marketplace is indisputably more robust today than in 1999, what would not have been good for America in 1999 would certainly not be good for America in 2014.

---

* Randolph J. May is President of the Free State Foundation, an independent, nonpartisan free market-oriented think tank located in Rockville, Maryland.

5.
Regulating Under the Influence:
The FCC's Title II Initiative for Broadband

Dennis L. Weisman *

Perspectives from FSF Scholars, **February 13, 2015,**
Vol. 10, No. 7

FCC Chairman Tom Wheeler is in a tough position. Notwithstanding the fact that the FCC is an independent federal agency, when the President weighs in on a policy matter – as is the case with net neutrality – it is difficult for the Chairman to say "thank you for your input Mr. President, but we are going to go in a different direction." It is widely recognized that "regulation is a political act" and no extant issue attests to this fact more than net neutrality.[1] Mr. Wheeler's claim, therefore, that economics ("long-standing regulatory principles") carries the day on net neutrality regulation is more than a bit disingenuous. Indeed, as I argue below, the "economic fig leaf" that the FCC dons to rationalize its actions with respect to Title II regulation for broadband is particularly ill fitting – Mr. Wheeler's wardrobe malfunction *du jour*.

The FCC's Title II initiative reclassifies broadband as a telecommunications service rather than an information service and broadband providers would become common carriers with all of the myriad obligations this entails. Mr. Wheeler attempts in a recent *Wired* article to soften the blow by claiming that the FCC has no interest in imposing rate regulation on broadband providers or subjecting their last-mile facilities to unbundling obligations.[2] This defense has a certain Clintonesque quality to it – "Yes, but I did not inhale." The problem here is three-fold. First, Mr. Wheeler has a commitment problem of sorts because he cannot speak for future FCC administrations. There is no such thing as a little regulation; it is invariably subject to regulatory creep, as the venerable Professor Alfred Kahn astutely recognized when he turned off the lights at the Civil Aeronautics Board.[3] Second, if Mr. Wheeler is going to make the case that more *heavy-handed regulation* encourages deployment and investment in broadband infrastructure, it is the capital markets that he will have to convince and this is likely to be a tough sell. Third, a ban on paid prioritization is itself a form of rate regulation and this means that the FCC is going to be dragged into seemingly endless disputes over compliance with its rules.

There is a two-part standard to justify economic regulation.[4] The first part is that governmental intervention is presumptively unnecessary absent market conditions that (1) credibly establish that the abuse of market power poses a substantial, non-transitory risk to economic welfare; and (2) should be expected to significantly undermine the integrity of the competitive process.[5] The second part is that no governmental intervention can be justified unless the expected benefits of such intervention exceed the expected costs, appropriately defined. The fact that the FCC failed to ground its Title II initiative in any formal market power analysis resonated with Judge Silberman in his dissent in *Verizon v. FCC*.[6]

Two additional observations are noteworthy. First, the FCC cannot point to any non-transitory abuse of market power. The net neutrality violations that it can cite are preciously few in number and the misconduct was remedied expeditiously.[7] Hence, whatever regulatory oversight is called for is most assuredly of an *ex post* variety rather than the intrusive, *ex ante* sort that the FCC now contemplates.[8] Second, the FCC cannot point to any systemic pattern of consumer harm stemming from these transitory violations of net neutrality principles to justify its approach because no such evidence exists.

In his *Wired* article, Mr. Wheeler makes the unexceptionable point that commercial interests are not always aligned with consumer interests. This is a fair point, but seemingly works at cross purposes with his proposal to ban paid prioritization. According to the Chairman, society is better off when the government forces everyone to fly coach and partake of parcel post. Really? Bill Baxter, the esteemed Stanford law professor and architect of the AT&T divestiture accord, recognized long ago that consumers cannot be harmed by the introduction of new services.

> Finally, it should be noted that, if there is a tomorrow's product, it cannot be monopolized to the extent that we would be worse off than if we did not have that tomorrow's product. Tomorrow's product is, at any finite price, a net gain. Today's products remain available to compete with it.[9]

Mr. Wheeler would appear to see it differently, but as a matter of economics he would be wrong. Of course, there is the oft-stated concern that paid prioritization will favor large (edge) providers over small innovators toiling away in their garages. This is a vacuous argument – the FCC should not be in the business of designing industrial policy to compensate for the failure on the part of small innovators to convince venture capitalists of the value of their creations. Lest we forget that Apple, Google, and Microsoft were all yesteryear's garage innovators that somehow managed to develop *better mousetraps* without industrial policy being hijacked to handicap the race.

Broadband is an example of a two-sided market in which edge (content) providers represent one side of the market and consumers represent the other side of the market. Just as newspapers impose positive prices on both advertisers and subscribers, it is quite generally efficient in two-sided markets for both sides of the market to contribute to the total price. A ban on paid prioritization over broadband networks essentially requires consumers to pay the full freight.[10] To paraphrase the late Judge Robert Bork, one often hears of the baseball player who, although a weak hitter, was also a poor fielder.[11] Mr. Wheeler's ban on paid prioritization is a little like that. Although it is socially inequitable, at least it is economically inefficient.

The FCC's invocation of Section 706 of the 1996 Telecommunications Act to justify its Title II initiative for broadband is particularly curious. This section of the Act calls for the Commission "to encourage the deployment on a reasonable and timely basis of advanced telecommunications capability to all Americans . . . by utilizing price cap regulation, regulatory forbearance measures that promote competition in the local telecommunications market, or other regulating methods that remove barriers to infrastructure investment." The FCC previously invoked this section of the Act to justify its decision not to require incumbent providers to unbundle their fiber networks.[12] In addition, the Department of Justice, in deference to the principle that dynamic efficiency trumps static efficiency,[13] advised the Commission to refrain from invoking economic regulation for broadband services even if there were a paucity of providers.

> The Department recommends that the
> Commission monitor carefully those areas in
> which only a single provider offers – or even two
> providers offer – broadband service. Although
> enacting some form of regulation to prevent
> certain providers from exercising market power

> may be tempting with regard to such areas, care
> must be taken to avoid stifling the infrastructure
> investments needed to expand broadband access.
> In particular, price regulation would be appropriate
> only where necessary to protect consumers from
> the exercise of monopoly power and where such
> regulation would not stifle incentives to invest in
> infrastructure deployment.[14]

The key point is that more *light-handed regulation* is the avenue through which to encourage deployment and investment in broadband networks. With its Title II initiative, the FCC seeks to turn this principle on its head, arguing that more *heavy-handed regulation* will actually encourage the desired deployment and investment, but the Commission cannot have it both ways. Professor Jean Tirole, the winner of the 2014 Nobel Prize in economics, was asked by the *New York Times* whether he thought regulation was moving in the right direction. Mr. Wheeler would be wise to reflect upon his response.

> What we have been trying to do is to get regulation
> which is light enough in order to let innovation
> happen and to promote investment by the
> incumbents. Bad regulation can actually reduce
> growth quite a lot, can create a lot of problems.[15]

Finally, a firm's incentives for investment and innovation turn on its ability to appropriate the returns on that investment. It is therefore incumbent upon the FCC to explain how a ban on paid prioritization, which will truncate the returns on investment, can be expected to strengthen incentives for investment and innovation in a manner consistent with Section 706 of the 1996 Act.

The FCC put forward and the majority in *Verizon v. FCC*

accepted the theory of a "virtuous cycle of innovation" to rationalize its Title II initiative.[16] The basic idea is that a ban on paid prioritization and blocking or throttling of data will encourage innovation by edge (content) providers that in turn will stimulate usage of broadband networks and ultimately increase deployment of such networks. Of course, a theory is only as good as its empirical validity and this one smacks of the very same smoke and mirrors that the FCC once embraced in the form of the now discredited *stepping-stone hypothesis* to justify pervasive unbundling of incumbent providers' networks at artificially low prices.[17] At a minimum, it is necessary for the FCC to establish that the second-order effects that it relies upon in the form of its "virtual cycle of innovation" to spur investment are not dominated by the first-order, investment-repressing effects associated with common carrier regulation of broadband providers. That is to say, the FCC should be required to demonstrate that its proposal passes a cost-benefit test, a point not lost on Judge Silberman in his dissent in *Verizon*.

The FCC's Title II initiative is driven by two principal objectives, a ban on paid prioritization and a corresponding ban on blocking or throttling of data. Nowhere does the FCC seem to appreciate the fact that these objectives are potentially in conflict with one another. To the extent that the FCC limits the ability of broadband providers to engage in price differentiation,[18] say, by offering different speeds at different prices, the greater the incentive those providers will have to engage in non-price discrimination (including the blocking or throttling of data) in a manner that may not be directly observable by regulators. This will drag the FCC into the abyss of monitoring service quality and reliability because one form of regulation invariably begets other forms of regulation. Hence, at a minimum it is incumbent upon the FCC to establish that the economic regulation it seeks to impose through its Title II initiative will not aggravate the very problem its seeks to remedy.

To conclude, if Mr. Wheeler wants to move forward with Title II regulation of broadband, he should concede that this is largely a political issue and not ask economics to do his bidding for him. It is not uncommon for public policy decisions to be made predominantly on the basis of politics. The hopelessly inefficient, long-standing practice of regulators setting artificially high long-distance rates and correspondingly low local service rates is a case in point.[19] That said, in hanging his hat on economics to rationalize Title II regulation for broadband, Mr. Wheeler has embarked upon a fool's errand because *that dog won't hunt.*

* Dennis L. Weisman, a member of the Free State Foundation's Board of Academic Advisors, is a Professor of Economics, *Emeritus*, Kansas State University. He is grateful to Glen Robinson and Tim Tardiff for stimulating discussions. The Free State Foundation is an independent, nonpartisan free market-oriented think tank located in Rockville, Maryland.

Endnotes

1   Ronald R. Braeutigam, "Optimal Policies for Natural Monopolies" in Handbook of Industrial Organization, ed. by Richard Schmalensee and Robert Willig, Amsterdam: North-Holland, Vol. 2, Chapter 23 1989, p. 1299.

2   "FCC Chairman Tom Wheeler: This Is How We Will Ensure Net Neutrality," *Wired*, February 4, 2015, available at http://www.wired.com/2015/02/fcc-chairman-wheeler-net-neutrality/

3   Glen O. Robinson and Dennis L. Weisman, "Designing Competition Policy for Telecommunications," *The Review of Network Economics*, Vol. 7(4), December 2008, pp. 534-540.

4   Dennis L. Weisman, "A 'Principled' Approach to the Design of Telecommunications Policy," *Journal of Competition Law and Economics*, Vol. 6(4), 2010, pp. 927-956.

5   Market power is enhanced if it is likely to encourage one or more firms to raise price, reduce output, diminish innovation, or otherwise harm customers as a result of diminished competitive constraints or incentives. See the U.S. Department of Justice Horizontal Merger Guidelines available at http://www.justice.gov/atr/public/guidelines/hmg-2010.html

6   *Verizon v. FCC,* 740 F.3d 623 (D.C. Cir. January 14, 2014).

7   Dennis L. Weisman and Glen O. Robinson, "Lessons for Modern Regulators from Hippocrates, Schumpeter and Kahn," in NEW DIRECTIONS IN COMMUNICATIONS POLICY, ed. by Randolph J. May, Durham NC: Carolina Academic Press, 2009, pp. 3–37.

8   See, for example, Jonathan E. Nuechterlein, "Antitrust Oversight of an Antitrust Dispute: An Institutional Perspective on the Net Neutrality Debate," *Journal on Telecommunications & High Technology Law*, Vol. 7(1), Winter 2009, pp. 19-66.

9   William F. Baxter, "The Definition and Measurement of Market Power in Industries Characterized by Rapidly Developing and Changing Technologies," *Antitrust Law Journal*, October, Vol. 53, October, 1984, p. 724.

10   Two-sided markets are characterized by a *seesaw principle* in that a lower price on one side of the market tends to give rise to a higher price on the other side of the market. See, for example, Jean-Charles Rochet and Jean Tirole, "Two-Sided Markets: A Progress Report," *Rand Journal of Economics*, Vol. 37, 2006, pp. 645-667.

11   Robert H. Bork, The Antitrust Paradox, New York: The Free Press, 1978, p. 382.

12   *In the Matter of Unbundled Access to Network Elements, Review of the Section 251 Unbundling Obligations of Incumbent Local Exchange Carriers*, WC Docket No. 04-313, CC Docket No. 01-338, Report and Order and Order On Remand and Further Notice of Proposed Rulemaking, released August 21, 2003, ¶ 173.

13   Richard J. Gilbert, "New Antitrust Laws for the 'New Economy,'" Testimony Before the Antitrust Modernization Commission, Washington D.C., 2005.

14   *Ex Parte* Submission of the United States Department of Justice, Before the Federal Communications Commission, *In the Matter of Economic Issues in Broadband Competition: A National Broadband Plan for Our Future*, GN Docket No. 09-51, January 4, 2010, p. 28.

15   Binyamin Appelbaum, "Q. and A. with Jean Tirole, Economics Nobel Winner," *New York Times*, 15 November 2014, available at http://www.nytimes.com/2014/10/15/upshot/q-and-a-with-jean-tirole-nobel-prize-winner.html?_r=1&abt=0002&abg=0

16   The majority in *Verizon v. FCC* derides Verizon for its characterization of this theory as a "triple cushion shot." The majority observes that in pool "a triple-cushion shot, although perhaps more difficult to complete, counts the same as any other shot." This observation misses the point. The objective, of course,

is not to make a single shot, but to win the game. The "triple cushion shot" is of limited value if the other balls displaced in the course of making the shot render subsequent shots more difficult.

17   *See, for example,* Glen O. Robinson and Dennis L. Weisman, "Designing Competition Policy for Telecommunications," *The Review of Network Economics*, Vol. 7(4), December 2008, pp. 534-540.

18   Price differentiation typically refers to any deviation from a uniform price. Conversely, price discrimination refers to price differences that cannot be explained by cost differences. For example, "the sale of two or more similar goods at prices which are in different ratios to marginal cost" would constitute price discrimination. See George J. Stigler, THE THEORY OF PRICE, New York: Macmillan Publishing, 1966, p. 209.

19   Robert W. Crandall and Leonard Waverman, Who Pays for Universal Service?, Washington D.C.: Brookings, 2000.

6.
Regulating Net Neutrality:
Who Will the FCC Really "Protect"?

Robert W. Crandall *

Perspectives from FSF Scholars, March 26, 2015, Vol. 10, No. 14

The Federal Communications Commission's (FCC's) new net neutrality rules, released March 12, 2015, are justified by the Commission as necessary to protect an "open Internet" for small, innovative content providers. Without such rules, the FCC claims, large media, content, and applications purveyors will negotiate favorable access and interconnection arrangements with large Internet service providers (ISPs), thereby disadvantaging new digital content start-ups. Unfortunately, the new rules are not based on any empirical evidence that such a threat exists. And the general, vague nature of the rules surely provides the opportunity for intense political lobbying as they are implemented in a rapidly-changing market environment.

When It Comes to Regulation, Past Is Prologue

Almost all new exercises in regulation begin with what is claimed to be a "reasonable" attempt to protect someone from some kind of discrimination. The Interstate Commerce Commission (ICC) was established in1887 to protect agrarian interests from long-haul/short-haul railroad discrimination. The Civil Aeronautics Board (CAB) was entrusted with regulating airlines in a manner that would provide dependable service to small communities. The Federal Communications Commission (FCC), in concert with state regulators, used its regulatory authority to "protect" local telephone ratepayers and to limit competition in broadcasting so as to protect local programming. In each of these cases, the regulators ultimately held back progress and restricted new entry, claiming they were just assuring that consumers would continue to obtain "fair and reasonable" access to some relevant services.

The ICC evolved – with the help of Congress – into an agency that controlled not only railroad rates, but also entry into commodity-specific interstate trucking routes, thereby keeping trucking rates artificially high. This, in turn, kept rail rates high, allowing the ICC to force railroads to continue offering service on unprofitable rural routes. For decades the CAB attempted to maintain service to small communities by blocking all entry into major routes. And for decades the FCC itself attempted to protect its regulated clients from the effects of new entry and new technologies. For example, the Commission attempted to block access to new terminal equipment (1956), switched long distance services (1977), and pay-television services (1977). In each case, in an effort to maintain the *status quo* for existing services, the Commission sought to block entrants using new technologies from delivering new or enhanced services to consumers. This regulatory history is instructive in considering the FCC's actions in the net neutrality proceeding.

The FCC's Net Neutrality Rules

The net neutrality rules issued on March 12th appear to have been driven, in part, by an almost religious fervor to impose strict "neutrality" mandates on Internet service providers regardless of the absence of evidence of market failure. But they were also driven, at least in part, by the agency's response to technology-driven new entry. As high-speed broadband service has spread throughout the country, innovators such as Netflix, Amazon, Apple, and even HBO began to explore "over-the-top" distribution of video programming in competition with broadcast, cable, and satellite delivery of such programming. Given the potential congestion created by these data-intensive video streams, some market participants began to question the network pricing model that had developed in the early years of the Internet. Specifically, should Internet service providers be required to accept all traffic from content suppliers, or the networks delivering their content, at the same, zero price, even though some of this content creates much greater network congestion than other content? Alternatively, should the video streaming services be allowed to negotiate with ISPs for assured, high-quality delivery of their services? When Netflix entered into a deal with Comcast for the termination of its video traffic in February 2014, the political pressure for rules that would, among other things, ban such "paid prioritization" began to build ...surprisingly, even from Netflix.

As Gus Hurwitz, a member of the Free State Foundation's Board of Academic Advisors, has noted elsewhere, there is no empirical evidence supporting the notion that paid priority granted to Netflix or other large media companies is harmful to smaller content providers. Nor is there any evidence that such arrangements benefit the Internet service companies that must compete for customers with other providers. Collecting fees from content providers for better, more reliable connections is likely to induce the ISPs to compete more aggressively for customers, thereby reducing consumer subscriber fees. As a result, it is difficult to demonstrate that ISPs would profit materially from collecting interconnection fees from content networks or that such a practice in two-sided markets is economically less efficient than having ISPs rely solely on subscriber fees for their revenues.

Nevertheless, the FCC, prodded aggressively by the White House, decided to ban paid prioritization.

The FCC's final regulations require that Internet service providers not engage in: (i) "blocking," (ii) "throttling," (iii) "paid prioritization," and (iv) "unreasonable interference or disadvantaging" of end users or content providers. Conduct must be "reasonable" – surely, a reasonable-sounding mandate. But why should "disadvantaging" of content providers be prohibited? Surely, any improvement in the availability of various types of programming over the Internet, for which viewers pay a direct fee, disadvantages some content providers, such as, for example, those that deliver home shopping networks or infomercials over one of the hundreds of cable or broadcast channels that are available to viewers at no additional charge. The improvements in Internet download speeds and in digital compression technologies have upset the old order in the video programming marketplace. As the foregoing recital of regulatory history shows, regulators very often respond by protecting the old order they have created or in which they are complicit.

The meaning of these four stated prohibitions will only be fleshed out as antagonists and protagonists flood the Commission with complaints and pleadings. Indeed, the final regulations allocate more space to the pleading and complaint process than to the detail of the four prohibitions. Given the vagueness of the rules, the prospects for adjudication of these complaints that establish any meaningful and proper boundaries are not good. For the present, Netflix relies heavily on programming produced by the large traditional media companies. But what happens when and if attractive new content emerges from elsewhere, even from abroad? For example, soccer from the UK's Premier League or interactive video games from Asian countries could begin to succeed through direct digital feeds over the Internet. When this begins to occur, our media and "cultural" interests will begin to petition the FCC for protection from unfair or unreasonable competition from abroad, much as the Canadian content owners have done for decades. And they could easily succeed if they can persuade the FCC, or a sitting President, that the carriage of the new content "disadvantages" existing Hollywood producers.

Mark Cuban, an early developer of digital video, has even offered a prediction that the net neutrality rules eventually could invalidate the traditional cable/broadcast model of video distribution. His interview over CNBC on the day the rules were released was summarized as follows:

> The rules would mean that television as we know it is over, Cuban said. He asserted that the transmission of content over television is essentially the same as the transmission of content over the Internet. By that logic, he speculated that the FCC could determine television delivered by cable should be part of the open Internet.
>
> That would mean the same standards would apply to television content providers, including the ban on pay for prioritizing service, he said, so shopping channels such as QVC would run around those rules because they pay cable providers to carry their content.
>
> 'Bits are bits and if all bits are to be treated equally you can't give priority to delivery of a television stream in a managed service,' he said.

Surely, Mark Cuban's predictions cannot be dismissed out of hand. Already, some of the video-streaming services are apparently seeking "specialized" services – *i.e.,* high-speed lanes over separate cable channel bandwidth – from cable companies. If the FCC were to ban such arrangements, concluding that they are evasions of the paid prioritization prohibition, the video streamers likely would sue the Commission for allowing "paid prioritization" on traditional cable channels but not on "specialized service" channels.

Given the vagueness of the new regulations and the rapidly-changing technological environment that drives the Internet's evolution – and ultimate consumer choices – one cannot predict how the politics of Washington ultimately will drive implementation. This is even more true now given that the FCC seemingly has allowed itself to be in the position of following the President's dictates. But no one should necessarily expect that the small innovator, perhaps working diligently in his own garage, will prevail against the major media and communications interests that inhabit Washington.

Consumer Protection Is Advanced by Deregulation

We are fortunate that the 1970s deregulatory movement succeeded in abolishing the ICC and the CAB. Transportation markets are now essentially open to new entry, new technologies, and new business models. For instance, the U.S. airlines are currently trying to prevent the new Gulf-state carriers – Emirates, Etihad, and Qatar Airways – from competing with them on North Atlantic routes. Prior to 1978, they might have convinced the CAB that this competition should be banned because it would bring an end to scheduled airline services to such outposts as Ely (NV), Kalispell (MT), or Rockland (ME), but there is no longer a regulatory forum available for such anti-competitive lobbying. In Canada, by contrast, Air Canada has succeeded in protecting its extremely inefficient operations by persuading regulators to severely limit this "unfair" Gulf-state competition on Canadian routes.

Alternatively, imagine what oil prices would be today if the Federal Energy Regulatory Commission (FERC) had jurisdiction over production of oil and natural gas that is found on private property in the various states. The recent Keystone XL pipeline fiasco provides a clue. Given strong lobbying pressures from environmentalists (in this hypothetical, perhaps joined by established major oil companies with large reserves of these commodities), U.S. oil and gas production would surely have remained near its mid-2000s lows. Luckily, Congress has not given FERC the authority to assure "just and reasonable" exploitation of private oil and gas reserves, and its failure to do so thus has allowed the "fracking" revolution to begin. In addition, the lack of an ICC with regulatory authority over railroads has been instrumental in allowing the increased oil supplies to move across state lines by rail as the federal government succumbs to environmentalists and blocks incremental pipeline construction.

Conclusion

Deregulation has also served consumers well in the communications sector to the extent that it has been implemented. Driven by technological change, unregulated prices of ordinary voice and text messages have declined dramatically. The classification of broadband as an information service meant that the FCC, unlike its European counterparts, refrained from regulating Internet service providers. This unleashed a major wave of investment in broadband networks. Unfortunately, Congress has left the Communications Act of 1934 largely intact, so the Commission has now been able reverse course with likely disastrous effects on network investment – unless the Commission's action is reversed.

Given the massive economic stakes involved, future arguments over the meaning of the new Title II regulations as they are implemented inevitably will stimulate a major increase in litigation and Washington lobbying. Were I a hedge fund manager, I would not try to predict how technology will evolve and whether Google, Comcast, Verizon, Apple, Disney, or DISH will emerge as the winner in future battles over the meaning of the new Title II rules. Rather, I would hedge my bets by simply buying downtown Washington, DC, real estate.

* Robert W. Crandall, a member of the Free State Foundation's Board of Academic Advisors, is a Nonresident Senior Fellow at The Brookings Institution and the Technology Policy Institute. The Free State Foundation is an independent, nonpartisan free market-oriented think tank located in Rockville, Maryland.

Part II – The Problems with Public Utility Regulation Under the FCC's 2015 *Title II Order*

7.
Title II Reclassification *Is* Rate Regulation

Daniel A. Lyons *

Perspectives from FSF Scholars, February 25, 2015,
Vol. 10, No. 12

Like "Voldemort" to wizards, "rate regulation" is the name re-classification enthusiasts dare not speak when describing Title II. It conjures up images of government bureaucrats interfering in the market to decide which services providers can offer to customers and at what price—a politically unpopular image at odds with a dynamic Internet ecosystem. For this reason, since his eleventh-hour conversion under White House pressure, FCC Chairman Tom Wheeler has repeatedly insisted that "there will be no rate regulation" under his Title II reclassification plan.[1]

But these fervent protests cannot change the fact that Title II reclassification *is* rate regulation—a fact that FSF President Randolph May has made repeatedly throughout the net neutrality debate. This truth is self-evident even from the handful of details that Chairman Wheeler has released before the Commission's fateful vote. More fundamentally, Title II, at its heart, is a rate regulation regime: Section 201(b) requires common carriers to charge only just and reasonable rates. And Section 202(a) makes it unlawful to make any unjust or unreasonable discrimination in charges. The Commission may avoid the most onerous forms of rate regulation such as tariffing and unbundling. But as the arbiter of Section 201 and 202 violations, the Commission will be forced into accepting the mantle of America's *de facto* regulator of broadband rates—and its recent ham-handed decisions about broadband competitiveness will dramatically limit its flexibility in this role.

As an initial matter, the Commission's own Open Internet fact sheet belies the claim that it will not regulate rates for broadband service. One of the three primary pillars of the proposed order is a prohibition on "paid prioritization," meaning that "broadband providers may not favor some lawful Internet traffic over other lawful traffic in exchange for consideration."[2] While this prohibition is an essential tenet of most net neutrality proposals, its effect is to set a specific rate – namely $0 – for priority delivery over last-mile broadband networks. The fact sheet also claims authority to review and, if necessary, enjoin terms of interconnection agreements between broadband providers and other parts of the Internet ecosystem, which would presumably include review of rates that ISPs charge for paid peering or transit service.

Chairman Wheeler may respond that he meant the Commission would not regulate *retail* broadband rates, the price that consumers pay for broadband service. This is a somewhat artificial distinction, as Title II has long governed interconnection rates between networks as well as retail rates to consumers.[3] But even under this narrow consumer-focused definition of rates, reclassification will necessarily lead to rate regulation by the Commission, because Title II is fundamentally a rate regulation regime.

The heart of Title II common carriage is Sections 201 and 202. Section 201(b) mandates that "[a]ll *charges*, practices, classifications, and regulations for and in connection with [] communication service, shall be just and reasonable; and that any such *charge*, practice, classification, or regulation that is unjust or unreasonable is declared to be unlawful."[4] Similarly, Section 202(a) makes it "unlawful for any common carrier to make any unjust or unreasonable discrimination in *charges*, practices, classifications, regulations, facilities, or services for or in connection with like service" or to "make or give any undue or unreasonable preference to any particular person, class of persons, or locality."[5] Section 208 allows any aggrieved party to file a complaint alleging that a carrier violated a duty under the Act, including Sections 201 and 202. If the carrier fails to redress the complaint promptly, Section 208 declares that "it shall be the *duty* of the Commission to investigate the matters complained of."[6] The statutory language simply does not allow the Commission to be a disinterested observer of communications rates as Chairman Wheeler suggests. Rather, it not only invites but demands that the Commission intervene in the market, at least upon request, to pass judgment regarding whether individual carrier rates are just and reasonable.

Admittedly, the Commission has proposed forbearing from the most aggressive forms of rate regulation that would otherwise be at its disposal, such as tariffing and mandatory unbundling of network elements.[7] While these are welcome announcements, they should surprise no one. The Commission has aggressively opposed tariffing of most telecommunications services for several decades.[8] And a multiyear litigation battle over pricing of unbundled network elements[9] ultimately ended in regime widely considered a failure that no one should be eager to repeat.[10]

But courts and the Commission have repeatedly emphasized that forbearing from tariffing does not mean the Commission has foresworn oversight of carrier rates. The D.C. Circuit Court of Appeals discussed the distinction in *Orloff v. Federal Communications Commission*,[11] a case alleging that a Verizon Wireless rate constituted unreasonable discrimination. The court noted that historically, the Commission assessed whether a rate was just or reasonable "largely ... by reference to the carrier's tariff."[12] Through forbearance, Congress and the Commission "dissolved what the Supreme Court described as the 'indissoluble unity' between § 203's tariff-filing requirement and the prohibition against rate discrimination in § 202."[13] But even in an untariffed environment, carriers "still have duties," including compliance with Sections 201 and 202, meaning its rates were still subject to Commission review in the event of a complaint.[14] The Commission "emphasize[d]" that it "is not forbearing from applying section 202(a)" and that even in a light-touch regulatory regime "section 202 continues to act as a powerful protection for...consumers."[15] It vowed to that the Commission "will not hesitate to find that unreasonable discrimination violates section 202."[16]

Orloff is a helpful case study in part because it occurred in the context of the untariffed wireless market, which Chairman Wheeler has repeatedly analogized to his proposed broadband rules. In 2000, Verizon Wireless customer Jacqueline Orloff filed a complaint with the Commission alleging that the carrier violated Sections 201 and 202 by offering discounts and other inducements to certain wireless customers to entice them to join or stay with Verizon Wireless.[17] Orloff's complaint focused on the carrier's willingness to allow customers to haggle for better deals. In essence, she asserted that those who haggled got a better price than non-hagglers for the same service, which constituted unreasonable discrimination under Section 202(a) and therefore was an unjust or unreasonable practice under Section 201(b).[18]

Importantly, the Commission did not simply dismiss the complaint on the grounds that it did not regulate wireless rates. Rather, it applied the same three-part test developed during the era of tariffing to determine whether Verizon discriminated unjustly or unreasonably among its customers.[19] Under the first two steps, the complainant must show that the services at issue are "like" services, and if so, that there are differences in the terms and conditions pursuant to which the services are provided. In this case, the Commission found that by granting concessions to customers who haggle, Verizon Wireless effectively charged different rates for the same service and therefore that the company discriminated against customers like Orloff who did not haggle as effectively. The burden then shifted to Verizon Wireless under step three to prove that its discrimination was reasonable.

Orloff also helps illustrate the limits of wireless as an analogy to Chairman Wheeler's proposed reclassification of broadband. Ultimately, the Commission held that although Verizon's sales concessions resulted in discrimination, this discrimination was reasonable because of the competitiveness of the wireless market in Orloff's native Cleveland. The Commission explained:

> [W]e decline to find that Defendants' concessions practices violated section 202(a) of the Act, even if those practices allowed some consumers to negotiate better deals than other consumers... because we find that market forces protect Cleveland consumers from discrimination from these particular practices. We find that there is no evidence that any market failure prevented customers from switching carriers if they were dissatisfied. Accordingly, we find it unlikely that a carrier would have an incentive to engage in unreasonable discrimination where such conduct would result in a loss of customers.[20]

In other words, the Commission avoided a searching review of Verizon's wireless rates because of its faith that competition would discipline market players and prevent carriers from engaging in unjust or unreasonable behavior. The D.C. Circuit upheld the Commission's decision on this ground, noting that "the generality of these terms—unjust, unreasonable—opens a rather large area for the free play of agency discretion" and that the Commission was "entitled to value the free market" when deciding whether a practice is reasonable.[21]

Once the Commission reclassifies broadband under Title II, one can imagine a similar complaint arising in the broadband context. As in the wireless market, sales concessions are a common practice to entice broadband customers to join or remain on a particular company's network. Comcast, Verizon, and others often offer low introductory rates for broadband service or "triple play" bundles of broadband, cable, and telephone services which are unavailable to existing customers. And numerous websites are dedicated to helping customers whose service contracts are expiring to haggle in pursuit of a better deal than the company's standard packages. Under *Orloff*, the Commission is likely to find that these concessions constitute discrimination under Section 202(a). And even the company's standard rates could be vulnerable to a challenge that they are unjust or unreasonable under Section 201(b).

But the Commission's recent rhetoric about the lack of competition in broadband markets limits its ability to conclude, as it did in *Orloff*, that competition obviates the need for an aggressive Commission investigation to determine whether the challenged rates are reasonable. In January 2015, the Commission raised its definition of "broadband service" from 4Mbps down and 1Mbps up to 25Mbps down and 3Mbps up.[22] As Commissioner Pai noted in dissent, the report offered little justification for this benchmark, which few consumers purchase even when they have the opportunity to do so, and which is at odds with the Commission's own 10 Mbps down benchmark for subsidizing broadband to rural areas.[23] Under this new definition, 17 percent of America lacks broadband access, and 75 percent of those who have broadband access can choose only one provider. Chairman Wheeler has emphasized these statistics when advocating for reclassification, noting that "[w]here there is no choice, markets cannot work. American families need to be able to shop for affordable prices and faster speeds."[24]

In the absence of a finding of competitive markets, Chairman Wheeler's analogy to regulation of wireless service breaks down. *Orloff's* hands-off approach to wireless rates is explicitly predicated upon the Commission's faith that market forces will deter unjust or unreasonable rates and discrimination. A recent Commission order emphasized that "in the absence of competitive pressures, the default of cost-based regulation should apply."[25] In that proceeding, which invalidated telephone rates for interstate calls by prison inmates, the Commission explained that a cost-based approach "is consistent with Commission practice that typically focuses on the costs of providing the underlying service when ensuring that rates for service are just and reasonable under Section 201(b)." [26]

The Commission's decision to redefine broadband, and the subsequent conclusions Chairman Wheeler has drawn – wrongly, I think – as to broadband competitiveness, may provide useful talking points to support his Title II reclassification plan. But together, the one-two punch of redefining and then reclassifying broadband service will make it difficult to fulfill the Chairman's promises to avoid broadband rate regulation. Title II requires the Commission to assure carrier rates are just, reasonable, and nondiscriminatory. In markets that the Commission claims are uncompetitive, this requires a searching inquiry to determine whether the rates in question are supported by costs – an inquiry that has taken ten years in the relatively simple world of inmate telephone calls and will be immeasurably more complex when applied to broadband networks.

The Commission may forbear from tariffing and unbundling broadband service. But under Title II it will play a significant and active role in determining the nation's broadband rates. To deny this fact is foolish optimism at best, and at worst is deceiving the public as to the inevitable effect of reclassification.

* Daniel A. Lyons, a member of the Free State Foundation's Board of Academic Advisors, is an Associate Professor of Law at Boston College Law School. The Free State Foundation is an independent, nonpartisan free market-oriented think tank located in Rockville, Maryland.

Endnotes

1   Tom Wheeler, *FCC Chairman Tom Wheeler: This is How We Will Ensure Net Neutrality*, Wired Magazine, Feb. 4, 2015, available at http://www.wired.com/2015/02/fcc-chairman-wheeler-net-neutrality/.

2   Federal Communications Commission, *Fact Sheet: Chairman Wheeler Proposes New Rules for Protecting the Open Internet*, available at http://transition.fcc.gov/Daily_Releases/Daily_Business/2015/db0204/DOC-331869A1.pdf.

3   See, e.g., *In re Developing a Unified Intercarrier Compensation Regime*, 16 FCC Rcd. 9610 (2001) (discussing intercarrier compensation under Section 201).

4   47 U.S.C. § 201(b) (emphasis added).

5   *Id.* § 202(a) (emphasis added).

6   *Id.* § 208 (emphasis added).

7   See Fact Sheet, supra note 2.

8   See, e.g., MCI Telecomm. Corp. v. AT&T, 512 U.S. 218 (1994).

9   See, e.g., Verizon Comm'cns v. FCC, 535 U.S. 467 (2002).

10 See, e.g., Larry F. Darby, Jeffrey A. Eisenach, and Joseph S. Kraemer, *The CLEC Experiment: Anatomy of a Meltdown*, Progress and Freedom Foundation Progress on Point Paper, Vol. 9, No. 23 (2002).

11 Orloff v. FCC, 352 F.3d 415 (2003).

12 *Id.* at 419; *see also id.* at 418 ("As in the Interstate Commerce Act, 'rate filing was Congress's chosen means of preventing unreasonableness and discrimination in charges' by common carriers.") (citing *MCI*, 512 U.S. at 230).

13 *Id.*

14 *Id.* at 420.

15   Orloff v. Vodafone Airtouch Licenses LLC, 17 FCC Rcd. 8987, 8997 (2002).

16   *Id.* at 8998.

17   *Id.* at 8988.

18   *Id.*

19   *Id.* at 8993.

20   *Id.* at 8996.

21   *Orloff*, 352 F.3d at 420, 421 (internal quotation marks and citations omitted).

22   Federal Communications Commission, *2015 Broadband Progress Report and Notice of Inquiry of Immediate Action to Accelerate Deployment*, No. 14-126, Feb. 4, 2015, at ¶ 3, available at http://transition.fcc.gov/Daily_Releases/Daily_Business/2015/db0206/FCC-15-10A1.pdf.

23   See Dissenting Statement of Commissioner Ajit Pai, available at http://transition.fcc.gov/Daily_Releases/Daily_Business/2015/db0204/FCC-15-10A6.pdf.

24   Remarks of FCC Chairman Tom Wheeler, Silicon Flatirons Center, Feb. 9, 2015, available at http://transition.fcc.gov/Daily_Releases/Daily_Business/2015/db0209/DOC-331943A1.pdf.

25   In re Rates for Interstate Inmate Calling Services, No. 12-375, Oct. 22, 2014, ¶ 9.

26   *Id.*

8.
Usage-Based Pricing, Zero Rating, and the Future of Broadband Innovation

Daniel A. Lyons *

Perspectives from FSF Scholars, January 4, 2016, Vol. 11, No. 1

I. Introduction and Summary

The Open Internet movement began as a means of protecting consumer welfare in cyberspace. The Federal Communications Commission's Internet Policy Statement, first adopted in 2005, emphasized that consumers should have access to the lawful Internet content of their choice, to run applications and use services of their choice, to connect the devices of their choice to the network, and to benefit from competition among broadband and app providers.[1] Then-FCC Chairman Michael Powell introduced these themes at a policy speech in which he emphasized that "empowering consumers" was "critical to unlocking the vast potential of the broadband Internet."[2] *Consumer choice* originally was, and always should be, the guiding principle for policymakers when determining broadband policy.

But a funny thing happened on the path from idea to implementation. The Commission shifted its focus away from *consumers* and toward *edge providers*. When President Obama pushed the

Commission to reclassify broadband providers as Title II common carriers, he emphasized the need to protect a "level playing field" for edge providers and to reduce barriers for the hypothetical "next Facebook" – themes that are echoed in the Commission's recent net neutrality order. The order emphasizes the risk that broadband providers might interfere anticompetitively in upstream markets for Internet-based content and applications. The Commission explained that rules were necessary because broadband providers have "the economic power to restrict edge-provider traffic and charge for the services they furnish edge providers,"[3] which might "reduce the rate of innovation at the edge."[4]

While many might assume that, in theory, what's good for Netflix is good for consumers, the reality is more complex. To protect innovation at the edge of the Internet ecosystem, the Commission's sweeping rules reduce the opportunity for consumer-friendly innovation elsewhere, namely by facilities-based broadband providers. Consumers in Chile recently felt the real-world impact of this tradeoff, as that nation's telecommunications regulator applied similar rules to outlaw wireless plans that included free access to selected online services such as Facebook, Wikipedia, or Twitter.[5] These wildly popular plans were aimed at prepaid customers and those with older phones, who could not afford, or otherwise did not want to purchase, a traditional unlimited-access wireless plan. Now, those customers are limited to purchasing a more expensive traditional plan, or none at all. Like the archetypal village in Vietnam, regulators felt they had to destroy consumer choice in order to save it.

Thus the *Open Internet* order allows the FCC to deprive consumers of services they want, in order to protect edge provider markets. Advocates have asked the agency to do just that with regard to two related policy issues: usage-based pricing and zero-rated services. Despite strong arguments that these alternative business models can enhance competition and consumer choice, many net neutrality advocates nevertheless have called for rules prohibiting these practices and limiting consumers to a homogenous "dumb pipe" broadband service. Ominously, the FCC has responded with inquiries targeting AT&T's Sponsored Data and Data Perks, T-Mobile's Binge On, and Comcast's Stream TV programs for further scrutiny. While Chairman Tom Wheeler has stated that these inquiries do not constitute an "investigation" or "an enforcement," they nonetheless are likely to put a damper on Internet providers' efforts to meet evolving consumer demand though zero-rating and sponsored data programs. The Commission's next steps in this inquiry, and its response to advocates' continuing pressure to impose a uniform "dumb pipe" model on the broadband industry, may determine how far the agency will go to sacrifice consumer choice out of fear that consumer preferences may somehow harm Internet-based edge provider companies.

II. Open Internet, Closed Mind (to Broadband Innovation)

The *Open Internet* order imposes structural rules that limit broadband providers' ability to offer differentiated services, even in partnership with upstream edge providers. Embedded in these rules is an unjustified bias in favor of existing broadband service models. The 2010 rules made this quite explicit: "These rules are generally consistent with, and should not require significant changes to, broadband providers' current practices, and are also consistent with the common understanding of broadband Internet access service as a service that enables one to go where one wants on the Internet and communicate with anyone else online."[6] In the 2015 rules, the Commission seems willing to entertain the notion that some innovation is permissible within the broadband space, cabined by its awkward and amorphous "no unreasonable interference/disadvantage" standard.[7] But it has also emphasized the need to "protect" and "preserve" the "Open Internet," rhetoric that suggests a bias toward the status quo. Indeed, homogenization of the broadband product seems to be the obvious and intended result of the Commission's decision to re-label Internet service providers as "common carriers."

But this assumption about the need for a homogenized broadband experience is at odds with an increasingly heterogeneous customer base. Some of us are light users, and some are heavy. Some visit many websites, and some only use a handful on a regular basis. Some consumers cannot justify paying high prices for a mobile plan that largely duplicates the access they already have at home or at work, but they might pay less for access to a handful of services. And some may not wish to pay for content, but they would gladly enjoy it if the content provider wished to give it to consumers for free. In short, a "one-size-fits-all" broadband model is ill-fitted to today's diverse user population.

Given this evolution, the Commission's imprimatur of approval for "current practices" at one moment in time is myopic and potentially harmful. As the market becomes saturated and consumer tastes diversify, providers should innovate to deliver increasing value to customers inadequately served by the traditional model.[8] Christopher Yoo, a member of the Free State Foundation Board of Academic Advisors, has explained that companies often test new business models without a definitive understanding of the new model's benefits or drawbacks. Instead they rely on a trial-and-error process to identify better methods of delivering value to consumers.[9] To protect consumer welfare in the Internet ecosystem, it is insufficient to promote innovation simply among edge providers; the Commission must recognize the value of innovation in broadband service markets as well.

As I have discussed in depth elsewhere,[10] international markets are vividly demonstrating the value of broadband-level innovation. In Latin America and many developing countries, broadband providers offer social media plans that include talk, text, and access to selected social media services such as Facebook or Twitter, at a lower price than a traditional mobile data plan.

In Canada, upstart wireless provider TELUS has partnered with Microsoft to offer a Skype-optimized mobile plan. And French provider Orange sought to expand in the United Kingdom by bundling Internet access with the customer's choice from a menu of available online services such as news, streaming video, or music. A rule limiting consumers to a "dumb pipe" connection would inhibit American consumers' ability to partake of this global revolution currently taking place for broadband services, particularly in the mobile space.

Given increasingly diverse consumer needs and the growth of international models showing alternative ways to serve customers more effectively, it is odd to see advocates pushing for *less* diversity and *less* choice among American broadband providers – yet that has been the goal of the net neutrality movement. And having successfully limited American broadband innovation in the *Open Internet* order, advocates are now pushing the FCC to close two of the few remaining avenues that the order left open: usage-based pricing and zero-rated services. The Commission has acknowledged strong arguments both for and against both practices. Admittedly, each is susceptible to anticompetitive abuse, as are many other business decisions by providers throughout the Internet ecosystem. But it would be a mistake to counter that risk with per se rules that would pull the reins of innovation even tighter and deprive consumers of alternatives to the status quo.

III. Usage-Based Pricing

Usage-based pricing has become a flashpoint in post-*Open Internet* order broadband policy discussions (where it often goes by the loaded and inaccurate term "data caps"). It has emerged as an alternative pricing strategy to the traditional unlimited flat-rate model. Its growth has been most prominent in the mobile sector, where tiered service plans helped solve the capacity problems created by the smartphone revolution. But several fixed broadband providers are also finding usage-based pricing to be a tool to segment their customer bases more intelligently.

I have discussed usage-based pricing at length in an earlier Free State Foundation *Perspectives* publication.[11] There is nothing inherently anti-consumer or anticompetitive about the practice. It simply represents a different way that a provider might spread its network costs across its customer base. The unlimited flat-rate model charges each customer the same amount regardless of use. As the Commission noted in its 2010 rules, "[r]equiring all subscribers to pay the same amount for broadband service, regardless of the performance or usage of the service, would force lighter end users of the network to subsidize heavier end users."[12] Usage-based pricing mitigates this problem by shifting more network costs onto those who use the network the most.

Critics charge that usage-based pricing can be a tool for anticompetitive behavior. Specifically, they fear that cable companies may adopt usage-based pricing to deter competition from over-the-top video providers such as Netflix and Hulu. Because Internet-based video consumes significant amounts of data, a customer that replaces traditional cable with an Internet-based alternative would experience a significant increase in monthly data consumption – and may not make the switch if this meant a significant increase in the monthly broadband bill.

These critics are correct that some broadband providers may have incentives to engage in anticompetitive behavior – though it's worth noting that many broadband providers (including DSL and wireless companies) do not have cable affiliates, and many that do (such as Verizon) do not engage in usage-based pricing. But the mere risk of anticompetitive harm alone is insufficient to ban a practice, especially in light of the procompetitive justifications for such a practice. What matters is whether the practice *actually* causes consumer harm. If, for example, a fixed broadband provider enforced a hard monthly limit – a true "data cap" – set near or below the amount of data a typical Netflix consumer would use, and if the consumer had no other alternatives for broadband service, the practice might warrant investigation. But most fixed usage-based plans are far more mild. Comcast, for example, is test marketing a 300GB monthly plan, with a modest $10 charge for each 50GB above that initial amount. This is hardly a "cap" on monthly service. It is, instead, a use-agnostic way to assure that those who use more data assume a greater share of the network's total cost.

The real culprit in the anticompetitive scenarios spun by critics is not usage-based pricing; it's market power. A broadband company with market power does not need usage-based pricing to punish cord-cutters; it could simply raise the price of the traditional flat-rate plan to compensate for the lost revenue. Similarly, a company using speed tiers (a practice that Public Knowledge and others have endorsed as an acceptable form of price discrimination) could set the basic tier below the speed necessary for HD streaming, and charge a significant premium for HD-capable speeds. In each case, the effect on competition would turn on a highly fact-specific inquiry into the broadband provider's market power and the effect that the pricing strategy has on various parts of the provider's customer base.

But absent proof of anticompetitive harm, broadband companies should be free to experiment with alternative pricing strategies. Consumers benefit from having a variety of broadband access models from which to choose. Consider, for example, the tiered pricing structure of most major postpaid wireless plans. Heavier users can choose plans with higher thresholds before overage charges occur, which translates to a lower price per gigabyte. Lighter users, by comparison, can choose smaller plans with a lower monthly fee. Forcing them both into a one-size-fits-all access plan could be detrimental to both and could increase the digital divide, as some cost-conscious customers would reject an unlimited plan at the unlimited price yet would be willing to pay a smaller price for limited monthly access.

IV. Zero-Rated Traffic

Similarly, several net neutrality advocates seek to prohibit zero-rating of broadband traffic. "Zero-rating" is the practice of allowing customers to consume particular Internet content or services without incurring charges against their monthly data plans. The idea is popular with some edge providers eager to distribute their content to a wider range of consumers. Wikipedia, for instance, has been an unabashed champion of zero-rating, forging partnerships with carriers in several developing countries to make its knowledge base available for free to anyone with an Internet-ready phone. The Wikipedia Zero project, modeled on a similar initiative by Facebook, won a 2013 SXSW Interactive Award for activism.[13]

Net neutrality advocates fear zero-rated traffic for the same reason they sought net neutrality regulation. They fear that the ability to partner with carriers to better deliver edge content to consumers will favor well-capitalized edge providers. According to this theory, companies that can afford to zero-rate their services will gain a competitive advantage over those that cannot. And as with usage-based pricing, broadband providers might use zero-rating to give their affiliated services an advantage over Internet-based competitors.

Of course, zero-rating of traffic is hardly the most significant part of the Internet ecosystem where well-capitalized companies have an advantage over their competitors. For example, large companies such as Google and Microsoft have built huge server farms to cache and distribute their content locally rather than deliver their services over the public Internet. Others like Netflix rely upon private content-delivery networks (or construct their own CDNs). By paying to bypass the public Internet, these companies gain more control over delivery of their product and are less susceptible to congestion, packet loss, and other pitfalls that plague their competitors who cannot afford these alternative delivery models. More basically, Netflix and Amazon are paying millions to develop their own content and to be the exclusive online provider of certain third-party content, striking deals that other video delivery services simply cannot afford to pay. These give them an advantage – but few would say such deals "skew edge provider competition." Rather, most would simply call this "competition."

Similarly, zero-rating plans can improve consumer choice and increase competition. Zero-rating of traffic enhances a consumer's broadband plan. Rather than purchasing a bucket of minutes each month, the consumer gets a bucket of minutes *plus* unlimited access to zero-rated content for the same price. By zero-rating certain traffic, a broadband provider can differentiate itself from its competitors, thus increasing the number of planes of competition among carriers. A carefully-targeted zero-rating plan can target niche customers whose needs are imperfectly met by traditional plans, and who are better off with free unlimited access to the content they value most.

And importantly, zero-rating can improve competition among edge providers as well. AT&T offers a sponsored data program, where any interested edge provider can include an API ("application program interface") that zero-rates app traffic by allowing the edge provider to pay the charges the customer would otherwise incur – a practice that Professor Babette Boliek has likened to couponing in cyberspace. Zero-rated agreements are not the exclusive prerogative of richer edge companies. They can also provide opportunities for newer or smaller startups to make a significant promotional splash. For example, when French streaming music service Deezer sought to enter the British market, it partnered with smaller wireless provider Orange, making Deezer one of the options in Orange's Swapables service. As noted above, the agreement gave Orange a point of differentiation over its wireless rivals. But it also gave upstart Deezer built-in delivery over the Orange network, easy access to Orange's customer base, and low-cost promotional marketing as part of the Swapables program.[14] The partnership allowed Deezer the foothold that it needed to begin taking on market leader Spotify.

T-Mobile: Music Freedom, Binge On

T-Mobile has been the most active American carrier to explore the benefits of zero-rating, and its experiments offer keen insight into the potential benefits of the practice. T-Mobile is smaller than rivals AT&T and Verizon and lacks many advantages that scale can bring, such as greater network capacity and spectrum licenses. In a head-to-head battle for customers over a homogenous product, it is likely to lose, because it cannot match its rivals' lower costs of business (a fact that Sprint is perhaps demonstrating). So to grow, the company has diversified its product to attract customers dissatisfied by traditional offerings from the larger carriers – most notably by zero-rating traffic from streaming music providers. The company recognized that a large niche of consumers regularly stream music to mobile devices and would be attracted to a plan that allows them to do so free. More recently, the company has extended the idea to streaming video through its Binge On promotion, using an algorithm that compresses video to SD quality to optimize delivery over the T-Mobile network.[15]

Although many advocates have condemned T-Mobile's innovative business model, none has yet accepted the FCC's invitation to ask whether the service violates the awkwardly-worded "no unreasonable interference/disadvantage" standard. This is likely because the Commission would almost certainly find the practice reasonable. T-Mobile is the third-largest provider in a scale-driven industry. It lacks market power and is in no position to extract super-competitive profits or otherwise harm consumers. Unlimited streaming music (or video) is appealing to a large niche of consumers, who are better off with this option than without. Consumers uninterested in the options available (or uninterested in cross-subsidizing the binge viewing of their fellow customers) can choose a different plan or a different carrier. T-Mobile now offers a product that its rivals do not, which enhances competition among wireless providers. Moreover, the Commission noted that the CEO of upstart streaming service Grooveshark praised T-Mobile's program for helping make little-known offerings available to a wider customer base.[16] Perhaps for this reason, Chairman Tom Wheeler described T-Mobile's offering as "highly innovative and highly competitive" and therefore "clearly" permissible under the *Open Internet* order.[17]

Comcast: Stream TV

Comcast's Stream TV offers a different permutation on the zero-rating issue. Stream allows Comcast Internet customers access to live television from a dozen networks on laptops, tablets, and mobile devices within the customer's home for $15/month.[18] The service appears to target millennial "cord nevers" who are unlikely to sign up for traditional cable service and who increasingly prefer to watch video on Internet devices rather than on a traditional television set. A Comcast spokesperson recently clarified that in those markets where Comcast offers usage-based pricing, Stream TV consumption does not count against the customer's monthly data limits.[19]

Initially, it's important to note that Stream TV likely complies with the *Open Internet* order. As Comcast explained, Stream TV is not a video service delivered over the Internet, like Netflix or Hulu. Rather, it is an IP cable service delivered over the company's managed cable network. The Commission explicitly exempted from the *Open Internet* order IP cable, facilities-based VoIP, and other application-level services that share capacity with broadband access, although it retained jurisdiction to examine whether individual offerings undermine investment, innovation, competition, or end-user benefits.[20]

Nonetheless, critics argue that the Stream TV offering could "unfairly crush competitors and make it hard for consumers to get rival services from Netflix."[21] But the fact that some may choose Stream over Netflix is not alone sufficient reason to ban it. The question is not whether Stream is competitive, but whether it is unfairly competitive.

If one considers Stream a substitute for online video like Netflix, then the objection seems obvious. Netflix video counts toward the customer's monthly limit. Stream video does not. Therefore, given the choice, customers will choose Stream, which penalizes Netflix for not being zero-rated.

But if Stream is instead a substitute for traditional cable, as Comcast suggests, the analogy begins to break down. After all, traditional cable viewing has never counted against a customer's monthly data limit, and few, if any, critics argue it should be. And there is much to suggest that Stream is more like traditional cable than Netflix. Like cable, Stream offers a handful of linear cable channels, whereas Netflix and most online video rivals rely upon an on-demand model. Like cable, Stream uses a separate part of the Comcast network for delivery, rather than the channels dedicated to broadband Internet access. And like cable, Stream is only available within the subscriber's home, whereas most over-the-top video can be consumed wherever the customer has Internet access.

Netflix and other over-the-top providers have long thrived alongside traditional cable offerings, despite being subject to monthly data limits. Customers like that Netflix is cheaper than cable and available on multiple devices. Comcast has found a way for cable to match those advantages to meet the tastes of the next generation of video consumers. This new option is a boon, not a curse, for consumers, who now have more options to choose from. Importantly, customers who choose not to watch cable and rely entirely upon Netflix are no worse off now than they were before Stream appeared in the marketplace. But the competitive pressure of an improving cable product will push Netflix to continue to in-novate and improve. While Comcast benefits from delivery over a dedicated network, that benefit stems from billions of dollars in infrastructure investment building networks to the home that its non-facilities-based competitors did not incur.

V. Conclusion

Usage-based pricing and especially zero-rating of traffic challenge the long-asserted notion that what's good for edge providers is good for consumers. Some actions by broadband providers, or agreements between broadband and edge providers, might fore-close competition in the edge space. But antitrust scholar Herbert Hovenkamp notes that most vertical integration is "either com-petitively neutral or affirmatively desirable because it promotes efficiency."[22] Some may promote competition in the edge space, as Deezer and Grooveshark would testify. Others may promote greater competition in the broadband provider sector, as Music Freedom does. Or they may offer consumers more options, as Stream TV does. One cannot pass judgment on a class of business innovations based simply upon the generic effect it may have on one company. The regulator must instead engage in a careful study, on a case-by-case basis, of the overall effects that a particu-lar practice may have on the market overall.

This is perhaps why the Supreme Court has long warned that antitrust law protects "competition, not competitors."[23] Contrary to what often appears to be the FCC's objective, the protection of edge providers should not be a goal in itself. It should be pursued only as a tool to protect consumers from harm. The Commission should allow broadband companies to experiment with innovative new offerings such as usage-based pricing and zero-rated traffic, because this experimentation is likely to give rise to consumer-beneficial alternatives to traditional broadband access models. Absent proof of anticompetitive harm, policy should promote innovation that enhances consumers' ability to access the content and services they desire – no matter where in the Internet ecosystem this innovation occurs.

* Daniel A. Lyons, an Associate Professor of Law at Boston College Law School, is a Member of the Free State Foundation's Board of Academic Advisors. The Free State Foundation is an independent, nonpartisan free market-oriented think tank located in Rockville, Maryland.

Endnotes

1   Appropriate Framework for Broadband Access to the Internet over Wireline Facilities, CC Docket No. 02-33, FCC 05-151, ¶ 4 (Sept. 23, 2005) (emphasis added).

2   Michael K. Powell, Chairman, Federal Communications Commission, Preserving Internet Freedom: Guiding Principles for the Industry 3, Remarks at the Silicon Flatirons Symposium (Feb. 8, 2004), available at https://apps.fcc.gov/edocs_public/attachmatch/DOC-243556A1.pdf.

3   In re Protecting and Promoting the Open Internet, GN Docket No. 14-28, ¶ 80 (Feb. 26, 2015), available at https://apps.fcc.gov/edocs_public/attachmatch/FCC-15-24A1.pdf (hereafter "2015 rules").

4   *Id.*¶ 20.

5   See Leo Mirani, When Net Neutrality Backfires: Chile Just Killed Free Access to Wikipedia and Facebook, Quartz, May 30, 2014, available at http://qz.com/215064/when-net-neutrality-backfires-chile-just-killed-free-access-to-wikipedia-and-facebook/.

6   *Preserving the Open Internet: Broadband Industry Practices*, GN Docket No. 09-191, WC Docket No. 07-52, Report and Order, 25 FCC Rcd. 17905 ¶ 43 (2010) (hereafter "2010 Rules").

7   2015 Rules, supra note 3, at ¶ 21.

8   Comments of Christopher S. Yoo, In re Preserving the Open Internet: Broadband Industry Practices, GN Docket No. 09-191, WC Docket No. 07-52, at 13.

9   *Id.*

10   See Daniel A. Lyons, *Innovations in Mobile Broadband Pricing*, 92 U. Denv. L. Rev. 453 (2015), available at http://papers.ssrn.com/sol3/papers.cfm?abstract_id=2418563.

11 See Daniel A. Lyons, *Why Broadband Pricing Freedom is Good for Consumers*, Free State Foundation *Perspectives*, Vol. 7, No. 32 (2012), available at http://www.freestatefoundation.org/images/Why_Broadband_Pricing_Freedom_Is_Good_For_Consumers_111612.pdf.

12 2010 Rules, *supra* note 6, at ¶ 72.

13 Monica Riese, SXSW Interactive Awards Announced, Austin Chronicle, Mar. 12, 2013, available at http://www.austinchronicle.com/daily/sxsw/2013-03-12/sxsw-interactive-awards-announced/.

14 *See* Tim Bradshaw, *Deezer Takes On Spotify with Orange Deal*, Financial Times (Sept. 7, 2011), available at http://www.ft.com/cms/s/2/66bdfd5c-d939-11e0-bd7e-00144feabdc0.html#axzz3p1nlygDb.

15 Eli Lubitch, T-Mobile's Bold "Binge On" Promise Compresses the Competition, BEAMR Blog, Dec. 10, 2015, available at http://blog.beamr.com/blog/2015/12/10/t-mobiles-bold-binge-on-promise-compresses-the-competition/.

16 2015 Rules, supra note 3, at ¶ 151 n. 362.

17 Jon Brodkin, T-Mobile's Data Cap Exemption for Video Gets FCC Chairman's Approval, ArsTechnica, Nov. 19, 2015, available at http://arstechnica.com/business/2015/11/t-mobiles-data-cap-exemption-for-video-gets-fcc-chairmans-approval/.

18 See Press Release, July 12, 2015, available at http://corporate.comcast.com/comcast-voices/a-new-streaming-tv-service-from-comcast.

19 Jon Brodkin, Comcast Launches Streaming TV Service that Doesn't Count Against Data Caps, ArsTechnica, Nov. 19, 2015, available at http://arstechnica.com/business/2015/11/comcast-launches-online-tv-service-that-doesnt-count-against-data-caps/.

20 2015 Rules, supra note 3, at ¶210.

21   Brian Fung, Comcast's Stream TV is Sparking
     a Controversy Over the Future of the Internet,
     Washington Post, Nov. 20, 2015, available at https://www.
     washingtonpost.com/news/the-switch/wp/2015/11/20/
     does-comcasts-streaming-tv-service-run-afoul-of-net-neutrality/.

22   Phillip E. Areeda & Herbert Hovenkamp, 3B Antitrust Law: An
     Analysis of Antitrust Principles and Their Application ¶ 756a, at 9
     (3d ed. 2008).

23   Cargill, Inc. v. Monfort of Colo., Inc., 479 U.S. 104, 110 (1986)
     (quoting Brown Shoe Co. v. United States, 370 U.S. 294, 320
     (1962)) (internal quotation mark omitted).

9.
Wireless Report Data Undermine the FCC's Rationale for Regulation

Seth L. Cooper *

Perspectives from FSF Scholars, January 22, 2016, Vol. 11, No. 5

Introduction and Summary

Amidst the 2015 holiday season, the Federal Communications Commission released its *Eighteenth Wireless Competition Report*. Considering the FCC's less-than-stellar track record in timely producing some of its statutorily-required reports, perhaps the Commission simply hoped to release the report before year's end. Then again, the December 23 release of *Eighteenth Report* all but guaranteed reduced public attention.

What the Commission might prefer the public overlook is this: The *Eighteenth Report* contains evidence that undermines the Commission's rationale for imposing public utility-style regulation on mobile broadband services as it did in its recent *Open Internet Order* (2015). One obvious line of evidence is supplied by the large scale of competing wireless broadband provider coverage. Another line of evidence consists of market trends toward no-contract wireless services and elimination of early Termination Fees (ETFs), thereby reducing consumer switching costs.

A highly dubious premise of the *Open Internet Order* was that "broadband providers have both the incentive and the ability to act as gatekeepers standing between edge providers and consumers." The *Order* claimed that broadband providers – including mobile broadband providers – can "block access altogether," "target competitors, including competitors to their own video services," and "extract unfair tolls." Of course, effective market competition provides a strong check against any such incentives or the ability to engage in such anti-consumer behavior. Service providers in competitive markets risk losing subscribers to rival providers.

The Commission's dubious mobile broadband gatekeeper premise is refuted by data cited in the *Eighteenth Report* concerning competing wireless provider coverage. As of the middle of last year – around the time the FCC issued its *Open Internet Order* – 91.5% of the U.S. population lived in census blocks with 4G LTE network coverage provided by three or more wireless providers. At that same time, 82.2% lived in census blocks with four or more LTE providers. The existence of the scale of such competing mobile coverage was widely recognized when the *Open Internet Order* was released. But the Commission ignored it. Even so, updated numbers in the *Eighteenth Report* mark a significant advancement in LTE capabilities. This fresh data points up the reality of wireless consumer choices and the emptiness of the *Order*'s gatekeeper label for mobile broadband.

Another shaky premise of the *Open Internet Order* was that "[s]witching costs are a significant factor in enabling the ability of mobile broadband providers to act as gatekeepers." Wireless provider-imposed ETFs were singled out as one such barrier. Yet the *Eighteenth Report*'s observations of pro-consumer marketplace trends in wireless service and pricing options also challenge this underpinning of the *Order*. Those trends indicate that wireless consumers enjoy competitive choices among a variety of service plans, along with easier ability and incentives to switch providers. The *Eighteenth Report* identifies "a rapid shift from traditional postpaid contract plans to no-contract plans." Bring your own device ("BYOD") and handset leasing options are now widely available to consumers. Also, "marketing tactics have increasingly focused on Early Termination Fee ("ETF") buyouts to encourage customers to switch from rivals."

Needless to say, the *Eighteenth Report* contains further data – highlighted below – that shows the competitive state of the wireless market. But were the Commission to expressly conclude that there is effective competition in the market, it would be tantamount to admitting its rationale for imposing public utility regulation on mobile broadband is faulty. Making such a concession would put the Commission's public utility regulatory policy for mobile broadband into further legal jeopardy. Unfortunately, the Commission appears locked into its public utility agenda, regardless of the reality of the wireless market data.

The Commission continues to kick up obstructionist dust over the answer to whether or not there is effective competition in the wireless market. But a clear-sighted view of the data contained in the *Eighteenth Report* supports the conclusion that – yes – there is effective wireless competition. A clear sighted view of 4G LTE provider coverage and pro-consumer trends toward reduced switching costs also supports the conclusion that the Commission's rationale for imposing public utility regulation on mobile broadband was wrongheaded.

The Data Demonstrate the Existence of Effective Competition

Section 332(c) of the Communications Act requires the FCC to annually prepare a report that includes an analysis of "whether or not there is effective competition" in the wireless market. The *Eighteenth Wireless Competition Report* is chock full of evidence to support a positive finding of effective competition in the wireless market:

- Over the past five years, wireless providers' capital investments totaled $146 billion. Carriers spent between $31 and $32 billion in capital investment in 2014 alone;

- Total mobile wireless connections grew from between 336-340 million in December 2013 to between 355-357 million in December 2014 – an annual growth rate of 5%-6%;

- 97.2% percent of the U.S. population lived in census blocks with coverage by at least three wireless providers as of July 2015, and 91.7% lived in census blocks with four or more providers;

- 91.5% of population lived in census blocks with 4G LTE network coverage provided by three or more wireless providers as of July 2015, and 82.2% lived in census blocks with four or more providers offering LTE coverage;

- Three major wireless providers – Verizon Wireless, AT&T, and T-Mobile – have already begun deploying voice-over-LTE (VoLTE) service across their networks, while Sprint and U.S. Cellular are planning or testing future VoLTE deployments;

- "[T]he price (in constant dollars) of wireless service has continued to decline." From December 2013 to December 2014, the annual Wireless Telephone Services consumer price index (CPI) decreased 2.1% while the overall CPI increased 1.6%;

- "Smartphone use has continued to increase over the last three years…although smartphone use flattened out in 2015." About 77% of mobile subscribers had a smartphone in the third quarter of 2015, compared to

51% in the third quarter of 2012. And the smartphone penetration rate among new phone purchases was 88% in the third quarter of 2015, up from 67% just three years earlier;

- In 2014, the Apple App Store generated about $10 billion in revenue to developers, while the Google Play marketplace paid out $7 billion to app developers. App revenue from both app stores is expected to double by 2018;

- "[T]he number of American homes with only wireless telephones continues to grow." As of June 2015, 46.7% of adults live in a household that is wireless-only and 55.3% of children live in a wireless-only household;

Regrettably – but not unexpectedly – the *Eighteenth Wireless Competition Report* excuses itself from making any finding or conclusion about "whether or not there is effective competition" in the wireless market. That makes the fifth consecutive report in which the Commission has dodged the question underlying its mandated analysis. (On prior occasions I have explained that Section 332(c) is best understood as requiring a "yes" or "no" finding. And earlier reports made such a finding.) Instead, the *Eighteenth Report* repeats some now-familiar but misguided boilerplate. That is, the *Report* claims that any conclusion about "whether or not there is effective competition" somehow would be misleading and that no accepted definition of "effective competition" exits among antitrust authorities.

A Competing Provider Analysis Brings Effective Wireless Competition Into Focus

In truth, the FCC already has a standard for measuring effective competition, which it uses in the local cable services context. As

I have previously written, the "FCC Should Be Clear and Consistent on Effective Competition in the Wireless Market." The Commission's wireless report analysis of the wireless market should include a "competing provider test" analysis similar to the one it applies pursuant to Section 623 concerning whether effective competition exists in local video markets.

An analogous application of the Section 623 competing provider test to wireless would presume that there is effective competition in a metropolitan statistical area if: (1) it is served by at least two competing wireless providers, each of which offers wireless voice and broadband services to at least 50% of all area households; and (2) the number of subscribers other than the area's largest provider exceeds 15 percent of area households.

The Commission should also consider nationwide population coverage by multiple wireless providers in light of competing provider test thresholds. Effective competition in the wireless market is clearly evident according to this type of metric. As indicated above, estimates cited by the *Eighteenth Report* reveal that 97.2% percent of the U.S. population lived in census blocks with coverage by at least three wireless providers as of July 2015, and 91.7% lived in census blocks with four or more providers. As of that same date, 91.5% of population lived in census blocks with 4G LTE network coverage provided by three or more wireless providers, and 82.2% lived in census blocks with four or more LTE providers.

There is also agency precedent for applying an analysis similar to the competing provider test for purposes of determining whether or not effective competition exists in the wireless market. As my above-cited *Perspectives from FSF Scholars* paper pointed out:

> The *Ninth, Tenth,* and *Eleventh Wireless Competition Reports* pointed to the percentage of the total U.S. population living in counties with

access to multiple providers as one indicator of "effective competition" in the wireless market. Additionally, the *Tenth* and *Eleventh Reports* pointed to the absence of any one provider having a dominant share of the market.

The Commission's *Effective Competition Order* (2015) offers yet another precedent, this one very recent, for the Commission to build on. Based on its competing provider analysis, the *Order* established a rebuttable presumption that local cable markets are subject to effective competition. Positive findings of effective competition for wireless services should similarly lead the Commission to adopt a rebuttable presumption that there is effective competition in national and local wireless markets. Such an approach would bring into sharper focus the strong competition that characterizes today's wireless market. And it should prompt the Commission to demand actual evidence of consumer harm before it intervenes in the market with new regulation.

Wireless Provider Coverage Data Undermine the Rationale for Public Utility Regulation

Unfortunately, the Commission is now beset by a conflict-of-interest concerning the status of wireless competition. That conflict-of-interest centers on the Commission's policy agenda for subjecting mobile broadband Internet access to Title II public utility-style regulation. Any path to admitting there is effective competition in the wireless market would call into question the validity of the Commission's application of public utility regulation to wireless services. The *Open Internet Order* was premised on wireless broadband providers possessing a monopoly-like gatekeeper power over wireless broadband network traffic.

The validity of the Commission's wireless gatekeeper premise is significantly undermined by data cited in the *Eighteenth Report* concerning competing provider coverage. Availability of other alternative broadband providers and platforms calls that premise into further question.

Pro-Consumer Trends Undermine the Rationale for Public Utility Regulation

The *Eighteenth Report* also contains another line of evidence that casts serious doubt on the viability of the Commission's premise for subjecting wireless to public utility regulation – the observations of pro-consumer marketplace trends in wireless service and pricing options. Those trends indicate that wireless consumers enjoy competitive choices among a variety of service plans, along with easier ability and incentives to switch providers. Pro-consumer trends in the wireless market also undermine a significant aspect of the Commission's rationale for imposing public utility regulation on wireless services.

Until 2013 most wireless subscribers to postpaid plans signed two-year service contracts in exchange for discounted or subsidized handsets that consumers paid for through higher monthly fees. Consumers who wanted out of their two-year contracts were typically subject to early-termination fees. But as the *Eighteenth Report* points out, since 2013 there has been "a rapid shift from traditional postpaid contract plans to no-contract plans." Bring your own device ("BYOD") and handset leasing options are now commonplace in wireless service offerings. Further, "marketing tactics have increasingly focused on Early Termination Fee ("ETF") buyouts to encourage customers to switch from rivals. ETF buyouts typically include a cash payment or credit to reimburse ETFs for customers on traditional contract plans, or alternatively, to pay off the remaining balance of an EIP, plus a separate device credit for trading in a customer's current handset."

This rapid market trend toward no-contract options and away from ETFs drastically undercuts concerns about wireless consumer lock-in or barriers to switching providers. In critical respects, the *Eighteenth Report*'s observations about wireless switching costs and incentives undermines one of the Commission's pretenses for subjecting mobile broadband Internet access to Title II public utility regulation. As the Commission stated in its *Open Internet Order*: "[W]e agree with those commenters that argue that mobile broadband providers have the incentives and ability to engage in practices that would threaten the open nature of the Internet, in part due to consumer switching costs. Switching costs are a significant factor in enabling the ability of mobile broadband providers to act as gatekeepers." The *Order* continued: "[C]ustomers may face a variety of hassle-related and financial switching costs. Disconnecting an existing service and activating a new one may involve early termination fees (ETFs), coordinating with multiple members of a family plan, billing set-up, transferring personal files, and porting phone numbers, each of which may create delays or difficulties for customers."

Switching nearly any service will typically impose some minimal costs on a consumer, whether in time or money. Those holds true even for free services, such as email, where a user might have to migrate old e-mail address books or messages to a new service account. It is a serious fact-specific question as to when switching costs for a given service might become so onerous as to produce consumer harm and require regulation to alleviate. In the *Open Internet Order*, ETFs were cited by the Commission as factors that ostensibly made wireless providers into "gatekeepers" and made wireless services uniquely subject to switching costs. Even assuming the Commission was correct, with the rise of no-contract postpaid wireless options and ETF buyouts its concerns appear grossly exaggerated. And they can scarcely constitute a sound basis for subjecting mobile broadband to public utility regulation.

The timing of the wireless market's trending toward no-contract services and away from ETFs makes even more pronounced the wrongheadedness of the *Open Internet Order*'s imposition of public utility regulations on mobile broadband on account of switching costs. The *Order's* depiction of the market was at odds with market reality on the day it was released. The *Eighteenth Report* covers the second half of 2014 and the first half of 2015 – the very same timeframe in which the Commission prepared and issued its *Order*.

Worse still is the fact that the Commission relied on a static picture of the mobile broadband market's service and pricing in imposing public utility regulation on mobile broadband. In just a handful of years, the wireless market has transformed from inter-connected analog voice services to a myriad of digital high-speed data communications services. The wireless market is a dynamic one, not a static one. The Commission should know better. The *Eighteenth Report* suggests it does know better, as it recognizes that "there is wide variety of pricing plans offered by the different mobile wireless service providers that vary along several dimensions, and that may frequently change."

Conclusion

A clear-sighted view of the data contained in the *Eighteenth Wireless Competition Report* demonstrates that there is effective competition in the wireless market. A clear-sighted view of 4G LTE provider coverage and pro-consumer trends toward reduced switching costs also supports the conclusion that the Commission's rationale for imposing public utility regulation on mobile broadband was wrongheaded. The Commission may continue to duck or downplay these developments in the wireless market, out of concern for defending its own regulatory preferences. But consumers more closely connected to marketplace reality are enjoying the variety of choices and sources of value offered by mobile broadband services in a wireless market that is effectively competitive.

* Seth L. Cooper is a Senior Fellow of the Free State Foundation, an independent, nonpartisan free market-oriented think tank located in Rockville, Maryland.

Further Readings

Randolph J. May and Michael J. Horney, "Mobile Broadband is a Substitute for Fixed Broadband," *FSF Blog* (January 14, 2016).

Comments of the Free State Foundation, *Annual Report and Analysis of Competitive Market Conditions with Respect to Mobile Wireless, Including Commercial Mobile Services*, WT Docket No. 15-125 (June 29, 2015).

Seth L. Cooper, "FCC Should Be Clear and Consistent on Effective Competition in the Wireless Market," *Perspectives from FSF Scholars*, Vol. 10, No. 21 (June 22, 2015).

Randolph J. May, "Dealing Effectively With Effective Competition," *FSF Blog* (April 17, 2015).

Seth L. Cooper, "FCC Should Adopt the Deregulatory Proposal for Local Cable Rates," *Perspectives from FSF Scholars*, Vol. 10, No. 15 (April 9, 2015).

Randolph J. May, "It's the Consumer, Stupid! – Part III" *FSF Blog* (January 13, 2015).

Randolph J. May, "Thinking the Unthinkable – Part III" *FSF Blog* (November 3, 2014).

Reply Comments of the Free State Foundation, *Protecting and Promoting the Open Internet*, GN Docket No. 14-28 (September 15, 2014).

Randolph J. May, "Net Neutrality vs. Consumers," *Perspectives from FSF Scholars*, Vol. 9, No. 29 (August 26, 2014).

Comments of the Free State Foundation, *Protecting and Promoting the Open Internet*, GN Docket No. 14-28 (July 15, 2014).

Comments of the Free State Foundation, *Annual Report and Analysis of Competitive Market Conditions with Respect to Mobile Wireless, Including Commercial Mobile Services*, WT Docket No. 13-135 (July 1, 2013).

Seth L. Cooper, "Convergent Market Calls for Serious Intermodal Competition Assessments," *Perspectives from FSF Scholars*, Vol. 8, No. 12 (May 2, 2013).

Seth L. Cooper, "FCC Report Reconfirms the Reality of Wireless Innovation and Competition," *FSF Blog* (March 27, 2013).

10.
FCC's Vague "General Conduct" Standard Deserves Closer Legal Scrutiny

Seth L. Cooper *

Perspectives from FSF Scholars, July 6, 2016, Vol. 11, No. 23

The June 14 decision in *US Telecom v. FCC* counts as a sweeping victory for government regulation of the Internet. Surprisingly, a 2-1 majority of the D.C. Circuit panel upheld every aspect of the *Open Internet Order*.

The FCC's Title II reclassification of broadband services was the lead legal issue of the case. But secondary issues also at stake are important too. The *Open Internet Order*'s "general conduct" standard governing broadband services was challenged as unconstitutionally vague. From a rule of law standpoint, the D.C. Circuit's legal validation of the "general conduct" standard is particularly troublesome. And, as a matter of policy, this aspect of the court's decision likely will lead to severe restrictions on Internet innovation.

I. The General Conduct Standard

The Commission's "general conduct standard" poses a serious regulatory certainty problem. It is unclear what kind of conduct the standard allows and what kind of conduct it prohibits. The D.C. Circuit's light-touch review of a heavy-handed regulatory order offered an unsatisfying analysis of the general conduct standard, too eagerly downplaying its vagueness.

In its *Open Internet Order*, the Commission supplemented its bright line rules restricting blocking, throttling, and paid prioritization with a "general conduct" or "no-unreasonable interference/disadvantage" rule. The "general conduct rule" provides that broadband service providers:

> [S]hall not unreasonably interfere with or unreasonably disadvantage (i) end users' ability to select, access, and use broadband Internet access service or the lawful Internet content, applications, services, or devices of their choice, or (ii) edge providers' ability to make lawful content, applications, services, or devices available to end users. Reasonable network management shall not be considered a violation of this rule.

The Commission says it will apply the standard on case-by-case basis, considering the "totality of the circumstances." To guide that case-by-case analysis, the Commission adopted what it conceded is "a non-exhaustive list of factors" to be considered. And the Commission also conceded it will attach different relative weight to the factors, whenever and however it deems fit. It's useful here to recall what the late Justice Antonin Scalia once called the "ol' totality of circumstances test." In *United States v. Mead Corp.* (2001), he said, "applications of this test…are of little use to bench and bar."

In the D.C. Circuit, the general conduct standard was subject to a facial challenge under the "void for vagueness" doctrine. Modern Supreme Court jurisprudence grounds the doctrine in the Fifth Amendment Due Process Clause. Two concerns animate the "void for vagueness" doctrine: first, regulated parties should know what is required of them; second, precision and guidance are needed to prevent arbitrary or discriminatory enforcement. And when government "regulates business conduct and imposes civil penalties" due process of law is satisfied if the regulation is "sufficiently specific that a reasonably prudent person, familiar with the conditions the regulations are meant to address and the objectives the regulations are meant to achieve, would have fair warning of what the regulations required."

For its part, the D.C. Circuit majority concluded in cursory fashion that the general conduct standard provides a good enough indication regarding its application to satisfy the void for vagueness doctrine. The D.C. Circuit pointed to the Commission's regulatory objectives: to complement the bright-line rules and to protect consumers' ability to access Internet content of their choice. The court also declared that the role of the advisory opinion process "cures it of any potential lingering constitutional deficiency."

However, it is hardly persuasive that a stated objective of the general conduct standard is to serve as an appendage or backstop to the bright-line rules. The net effect of this view is that the named and yet-to-be-named factors will collectively function like blurred lines. Moreover, although the D.C. Circuit praised the advisory process as a cure for constitutional defects, in truth it's more like a placebo. Advisory opinion authority is delegated to the Commission's Enforcement Bureau, which retains absolute discretion on whether or when to issue such opinions. And, significantly, the *Open Internet Order* acknowledges they are non-binding on the Commission.

According to the D.C. Circuit, the Commission's specification of the seven factors and description of how they will be interpreted and applied mitigated against any finding of unconstitutional vagueness. The D.C. Circuit contended that "[a]ny ambiguity in the General Conduct Rule is therefore a far cry from the kind of vagueness this court considered problematic in *Timpinaro v. SEC* [1993]." In *Timpinaro*, the D.C. Circuit struck down the SEC's multi-factor rule defining a professional trading account as unconstitutionally vague. A key supposed difference in the SEC case is that "'five of the seven factors…are subject to seemingly open ended interpretation.'"

II. An Open-Ended Multi-Factor Test That Is Inherently Vague

Not so fast. A closer reading of the *Open Internet Order* and its description of the factors – footnotes and all – suggests that at least five of the seven factors at issue in *US Telecom v. FCC* are likewise subject to open-ended interpretation. Indeed, when considered in light of the entirety of the *Order* and the Commission's rationale, several factors become downright fuzzy:

End user control – According to the Commission, a practice that allows end-user control is deemed less likely to violate the general conduct standard. However, "we are cognizant that user control and network control are not mutually exclusive and that many practices will fall somewhere on a spectrum from more-end-user-controlled to more broadband provider-controlled." Also, "there may be practices controlled entirely by broadband providers that nonetheless satisfy" the standard. Clear? I don't think so.

Competitive effects – The Commission says that practices that have anti-competitive effects "that would have a dampening effect on innovation, interrupting the virtuous cycle" will likely violate the general conduct standard. The Commission "will also review the extent of an entity's vertical integration as well as its relationships with affiliated entities." But the *Open Internet Order* eschewed reliance on antitrust-like market power analysis of competitive conduct. That leaves unanswered what set of principles one could derive a competitive analysis from. Clearer? I don't think so.

Effect on Innovation, Investment, or Broadband Deployment – "[P]ractices that stifle innovation, investment, or broadband deployment" likely violate the general conduct standard. This factor sounds like it is in part a protection for broadband providers from self-harm. In any event, the *Order* nowhere identifies a criterion for measuring or anticipating such effects. Clear now? I don't think so.

Application agnostic – Practices that "do[] not differentiate in treatment of traffic, or if it differentiates in treatment of traffic without reference to the content, application, or device" will likely not violate the general conduct standard. "We note, however, that there do exist circumstances where application-agnostic practices raise competitive concerns, and as such may violate our standards to protect the open Internet." Also, left unclear is whether there might be instances where reasonable network management might allow for departures from application-agnostic practices. Helpful? I don't think so.

Standard practices – The Commission "will consider whether a practice conforms to best practices and technical standards adopted by open, broadly representative, and independent Internet engineering, governance initiatives, or standards-setting organization" [sic]. In other words, the general conduct standard will be based in part on a factor that will consider but not necessarily rely on another standard adopted by other bodies. Got that? I don't think so.

Those five factors are much too open-ended to provide fair warning about what is required. As Senior Judge Williams wrote in dissent, "these factors themselves are vague and unhelpful at resolving the uncertainty." They contain no safe harbor "numerical thresholds" as the D.C. Circuit suggested might save the regulation in *Timpinaro*. Remember also they are "nonexhaustive factors" – the Commission can add new factors as it suits them. That's hardly the precision and guidance required to guide against arbitrary and capricious enforcement.

The general conduct factor concerning consumer protection against unfair and deceptive billing practices, including cramming and spamming, may offer more clarity than the rest. So too, the free expression factor may offer more clarity than the factors just listed. Even so, it is difficult to see how the free expression factor improves upon protections from the no blocking and no throttling bright-line rules. Indeed, even in their pro-Title II amicus brief, the Electronic Frontier Foundation and the ACLU expressed constitutional free speech concerns with the general conduct standard "because of its sheer complexity." Wrote EFF-ACLU: "The burden on regulated providers in litigating such cases *ad hoc* would discourage innovation and impede the Internet's continued growth as a platform for speech, commerce, and social activity." To no avail, EFF-ACLU even urged the D.C. Circuit to consider a limiting construction of the standard to avoid the vagueness problem.

III. Conclusion

It's especially regrettable that the vagueness problems with the general conduct standard received so little attention in the rulemaking process and in the litigation thus far. The Notice of Proposed Rulemaking proposed only a less intrusive "commercially reasonableness" standard for network management – which it later jettisoned. The D.C. Circuit concluded, again in cursory fashion, that the Commission's request for "comment on whether [it] should adopt a different rule to govern broadband providers' practices to protect and promote Internet openness" was sufficient notice of the general conduct standard.

Understandably, the Commission's mistaken Title II reclassification has consumed the most attention in this case. Often in litigation the lead issue effectively becomes *the* issue. And in wide ranging and complex cases – like *US Telecom v. FCC* – other momentous legal issues that would normally receive significant attention from litigants and judges receive curtailed treatment.

The general conduct standard shouldn't be let off the hook so easily. It is possible that the vagueness issue will receive closer scrutiny in a possible future appeal – and it should. Or a future facial challenge to the standard or as-applied challenge may be the vehicle for finally giving the issue a full vetting. In any event, the rule of law deserves no less.

* Seth L. Cooper is a Senior Fellow of the Free State Foundation, an independent, nonpartisan free market-oriented think tank located in Rockville, Maryland.

Further Readings

Tim Brennan, "Is the Open Internet Order an 'Economics-Free Zone'?" *Perspectives from FSF Scholars*, Vol. 11, No. 22 (June 28, 2016).

Daniel A. Lyons, "Net Neutrality's Path to the Supreme Court: Chevron and the 'Major Questions' Exception," *Perspectives from FSF Scholars*, Vol. 11, No. 21 (June 24, 2016).

Seth Cooper, Gus Hurwitz, Daniel Lyons, and Richard Epstein, "Free State Foundation Scholars React to the D.C. Circuit's Decision on the Open Internet Order," *Perspectives from FSF Scholars*, Vol. 11, No. 18 (June 15, 2016).

Randolph J. May and Seth L. Cooper, "The FCC Threatens the Rule of Law: A Focus on Agency Enforcement," *The Federalist Society Review*, Vol. 17, Issue 2 (May 24, 2016).

Seth L. Cooper, "Wireless Report Data Undermine the FCC's Rationale for Regulation," *Perspectives from FSF Scholars*, Vol. 11, No. 5 (January 22, 2016).

Enrique Armijo, "Net Neutrality, Administrative Procedure, and Presidential Overreach," *Perspectives from FSF Scholars*, Vol. 10, No. 39 (November 19, 2015).

Randolph J. May, "Regulatory Uncertainty Harms Broadband Investment and the Economy," *FSF Blog* (December 10, 2015).

Daniel A. Lyons, "Title II Classification *Is* Rate Regulation," *Perspectives from FSF Scholars*, Vol. 10, No. 12 (February 25, 2015).

Randolph J. May, "Is the FCC Lawless?" *The Hill* (February 25, 2015).

Robert W. Crandall, "Regulation Won't Preserve a Dynamic and 'Open' Internet," *Perspectives from FSF Scholars*, Vol. 10, No. 10 (February 20, 2015).

Justin (Gus) Hurwitz, "Regulating the Most Powerful Network Ever," *Perspectives from FSF Scholars*, Vol. 10, No. 9 (February 19, 2015).

Dennis L. Weisman, "Regulating Under the Influence: The FCC's Title II Initiative for Broadband," *Perspectives from FSF Scholars*, Vol. 11, No. 7 (February 13, 2015).

Part III – Economic Perspectives Regarding Public Utility Regulation Under the FCC's 2015 *Title II Order*

11.
Is the Open Internet Order an "Economics-Free Zone"?

Tim Brennan *

Perspectives from FSF Scholars, June 28, 2016, Vol. 11, No. 22

Hi. I'm the "economics-free zone" guy.

For those of you not deep in the weeds of net neutrality policy in the United States, I'm the former chief economist of the Federal Communications Commission who used that line as part of a self-deprecating joke I told to defuse tensions at a small but contentious conference on the FCC's *Open Internet Order*. In the Order, the FCC controversially redefined broadband provision as a service subject to "Title II" common carrier regulation. It claimed it was doing so to prevent broadband providers – cable, fiber, wireless – from charging content suppliers for delivery at all or for higher quality service, a practice known in the trade as "paid prioritization."

The phrase "economics-free zone" ended up in a Wall Street Journal op-ed and went somewhat viral, to my regret and chagrin. A panel of the D.C. Circuit Court of Appeals recently upheld the *Open Internet Order* by a 2-1 vote, but the dissenting judge, unfortunately from my perspective, made reference to what was part of an off-hand joke.

I do not deny saying the *Open Internet Order* was an "economics-free zone," although I did not say it intending to slap the FCC. As will be apparent, I do disagree with the Order. But I do so in the belief that the FCC was pursuing its genuine view of the public interest. But now with allusions to this phrase in a judicial opinion, I want to set the record straight.

Not Economics-Free, But …

Economics was in the *Open Internet Order,* but a fair amount of the economics was wrong, unsupported, or irrelevant. Some examples:

Wrong. Even if broadband providers have market power because subscribers are slow to switch broadband services, as the FCC claims, the FCC incorrectly found such providers lack an incentive to provide high-quality service. Broadband providers, in the FCC's scenario, will raise their prices up to where subscribers will consider switching. The better the broadband service, including content "neutrality" if that's what consumers want, the higher that switching price will be – establishing the incentive that the FCC denies.

Unsupported. The FCC claims that a "virtuous circle" preventing broadband providers from charging content suppliers for delivery will lead to more content suppliers, driving up demand for broadband. But the circle can work in reverse – charging content suppliers for delivery creates incentives to attract subscribers by cutting retail rates. The FCC didn't use its best supporting evidence – that broadband providers had already largely adopted net neutrality – as that would have undermined the necessity of regulation.

Irrelevant. In arguing against "paid prioritization," the FCC cited articles on what economists call "price discrimination" to suggest possible harms when a broadband provider charges different prices to content providers that compete with each other. But paid prioritization isn't price discrimination; it's charging higher prices for better service. These price discrimination articles are relevant only if there is no cost to providing better service, such as guaranteed speeds or minimal transmission gaps. The only way this can be done at no cost is that the existing capacity can provide the best service anyone would ever want at any time – that is, that capacity can never be congested. While counterintuitive, especially for wireless, some nonetheless believe this premise.

Potentially Better Alternatives

Nevertheless, there could be economic reasons warranting some rules regarding the relationship between broadband providers and content suppliers. First, if broadband providers advertise content-neutral practices, they should be held accountable as a matter of consumer protection. It remains to be seen whether we are better served by the FCC taking over this responsibility from the Federal Trade Commission, which lost its authority over broadband following its reclassification by the FCC as a common carrier.

Second, if the value of broadband depends on confidence that others can open links I post (unless they lie behind a paywall, like The Wall Street Journal's), minimum-quality regulation may be warranted. While the FCC nominally rejected a minimum-quality rule, its "no throttling" rule implies minimum quality – the lower limit of what would presumably be acceptable quality, "unthrottled," to use the FCC's terminology. A minimum-quality rule would also address concerns that a broadband provider would diminish the quality of non-priority service. The theoretical appeal of a minimum quality does not make such a rule operational, enforceable, and worth any costs in additional congestion management.

A third possibility is regulating the price broadband suppliers charge for content delivery. The FCC effectively has done this. Its "no blocking" rule implies a regulated price of zero for content delivery, because broadband service cannot be denied to content suppliers who do not pay. But the novelty – and highly problematic nature – of this approach is not appreciated by some. The federal government has been reluctant to regulate sectors without a clear monopoly provider, because competition between only two firms is likely to lead to a better outcome than regulation. And regulation is even harder to justify when, as in this case, technological progress rapidly changes the definition of the product one is trying to regulate.

The D.C. Circuit Court of Appeals that sustained the FCC's *Open Internet Order* apparently believed that the agency properly took those difficulties into account in its decision to take this unusual step. I do wonder how the FCC's effective imposition of zero price regulation on content delivery was legally sustainable, when it denied that content delivery was a service that could be regulated. That denial could be taken to be a device to evade having to show that a zero delivery price is just and reasonable. I guess the Administrative Procedures Act prohibits arbitrary and capricious regulations, but perhaps not bizarre ones.

And on the Other Side

Opponents of the FCC's order had flawed arguments too. One often heard that these issues should be left for antitrust. Yet consumer protection, minimum quality standards, and price regulation all lie outside the scope of antitrust. Moreover, in a series of rulings since 2004, the Supreme Court has limited the role of antitrust in industries subject to federal regulation.

Opponents also claimed that but for President Obama's

support of Title II, the FCC would have adopted less stringent rules. I was not privy to discussions and phone calls, and I was not on the FCC's staff when the Order was adopted. But in my year as the FCC's Chief Economist, my sense was that more stringent intervention was always a serious and widely preferred option on the table.

What Might Be Going On?

If broadband providers had largely followed net neutrality principles, why did both sides fight so hard over this regulation? The broadband industry may have feared even stronger regulation. The FCC in 2005 had classified broadband as an unregulated "information service" so providers would not have to provide regulated wholesale service to competitors with no facilities of their own. Now that the FCC's Order has reversed this position, regulated wholesale service may be on the way.

Moreover, when the New York Times reports the D.C. Circuit's decision as "Court Backs Treating Internet as Utility," one has to ask when customer rates, untouched by the Order, will eventually be regulated as well.

From the government's side, a speculative possibility may be that if the U.S. government allows broadband providers to charge content suppliers for delivery, it will invite broadband providers in other countries to extract delivery fees from the dominant U.S. content suppliers, such as Google, Facebook, Amazon, and Netflix.

Finally, the FCC's motive may not involve economics and competition. It rather may be "public interest" civic and cultural populist values that the Internet "belongs to everybody." The *Open Internet Order* was not really an economics-free zone. But were those civic and cultural norms the real concern, perhaps it should have been.

* Tim Brennan is a member of the Free State Foundation's Board of Academic Advisors and a professor of public policy at the University of Maryland, Baltimore County. He was Chief Economist at the Federal Communications Commission (2014).

12.
Allow Paid Prioritization on the Internet for More, Not Less, Capital Investment

Theodore R. Bolema *

Perspectives from FSF Scholars, May 1, 2017, Vol. 12, No. 16

I. Introduction and Summary

Paid prioritization is an agreement between a broadband provider and an "edge provider," or provider of content or services over the Internet, that allows the edge provider to pay for priority treatment in a "fast lane" to jump around congestion on the Internet.

Net neutrality proponents argue that having a fast lane for those willing to pay for it would place their competitors in the "slow" lane at a disadvantage. Moreover, they sometimes claim that broadband providers have the incentive to make the slow lane even less attractive by avoiding investing in it, so that firms in the slow lane would eventually be forced to pay to move to the fast lane. Thus, they argue, regulatory intervention is needed to protect those left in the slow lane.

In its March 2015 *Open Internet Order*, the Federal Communication Commission's response was to prohibit broadband providers, on a blanket basis, from charging for paid prioritization. The 2015 Commission majority argued that by taking away this potential revenue source for broadband providers, the FCC would give them the incentive to increase their investment in broadband capacity.[1] Significantly, the FCC adopted the blanket ban on paid prioritization even though, to that point, under the Commission's previous light touch" regulatory regime, Internet service providers (ISPs) had not adopted in any meaningful way the paid prioritization practices that the agency decided to prohibit based on speculative potential harms.

The FCC will now be reexamining the existing net neutrality rules, including the blanket ban on paid prioritization, in the new rulemaking announced by Chairman Ajit Pai on April 26.[2] As FCC Commissioner Michael O'Rielly stated at the time of Chairman Pai's announcement: "Even ardent supporters of net neutrality recognize, as I've said before, that some amount of traffic differentiation or 'prioritization' must be allowed or even encouraged."[3]

My two previous *Perspectives* discussed the relationship between regulation and investment. The first, Understanding Why More Regulation Means Less Investment, showed how, as a general proposition across industries, more regulation has several negative implications for capital investment in an industry. The second, How Too Much Unnecessary Regulation Is Impeding Telecommunications Sector Investment, showed how accumulating regulatory burdens has led to less investment in the telecommunication sector, and applied the key principles to three current regulatory issues that have significant implications for telecommunications investment.

Now, this timely *Perspectives* applies this analysis to a specific regulatory restriction, the ban on paid prioritization in the FCC's 2015 *Open Internet Order*. It describes how, despite the claim by the FCC majority in 2015 that this restriction will lead to more capital investment in broadband infrastructure, banning paid prioritization, along with the other adverse effects of the *Open Internet Order*, has held back investment in broadband infrastructure.

This loss of infrastructure investment will only increase over time. This *Perspectives* then describes how similar paid prioritization practices in other industries have led to more capital investment and greater benefits for ultimate consumers. It also discusses certain industries that are likely to be held back in the future because they are prohibited from paying for the prioritization they will need to assure the quality of their service.

The FCC majority asserted in 2015 that unregulated broadband providers have an economic incentive to restrict end users and edge providers from freely connecting. Using paid prioritization to restrict access, the FCC argued, lets broadband providers (1) reduce their cost of making new capacity investment and (2) increase their profits by extracting payments from edge providers competing for limited capacity that has been restricted by the lack of investment. Thus, under the FCC's conjecture, banning providers from charging for faster access or other enhancements to their service was supposed to take away the incentive for ISPs to "choke" consumer demand for its product, and instead encourage them to invest more in broadband infrastructure.

The FCC's justification for banning paid prioritization is little more than the theory of how a monopolist protected from competition can restrict output in order to drive up prices. This theory does not apply, however, when a broadband provider does not have a large enough market share and faces current competition, because any attempts to extract high and inefficient tolls will be defeated when customers switch to a competing provider.

Moreover, if entry by other providers is reasonably easy, even a firm that is currently a monopolist will see that any inefficient tolls it imposes will only give other providers more incentive to enter the market and take its customers. When entry like this can occur, profits based on taking advantage of leverage from high market shares in a dynamic market are not sustainable because they attract new investment and entry by competitors.

Rather than address any possible concerns, however

conjectural, about consumer harm in ways that will encourage more competition, the FCC chose to take a regulatory approach that will only discourage new entry and investment by ISPs. Limiting the revenue streams and pricing arrangements for new entrants reduces their incentive to make the investments necessary to enter and compete effectively against current broadband providers.

Various forms of paid prioritization arrangements can be found in many different industries, including grocery stores, book store chains, air travel, sports stadiums, and package delivery services. Governments seeking to attract private investment for road construction are expanding their optional toll lanes for commuters willing to pay to avoid congestion. Having prioritization as a revenue source increases the incentive for providers in other industries to make capital investments needed to compete for customers willing to pay for priority service. These capital investments provide benefits to all customers, even the ones who are not paying for prioritization. In general, these pricing arrangements have not worked to exclude those who do not pay for prioritization, and more typically lead to lower prices and better service for the most cost-conscious customers.

Autonomous vehicles, interactive e-learning, and telemedicine are examples of applications in their early stages of development that require a high level of end-to-end reliability. Investors may be unwilling to take the risk of investing in these applications if they cannot be assured of reliable prioritized broadband connections. Some edge providers that are sensitive to delays may be better off paying extra, in the same way that some people shipping packages are willing to pay extra for priority mail services, while others will not see enough benefit from avoiding delays to justify paying more.

Governmental units in the future may find that Amber alerts, severe weather alerts, and Homeland Security warnings should be given priority over other Internet traffic. As emergency services evolve, governments may want to have paid prioritization available as an option for these and other highly time-sensitive functions.

Paid prioritization should not be treated as unambiguously pro-competitive or anticompetitive on a blanket basis. Less intrusive responses used to address market failures and inefficiencies in other industries, including antitrust, consumer protection laws, and minimum quality standards, may be sufficient to prevent the harms that could plausibly result from paid prioritization by broadband providers. These alternative approaches have the advantage of not destroying the real benefits and efficiencies that can be achieved using voluntary contracting arrangements, which will encourage more investment by both broadband providers and edge providers whose applications require fast and reliable broadband connections.

In the absence of much evidence of actual harm from paid prioritization on the Internet, the FCC should proceed with caution. Whatever policy the FCC develops, it should seek to address the specific harm that arises from clearly anticompetitive instances of paid priority, while encouraging the experimentation and innovation that will attract capital investment and provide benefits to consumers.

II. The FCC's Ban on Paid Prioritization

The FCC based its ban on paid prioritization on the Internet in large part on what it called the "virtuous cycle" theory:

> The key insight of the virtuous cycle is that broadband providers have both the incentive and the ability to act as gatekeepers standing between edge providers and consumers. As gatekeepers, they can block access altogether; they can target competitors, including competitors to their own

video services; and they can extract unfair tolls. Such conduct would, as the Commission concluded in 2010, "reduce the rate of innovation at the edge and, in turn, the likely rate of improvements to network infrastructure." In other words, when a broadband provider acts as a gatekeeper, it actually chokes consumer demand for the very broadband product it can supply.[4]

This questionable theory gave the FCC the basis for arguing that its restrictions on broadband providers would encourage investment by ISPs by taking away their incentive to restrict output and drive up their tolls. In doing so, the Internet would be divided into "fast lanes" for those who pay the tolls and "slow lanes" for those that don't. Thus, the FCC adopted the following prohibition:

> No Paid Prioritization. Paid prioritization occurs when a broadband provider accepts payment (monetary or otherwise) to manage its network in a way that benefits particular content, applications, services, or devices. To protect against "fast lanes," this Order adopts a rule that establishes that:

>> A person engaged in the provision of broadband Internet access service, insofar as such person is so engaged, shall not engage in paid prioritization. "Paid prioritization" refers to the management of a broadband provider's network to directly or indirectly favor some traffic over other traffic, including through use of techniques such as traffic shaping, prioritization, resource reservation, or other forms of preferential traffic management, either (a) in exchange

for consideration (monetary or otherwise) from a third party, or (b) to benefit an affiliated entity.[5]

III. How the FCC's Ban on Paid Prioritization Discourages Capital Investment

The FCC majority asserted in 2015 that unregulated broadband providers have an economic incentive to restrict end users and edge providers from freely connecting. Doing so, the FCC argued, offers broadband providers two benefits: They can avoid the cost of making new investments and they can increase their profits by extracting payments from edge providers competing for limited capacity that has been restricted by the lack of investment. Thus, under the FCC's conjecture, banning providers from charging for faster access or other enhancements to their service was supposed to take away the incentive for ISPs to "choke" consumer demand for its product, and instead encourage them to invest more in broadband infrastructure.

The 2015 FCC majority offered very little evidence that these conjectured harms were occurring, despite the history of the Internet having been allowed to develop to that point with only "light touch" regulatory oversight. As then-Commissioner Ajit Pai pointed out in his dissent to the *Open Internet Order*:

> Nevertheless, the Order ominously claims that "[t]hreats to Internet openness remain today," that broadband providers "hold all the tools necessary to deceive consumers, degrade content or disfavor the content that they don't like," and that the FCC continues "to hear concerns about other broadband provider practices involving blocking or degrading third-party applications." The evidence of these continuing threats? There is none; it's all anecdote,

hypothesis, and hysteria. A small ISP in North Carolina allegedly blocked VoIP calls a decade ago. Comcast capped BitTorrent traffic to ease upload congestion eight years ago. Apple introduced FaceTime over Wi-Fi first, cellular networks later. Examples this picayune and stale aren't enough to tell a coherent story about net neutrality. The bogeyman never had it so easy.

But the Order trots out other horribles: "[B]roadband providers have both the incentive and the ability to act as gatekeepers," "the potential to cause a variety of other negative externalities that hurt the open nature of the Internet," and "the incentive and ability to engage in paid prioritization" or other "consumer harms." The common thread linking these and countless other exhibits is that they simply do not exist. One could read the entire document—and I did—without finding anything more than hypothesized harms. One would think that a broken Internet marketplace would be rife with anticompetitive examples. But the agency doesn't list them. And it's not for a lack of effort.[6]

Apart from the thinness of evidence of actual harm from any existing Internet practices, the FCC's theory is little more than the standard economic analysis of the incentives of a monopolist or firm in a highly-concentrated market to restrict output in order to drive up prices. For this theory to be plausible, two conditions must be met: The broadband provider (1) must have a large market share and (2) must have some protection from new firms entering the market.

If, however, the broadband provider does not have a large market share and faces current competition, then any attempts to extract high and inefficient tolls will be defeated when customers switch to a competing provider. And if entry by other providers is reasonably easy, then even a firm that is currently a monopolist will see that any inefficient tolls it imposes will only give other providers more incentive to enter the market and take its customers.

Thus, profits based on taking advantage of leverage from high market shares in a dynamic market are not sustainable because they attract new entry and investment by competitors. More competition like this should be encouraged, because it defeats the incentive to restrict capacity described by the "virtuous cycle" theory, and also bring new firms into the market that can be the source of new innovation.

Rather than address any possible concerns, however conjectural, about consumer harm in ways that will encourage more competition, the FCC chose to take a regulatory approach that can only discourage new entry and investment. As Commissioner Michael O'Rielly pointed out in his dissent to the *Open Internet Order*:

> And yet, literally nothing in this Order will promote competition among Internet service providers. To the contrary, reclassifying broadband, applying the bulk of Title II rules, and half-heartedly forbearing from the rest "for now" will drive smaller competitors out of business and leave the rest in regulatory vassalage. Monopoly rules designed for the monopoly era will inevitably move us in the direction of a monopoly.[7]

By restricting how ISPs can benefit from their new investments, the FCC made entry and new capital investment by potential competing broadband providers less attractive for new providers. Unless incumbent providers can be confident that they are well-insulated from new competition or expansion by smaller providers, they do not have the incentive to restrict capacity to raise tolls, because other providers can provide that capacity through their investments.

The 2015 FCC majority's analysis of how banning paid prioritization will encourage more investment is contradicted by conventional economic analysis, and now is being exposed as misguided by the recent decline in capital investment. My previous *Perspectives*, How Too Much Unnecessary Regulation Is Impeding Telecommunications Sector Investment, described the growing evidence that accumulating regulatory burdens generally in the telecommunication sector have been accompanied by less capital investment in broadband capacity. There is also considerable evidence and analysis from other markets where paid prioritization has been used, which shows that the paid prioritization arrangements that develop without regulatory intervention generally benefit consumers and lead to more capital investment in their industries.

IV. Consumers Benefit from Paid Prioritization in Many Markets

Paid prioritization is used in many markets, regulated and unregulated. It takes a variety of different forms, so that it is possible to point out differences between the paid prioritization in different markets. Even so, it is striking how common the practice is, and how widely accepted different forms of paid prioritization have become in other markets. More to the point, these forms of paid prioritization do not lead to firms trying to choke off demand for their products. More typically, they lead to more investment and more choices that benefit customers.

Many states now offer optional "fast lanes" on highways, for a toll, as a way of attracting investment for highway projects.[8] Commuters who want to avoid the tolls are not excluded from the highway, while commuters willing to pay for a faster trip have that option. Virginia has used the optional toll system to attract private investment for highway construction, and recently announced that it had attracted new private investment to expand the optional toll network to another stretch of highway I-395. Terry McAuliffe, Virginia's Democratic governor, touted this expansion as "the latest step in our ongoing effort to move more people and provide more travel choices in one of the most congested corridors in the country."[9] Even the drivers who do not pay the toll benefit from the private investment and expansion of the highway, which reduces congestion in the non-toll lanes while giving them the option to use the faster toll lanes when they wish to use them.

One paid prioritization practice that has been extensively analyzed over many years by the U.S. antitrust agencies is the payment of slotting allowances at grocery stores, bookstores, and other retailers.[10] A supplier seeking to sell its merchandise at a retailer may agree to pay a slotting allowance to have its products placed on the most favorable shelf space, while other suppliers may be willing to accept less favorable shelf space. Rather than excluding new suppliers, paying for favorable slotting may be an effective strategy for introducing new products that would otherwise require more spending on advertising and other forms of marketing. Notably, some major retailers, including Wal-Mart, choose not to charge slotting allowances, while other retailers have charged them for decades. Former Federal Trade Commissioner Joshua D. Wright, in his review of the economic effects of slotting allowances, finds that the practice generally benefits consumers:

> My results show that slotting contracts are primarily associated with brand-shifting of sales within a product category, but not increases in category level prices or a reduction in category output or variety. To the extent that slotting

contract revenue is passed on to consumers in
competitive retail markets, an assumption generally
warranted in the grocery retail industry, the results
here imply that slotting contract competition is
likely to benefit consumers. In sum, my findings
are inconsistent with anticompetitive theories and,
in practice, demonstrate that such agreements
are likely procompetitive and consistent with the
promotional services theory.[11]

The paid prioritizations prohibited by the *Open Internet Order*, the slotting allowances charged by retailers, and optional toll fast lanes on highways all take the form of upstream parties paying the downstream distributors for favorable treatment. Final consumers in these markets are not directly involved in forming the paid prioritization arrangement, but they are still affected by the arrangements. In other markets, however, final customers have shown they are willing to enter into paid prioritization arrangements from the downstream side of the transaction, and usually are better off for it.

Airlines charge passengers extra for a variety of different enhanced services, including first class seats, priority boarding, seats with extra leg room, and seats near the front of the airplane. The airlines' goal is not to exclude passengers who do not pay for these services or force them to pay higher fares. In fact, the opposite is much more likely. Regular air travelers can see that airlines try to fill as many seats as they can, and even market "bare bones" fares that may not include any choice of seat, for example. The customers who do not pay extra for better service are unlikely to be made worse off by having other customers on the plane who choose to pay extra for better service. Instead, it is more likely that customers who pay less are better off if the airline chooses to offer more flights over more routes to attract customers willing to pay extra, and then offers lower fares to fill the remaining seats on those flights. Put another way, forcing airlines to charge the same fares for everyone will almost certainly lead to fewer flights and routes, as well as less investment for increasing capacity, all of which will raise fares and reduce choices for the most cost-conscious customers, leaving them worse off as a result.

Similarly, sports stadiums have luxury boxes and favorable seating available for higher prices, but that does not mean the stadium operators want to exclude other customers who are unwilling to pay for premium seating or amenities, or build smaller stadiums to restrict the supply of seats in order to drive up prices. Having some customers pay extra for better seats generates revenue that may be used to upgrade the stadium, to offer extra amenities that may be available to all customers, or to attract free agent professional players to make their teams more competitive, all of which may make seeing the games more enjoyable for all fans, even the ones paying the least.

Of course, the U.S. Postal Service also offers its own fast lane and slow lane for customers. Customers can pay for various forms of expedited delivery for packages and mail, or they can pay regular postage or bulk rates for mail that will be delivered on a slower schedule. Federal Express and other private delivery services offer similar expedited "fast lane" schedules, but that has not given them the incentive to slow down deliveries of packages for customers who do not pay extra for higher priority deliveries.[12]

These and other variations on paid prioritization have developed over time, as suppliers, distributors, and customers have experimented in the market to find the arrangements that provide the greatest benefits. So long as markets are reasonably competitive, arrangements that try to take advantage of other parties will not survive for long, because the parties at a disadvantage can find alternative arrangements.

V. When Paid Prioritization May Be Necessary for Attracting Investment.

Some specialized services for dedicated users require a high level of end-to-end reliability. The benefits from video phone calls and video streams from Netflix, for example, are reduced when they are delayed by slow buffering. Other Internet uses do not necessarily require a prioritized Internet connection. Email traffic, most file downloading, and many other uses lose little of their value if their transmission is delayed somewhat in a slow lane, although too long a delay could diminish their value.

Governmental units in the future may find that Amber alerts, severe weather alerts, and Homeland Security warnings should be given priority over other Internet traffic. As emergency services evolve, governments may want to have paid prioritization available as an option for these and other highly time-sensitive functions.

As capital investment in broadband capacity continues to decline and demand for Internet services increases, the ban on paid prioritization will affect both services that are sensitive to delays and services that are not. Those that are harmed may be better off paying extra, in the same way that some people shipping packages are willing to pay extra for priority mail services, while others will not see enough benefit from avoiding delays to justify paying more.

The analysis above describes how slotting allowances in retail stores are more likely to encourage entry by new suppliers rather than discourage them from entering. For many new suppliers, paying for favorable slotting may be a cost-effective strategy for introducing a new product. Similarly, paid prioritization could be cost effective for Internet start-ups to allow the new entrants to promote their services as being in the "fast lane," and therefore give them more incentive to invest in their own operations.

Many future web applications are unlikely to develop if their developers cannot be assured that they will have access to fast and stable Internet connections. Autonomous vehicles, interactive e-learning, and telemedicine are examples of applications in their early stages of development. Investors may be unwilling to take the risk of investing in these applications if they cannot be assured of reliable prioritized broadband connections.

The FCC's prohibition against charging for paid prioritization may well prevent these services from developing, as well as other new applications that no one is yet anticipating. Their loss is difficult to measure because we cannot easily anticipate what will never happen. Less intrusive responses used to address market failures and inefficiencies in other industries, including antitrust, consumer protection laws, and minimum quality standards, may be sufficient to prevent the harms that could plausibly result from paid prioritization by broadband providers. These alternative approaches have the advantage of not destroying the real benefits and efficiencies that can be achieved using voluntary contracting arrangements, and not driving off investment for the applications and new entrants that may require fast and reliable broadband connections.

VI. Conclusion

Paid prioritization should not be treated as unambiguously pro-competitive or anticompetitive on a blanket basis. Paid prioritization potentially can discourage investment, and can lead to harm to final customers when too little investment in infrastructure may give ISPs market power as they allocate limited capacity.

Addressing these situations with a sweeping regulatory ban on paid prioritization creates two problems that are likely to be worse than the problem the regulation is intended to address. First, such a ban prevents the paid prioritization arrangements that benefit final customers, who may want to pay extra for the reliability needed for their applications. Second, the ban on paid prioritization limits the return on investment by ISPs, so that they will invest less in situations where they do not have market power and protection from new entry.

Any concerns about broadband providers having market power and abusing it should be addressed in a more focused way on a case-by-case basis that does not throw out the baby with the bathwater. In the absence of much evidence of actual harm from paid prioritization on the Internet, the FCC should proceed with caution. Whatever policy the FCC develops, it should seek to address the specific harm that arises from clearly anticompetitive instances of paid priority, while encouraging the experimentation and innovation that will attract capital investment and provide benefits to consumers.

* Theodore R. Bolema is a Senior Fellow of the Free State Foundation, an independent, nonpartisan free market-oriented think tank located in Rockville, Maryland.

Endnotes

1   Federal Communications Commission, FCC-15-24, In Re Protecting and Promoting the Open Internet (hereinafter *Open Internet Order*), March 12, 2015 at ¶ 18 (footnotes omitted).

2   Ajit Pai, "Remarks of FCC Chairman Ajit Pai at the Newseum: "The Future of Internet Freedom," (Speech, Washington, DC, April 28, 2017), available at https://www.fcc.gov/document/chairman-pai-speech-future-internet-regulation.

3   Michael O'Rielly, "Remarks of FCC Commissioner Michael O'Rielly at the FreedomWorks and Small Business & Entrepreneurial Council Event (Speech, Washington, DC, April 28, 2017), available at https://www.fcc.gov/document/commissioner-oriilly-remarks-freedomworks-sbe-council-event.

4   *Id.* at ¶ 20 (footnotes omitted).

5   *Id.* at ¶ 18 (footnotes omitted).

6   Dissenting Statement of Commissioner Ajit Pai, *Open Internet Order* (footnotes omitted).

7   Dissenting Statement of Commissioner Michael O'Rielly, *Open Internet Order* (footnotes omitted).

8   Robert Krol, "Tolling the Freeway: Congestion Pricing and the Economics of Managing Traffic." Mercatus Working Paper, Mercatus Center at George Mason University, Arlington, VA, May 5, 2016, available at https://www.mercatus.org/publication/tolling-freeway-congestion-pricing-and-economics-managing-traffic.

9   Terry McAuliffe, "Governor McAuliffe Announces Acceptance of Private Sector Proposal to Deliver I-395 Express Lanes Extension, News Release, February 25, 2017, available at https://governor.virginia.gov/newsroom/newsarticle?articleId=19616.

10 *See, e.g.,* Federal Trade Commission Staff Study, "Slotting Allowances in the Retail Grocery Industry, Selected Case Studies in Five Product Categories," Nov. 2003, available at https://www.ftc.gov/reports/use-slotting-allowances-retail-grocery-industry.

11 Joshua D. Wright, "Slotting Contracts and Consumers Welfare, *Antitrust Law Journal,* Vol. 74, No. 2 (2007), 439, at 440.

12 *See* Kenneth Button and David Christiansen, "Unleashing Innovation: The Deregulation of Air Cargo Transportation." Mercatus on Policy, Mercatus Center at George Mason University, Arlington, VA, December 15, 2014, available at https://www.mercatus.org/publication/unleashing-innovation-deregulation-air-cargo-transportation.

13.
What Do Economists Know About Net Neutrality Regulation?

Quite a Lot, and the FCC Should Pay Attention

James E. Prieger *

Perspectives from FSF Scholars, September 6, 2017, Vol. 12, No. 29

The initial and reply comments from interested parties are in, the arguments have been made, and now the Federal Communications Commission will decide whether to move beyond its 2015 order that placed the Internet under public-utility regulation designed during the Great Depression. There have been many parties on both sides of the issue who have embraced the devolution of the discussion into sloganeering – Net Neutrality! Discrimination is bad! Or: Internet Freedom! Freedom is good!

Millions of comments have been filed with the FCC, albeit most with little understanding of the issues involved other than that many celebrities and the "cool" tech companies say that the FCC wants to "kill net neutrality." Nevertheless, there are serious policy debates to be had about the open Internet, and reasoned arguments to be made. I want to focus here on the economic

analysis of key net neutrality rules such as bans on paid prioritization of Internet traffic, blocking or throttling traffic, or disallow-
ance of fees to deliver traffic to the "edge" of the network. While
economic analysis is less headline-grabbing than the slogans, and
no academic discipline can perfectly predict the evolution of such
a rapidly changing technology such as the Internet, it is important
to look at what we already have learned as the FCC crafts its policy.

What do economists know about the issues surrounding
net neutrality and Internet regulation? I joined an ad hoc group
of academic economists headed up by Mark Jamison from the
University of Florida in putting together an objective compilation
of known results about net neutrality issues from the economic
literature.[1] Our goal was to set forth whether the economic
literature supports net-neutrality-type restrictions on Internet
service providers. To be transparent about which studies we
would discuss, we limited the pool to articles published in the
top 300[2] peer-reviewed economics journals. The restriction to
top journals is important, because not all peer-reviewed journals
have uniformly high standards for publication. We didn't feel that
a paper slipped into The Lower Slobobian Journal of Economics
(to make up a title to avoid offending any researchers) should be
treated with the same respect or weight as research that appeared
in American Economic Review or even Information Economics
and Policy.

The restriction to peer-reviewed journals is also highly
important, because (as the old saying goes) "figures don't lie but
liars figure." Since we reviewed theoretical rather than empirical
papers,[3] perhaps a more germane recasting of the saying would
be that "theorems follow logically from axioms and assumptions,
but people with varying motives and interests make the assumptions." The record of the contentious FCC proceedings touching
on net neutrality is filled with references to unpublished studies
of highly varying quality and white papers that did not undergo
peer review. Such studies can be useful to fill gaps in the literature,

but sometimes their choice of data, assumptions, modeling, and analysis are guided by narrow self-interest.[4] Before beginning a review of what we found, it is also important to note that I do not claim in this essay to speak for any of the other co-signers of our summary.

So, what did we find? Of surprise to none of us, we found that (as in most other areas of economic analysis of complex issues) most models predict a variety of possible outcomes. This is not to say that "anything can happen" or to throw up our hands and conclude that economic theory is useless. When a model predicts several outcomes, it is usually because the modeler admitted a range of assumptions about consumer behavior or the nature of competition among Internet providers. Therefore, it becomes important to examine which assumptions lead to which outcomes, rather than merely counting the number of articles that lead to one's desired conclusion.

The first question we looked at was the economic impact of prohibitions on Internet service providers offering enhanced features (such as "fast lanes") to content providers like Netflix or YouTube. The twelve articles we found that addressed this issue generally concluded that such prohibitions decrease economic welfare (the total benefits created by a market, whether accruing to consumers, content providers, or ISPs). Models yielding the opposite conclusion usually seemed to have unrealistic assumptions hard-wired into them, such as assuming that ISPs have fixed instead of varying bandwidth – a very short-term assumption – or assuming away content providers who might value lower-quality, lower-cost (or higher-quality, higher-cost) service. This result is not surprising; whether net neutrality proponents admit it or not, the Internet is already built upon fast lanes for content providers valuing high-quality higher cost arrangements in the form of "peering connections" and "content delivery servers" – because that is what these edge providers want.

The second question is whether those sorts of net neutrality prohibitions on ISPs' offerings hinder the ISPs' investment in networks. At first the answer seems like it should be obvious: the more freedom the ISPs have to design services that content providers want, the more profit they can make from the network, and therefore the more incentive they would have to invest in its maintenance and expansion. Indeed, several of the five papers we found demonstrate that logic: prohibitions lead to less investment. Other outcomes are theoretically possible, however, if (for example) fast lanes do not stimulate enough additional content by remaining content providers to make up for small content providers who might leave the network. The real-world relevance of such results appears to be limited, though, since the freedom to tailor offerings to content providers also gives freedom to find ways to keep such small providers profitably on the network. Keep these results in mind when the FCC Chairman says that to change his thinking about net neutrality, it would take credible economic analysis that shows that the 2015 regulations increased infrastructure investment. Given the expectations from the literature, the burden when turning to data is properly placed on those who wish to claim that onerous regulation does not harm investment.

Third, what do we know about how prohibitions on ISPs' enhanced features affect the variety of content and investment in its creation? Again there were a variety of answers in the seven articles we found, but many models concluded that the prohibitions lowered the value of some content, and therefore investment in content and its variety. This is a natural result: with the freedom to design fast lanes and other offerings that provide value to content providers, some types of content become more valuable to create and sell to Internet users. Would the Amazons, Netflixes, and Hulus of the Internet world invest millions in developing new original series if they could only be delivered over congested "slow lanes"? And not all the action happens on the "large and fast" side of the market, where the established content providers reside. Some newer, smaller content providers might prefer low-cost, relatively slow service. For example, a personal calendar organizer app may not require the same speed or quality guarantees as full-motion video would. Without higher-priced fast lanes, there are no lower-priced slower lanes, and content providers desiring slower service may be priced out of the market.

Fourth, do regulations that prevent ISPs from charging to deliver traffic to the edge increase economic welfare? This question has to do with whether an ISP can charge an edge provider to terminate traffic to it, the same way the local phone company on the receiving end of a cross-country call has to pay the originating phone company. The 2015 net neutrality regulations prohibited such payments. Not many papers look at this issue, but we found three. Interestingly, the answers are nuanced. One might think that such charges are necessarily bad for content providers. After all, how could paying to receive traffic be better than getting it delivered for free? In some cases, however, the answer is that paying to receive traffic gives more incentive to the network providers to invest in network quality. With higher quality networks, the edge providers receive more traffic – more clicks – and make more money on advertising, which can outweigh the disadvantage of having to pay the ISP to terminate the traffic. This is just one more example of a common theme to many of the varied results in the literature: the option to pay more to receive higher quality is valued by some content providers. This is not a general result, but each paper we found identified circumstances plausible to at least some settings under which allowing termination charges would increase economic welfare.

What about restrictions on blocking certain types of content? If the ISP is also the "phone company" (to use a dated term), it may wish to block competing services such as VoIP offered by edge providers. Is that always detrimental to economic welfare? Since such actions would appear mainly to stifle competition to the advantage of the incumbent, it is not surprising that the three papers we found conclude that blocking harms welfare under at least some circumstances. Even in this case, however, it remains to be emphasized that anything that lowers the profit from the network to the ISP necessarily lowers incentives to invest in its maintenance, improvement, and extension. It is also worth noting that the antitrust authorities in the U.S. outside the FCC already take a dim view of the legality of such "foreclosure" of essential inputs to rivals, leaving open a viable recourse to the courts should an ISP attempt such behavior.

So with what do these various results leave us? First, with the knowledge that a lot of serious work by scholars is available to help isolate the impact of the various practices prohibited by net neutrality rules. Second, with the impression that – my earlier cautions against "counting results" notwithstanding – the economic rationale against many net neutrality prohibitions is quite strong (with the important potential exception of blocking). Third, with the hope that the FCC will make use of this knowledge this time around...because last time it did not.

It is highly disappointing to recognize that this accumulated body of knowledge was largely ignored in the FCC's 2015 Open Internet Order. Some of the studies we reviewed were published after that time, but most were not. How many of these papers did the FCC cite in its order? Exactly zero. In fact, Michelle Connolly, a former two-time chief economist at the FCC (and with whom I worked there, briefly) and a co-signer of our summary, noted recently that the 2015 Order apparently cited only four peer-reviewed, published papers.[5] None of them were specifically on net neutrality. Three were from a single author – another former chief economist at the FCC, Michael Katz (professor at UC Berkeley and former advisor of mine from my graduate school days) – who has since noted that his papers have results that are the "opposite of the pro-net neutrality narrative" and that he suspects his papers were cited as an "inside joke" by the FCC staffers.[6]

Much has been written about the lowly status of economics at the FCC during the previous administration, and I will not rehearse those arguments. Suffice it to mention two salient points: lawyers at the FCC should not be in charge of picking and choosing which "results" from the economic literature to cite; and policymaking should proceed from analysis of facts, including economic analysis, to regulatory conclusions, not the other way around. Given the faulty reasoning in the 2015 Order, at least concerning the economic issues, I find it either amusing at best and disingenuous at worst that certain "pro net neut" parties claimed in the final round of comments in the FCC's proceedings that the current Commission is relying on "bad analysis," having pre-judged the issue on the basis of "feeble evidence." This, about the FCC Chairman who I heard a few months ago (after wading through the rent-a-protester moblet outside the venue) discuss plans for a new internal Office of Economics and Data to empower economists at the Commission to perform analysis and research to improve policies[7] and who has spoken elsewhere on the importance of economic analysis at the FCC.[8]

I hope and expect, along with many of my fellow economists, that this time around more than lip service will be paid to economic analysis. Politics, administrative feasibility, less-quantifiable social goals such as the "public welfare" – these will always have a place and play a role in policymaking. The solid foundation, however, should be provided by the underlying economics. And on balance, economic analysis gives many reasons to be suspicious of several aspects of the 2015 net neutrality regulations.

* James E. Prieger is Professor of Economics and Public Policy at the Pepperdine University School of Public Policy and a member of the Free State Foundation's Board of Academic Advisors. The Free State Foundation, an independent, nonpartisan free market-oriented think tank located in Rockville, Maryland.

Endnotes

1   Mark A. Jamison, Michelle P. Connolly, Gerald Faulhaber, Janice Hauge, and James Prieger, Economic Scholars' Summary of Economic Literature Regarding Title II Regulation of the Internet, comments filed Before the Federal Communications Commission in the Matter of Restoring Internet Freedom (WC Docket No. 17-108), 2017. The Summary is available at: http://warrington.ufl.edu/centers/purc/purcdocs/papers/1703_Jamison_Review_EconLit_TitleIIRegulationofInternet.pdf. No author received any compensation from any entity for this work.

2   As ascertained from the IDEAS/RePEc Aggregate Rankings for Journals, available at: https://ideas.repec.org/top/top.journals.all.html.

3   Despite the many numbers that have emerged from the various studies performed by interested parties in the record of the FCC proceedings over the last several years, peer-reviewed published empirical work that speaks directly to net neutrality issues is virtually nonexistent. I expect this state of affairs to change greatly during the coming decade as more data from varied experiences and practices becomes available for study.

4   Having participated in such research myself, I do not mean to suggest that self-interest alone or being compensated to perform research necessarily invalidates the findings. Far from it. But it takes much more time than we had, however, to sift through the dozens of white papers in the record. Consider this: when I peer-review a paper that has been submitted to a journal, I may spend anywhere from several hours to a few weeks going over the methodology, thinking about whether best-practice was followed and good research decisions were made, and whether the conclusions follow solidly and logically from the premises or data. Multiply that time by the two to four scholars reviewing any one paper for a journal. That doesn't even include the additional time spent by the editor of the journal assigned to the paper. The

total burden of time invested in checking the quality of articles published in a peer-reviewed journal quickly adds up.

5   "Bringing Economics Back into the Net Neutrality Debate", July 12, 2017, Forbes.com, available at https://www.forbes.com/sites/washingtonbytes/2017/07/12/bringing-economics-back-into-the-net-neutrality-debate/#62e32c3769da.

6   *Ibid.*

7   Ajit Pai, speech given at the American Enterprise Institute in Washington, DC, May 5, 2017, transcription available at https://www.aei.org/wp-content/uploads/2017/04/170505-AEI-A-New-Course-for-the-FCC-Ajit-Pai.pdf.

8   Ajit Pai, "The Importance of Economic Analysis at the FCC," speech given at the Hudson Institute in Washington, DC, April 5, 2017, available at https://apps.fcc.gov/edocs_public/attachmatch/DOC-344248A1.pdf.

14.
Net Neutrality Regulation, Investment, and the American Internet Experience

James E. Prieger *

Perspectives from FSF Scholars, October 25, 2017,
Vol. 12, No. 36

Introduction and Summary

Under what type of government oversight will the Internet eco-system flourish best? The Federal Communications Commission is currently wrestling with this question as it considers whether to move beyond its 2015 *Open Internet Order* that placed Internet service providers (ISPs) under heavy-handed public utility regulation. On one side, supporters of such strict net neutrality claim that the recently promulgated rules promote investment, encourage innovation, and create jobs.[1] On the other side, proponents of light-touch regulation that would allow ISPs more freedom claim the opposite. The latter group — including many academic economists (a group of which I am a member) — argues that letting Internet service providers manage their networks efficiently as they see fit and allowing them freedom to offer paid prioritization or other differential treatment of data will lead to the best outcomes. Permitting ISPs to offer a variety of practices, terms, and conditions in their contracts gives greater flexibility to satisfy the wants and needs of content providers and end users.

I joined a group of fourteen prominent economists recently in a review of the evidence that concluded that stricter regulation of ISPs would harm investment, innovation, and the economy, contrary to the claims of net neutrality boosters.[2] This group of economists has centuries of collective research experience studying exactly these issues. Having myself studied how regulation affects innovation in telecommunications and related industries for twenty years, I am highly skeptical of claims that strict net neutrality regulation will benefit the Internet ecosystem by spurring innovation. A lot of history at home and abroad suggests the opposite will occur. In this Free State Foundation *Perspectives*, I review that evidence, consider whether net neutrality rules outside the United States have encouraged innovation, and address some of the costs for the economy that would follow from hampering incentives to investment.

Allowing the rules in the *Open Internet Order* to remain in place would run counter to much research demonstrating that heavy-handed communications regulation threatens investment and innovation. Several econometric examinations of mine have shown that, in varied U.S. regulatory settings, increased regulation discourages the creation and introduction of new communications services.[3] Other economists studying the rate of telecommunications patenting and communications investment similarly conclude that heavier regulatory burdens are associated with less innovation and investment. The lessons from the economic literature on regulation apply to net neutrality rules such as the ban on paid prioritization of traffic and the saddling of ISPs with old-style public utility regulation. It is no surprise, then, that broadband investment has fallen in the U.S. since the *Open Internet Order* was imposed, during a period in which investment elsewhere in the economy was rising.

Those who foresee dire consequences for the future of the

American Internet seem to ignore the great success and continued growth of the Internet over the past two decades – growth that occurred (until 2015) in the absence of net neutrality regulation. Whether looking at growth in usage of the Internet, how ubiquitous usage is today, growth in the number and quality of broadband access lines, or the emergence and now dominance of the mobile broadband experience, the rapid ascendance of the Internet in the U.S. is nothing short of amazing. And yet somehow now the Internet ecosystem is supposed to be in peril without net neutrality regulation? It is hard to see how increasing the regulatory burdens on broadband service providers during the past two decades would have led to better industry performance or consumer satisfaction.

While the negative consequences for innovation and investment by ISPs is clear, it is also important to examine how net neutrality regulation affects innovation by content providers and app developers — the so-called "edge" of the network. The evidence — as opposed to the opining — here is scant. But one study comparing two European countries with differing net neutrality regimes concludes that lighter-touch regulation is associated with more innovation at the edge.

The stakes are large. Government actions that discourage broadband investment have significant deleterious effects. Broadband is highly important to the U.S. economy, the productivity of businesses, and the satisfaction of consumer wants. The investment that enables broadband services adds directly to the economy through spending on capital goods and the jobs involved with network installation and maintenance. Broadband investment also has a multiplied effect on the economy and job creation through stimulation of supplying industries. Among other things, this implies that regulatory impingement on investment behavior will also negatively affect the economy outside the communications industry.

For all of these reasons, which are addressed in much more

detail in the body of my *Perspectives*, the FCC should follow the empirical evidence and return to light-touch regulation in the Internet ecosystem.

Looking Back: Experience with Regulation, Investment, and Innovation

Investment and innovation is highly sensitive to changes in communications policy. Regulatory policy such as stringent net neutrality rules that restrict how investing firms can gain returns on their investment will push some potential projects into the red, so that businesses will not pursue these opportunities.[4] While the resulting social costs of such onerous regulation do not show up in any accountant's ledger, the negative impact on consumers and firms is nonetheless real. Here are some examples that illustrate the impacts of regulation on innovation.

In one of the earliest comparisons of telecommunications innovation rates under lighter and heavier regulatory regimes, I studied the experiences of the major telecom service providers in the 1990s (the "Baby Bells" and AT&T) when they were introducing then-new services such as voice mail and data services to their customers.[5] My study found that the number of services created during the period of lighter FCC regulation was 60-99 percent higher than the model predicted would have been introduced to consumers if stricter regulation had remained in place.

In other research, I examined the effect of allowing dominant telecom firms more freedom to profit from their investment and innovation, which increases the incentives to innovate. In one Midwestern state I studied, allowing the incumbent telephone companies more freedom to set prices and to escape long regulatory delays when attempting to introduce new services spurred innovation.[6] I estimated that the dominant company in the area created new services 2 to 4.5 times faster than it did under the previous heavy-handed regulatory regime. Moreover, the firm would have introduced up to twelve times as many services had reform been enacted at the beginning of the observed period.

Another study I co-authored assessed how differences in state communications regulation affected investment in broadband infrastructure in the early 2000s.[7] We found evidence consistent with stricter regulation dampening the incentive to deploy broadband infrastructure and service, compared to alternative, lighter-touch regulation.

Many other economists have also studied how regulatory stringency can decrease investment and innovation.[8] One study compared the United States and Japan in the 1980s and 1990s, a time of deregulation in telecommunications in these countries, with Germany, France, and the United Kingdom, which maintained stricter telecom regulation in place.[9] In the U.S. and Japan, the growth rate of new communications patents was higher than in the European countries. In other research, several economists studied a multi-country sample and concluded that the stricter the regulatory regime, the lower the investment in the communications industry and in the economy at large.[10]

While each regulatory regime examined in these studies is unique, the basic message that increased communications regulation discourages investment and innovation appears to be a consistent theme. Whether looking at old-style rate-of-return regulation from the 20th century or the heavy-handed net neutrality regulation under discussion today, the fundamental economic fact remains – the more onerous the regulation in the communications sector, the less investment and innovation there is likely to be.

We can see another example of this principle illustrated by the differing treatment of cable modem and DSL service between 1996 and 2005 in the U.S. This example is particularly germane to the *Open Internet Order*, because, by virtue of a regulatory quirk, DSL service providers were subject to heavy-handed "Title

II" regulation (the 20th Century public utility obligations that the 2015 Order imposed on all ISPs) but cable service providers were not. One recent econometric study showed that the application of Title II regulation retarded investment by DSL service providers by about $1 billion per year, a reduction of about a 5.5 percent.[11]

That study is new but the message is not. That the regulatory disparity between DSL and cable was responsible in part for the early market dominance of cable modem service in the Internet access market has been known at least since the work of MIT economist Jerry Hausman and his co-authors examining the early Internet period.[12]

Given all these empirical links between heavier regulatory burdens and lower investment and innovation, the experience of the U.S. broadband industry after the *Open Internet Order* is no surprise. Since Title II was imposed, U.S. broadband investment has dropped. Theodore R. Bolema explains in another Free State Foundation *Perspectives* why the ban on paid prioritization in the FCC's 2015 *Open Internet Order* has held back investment in broadband infrastructure.[13] Another examination shows that broadband investment in 2016 declined by $3.6 billion compared to 2014 levels.[14]

Now, investment may rise and fall in industries for many reasons, but it is important to note that capital expenditure in the aggregate in the U.S. has been rising every year since the end of the recession in 2009.[15] Clearly, something diminished the incentives to invest in broadband infrastructure that did not affect other industries across the board. Dr. Bolema also discusses why this prohibition on ISPs offering "fast lanes" to content providers who wish them will hold back future investment and innovation in certain industries for which high levels of end-to-end reliability are critical.

Looking at Today: Did Lack of Net Neutrality Regulation Stunt the Growth of the Internet?

We can also consider the great success of the development, provision, and continued growth of the Internet in the United States in the past two decades. Until 2015, when the FCC's *Open Internet Order* imposed burdensome net neutrality rules on the industry, there were no formal rules restricting ISPs' ability to manage networks efficiently and contract freely with content providers. Thus, the strong growth of fixed and, more recently, mobile Internet access, usage, and content occurred under exactly the conditions that critics claim will stymie innovation and freedom on the Internet. Given that present-oriented bias always threatens to skew the picture of the current Internet landscape, it is important to remember how far we have come in such a short time.

Starting from the introduction of the World Wide Web in 1993, Internet usage in the U.S. grew at an explosive rate.[16] Within ten years, 62% of Americans were using the Internet – a rate of adoption almost without precedent in the history of technology. The number of people online has risen and today about 88% of Americans use the Internet in some fashion.[17] One recent study found that an average of 92 percent of adults in the U.S. connect to the Internet over the course of the day.[18] In short, the eager adoption of the Internet in this country in such a brief period has been nothing less than amazing.

To serve this rapidly growing market, ISPs and network operators expanded Internet infrastructure and provision at equally brisk rates. Since 1999, the compound growth rate in broadband lines has averaged an astounding 33.3% per year in the nation. By midyear 2016, there were 370 million broadband Internet access connections, up from only 380,000 in 2005.[19] Virtually every census block (the smallest unit of geography at the Census Bureau) where people live has fixed broadband service available at some speed, even without counting mobile or satellite-based services.[20] About 72% of all broadband Internet access lines were mobile broadband connections, which did not even exist as a consumer service when the FCC first began collecting broadband statistics in 1999.

Merely counting lines obscures the great quality improvements ISPs have made. In 2010, only one in seven fixed broadband lines exceeded 6 Mbps, while in 2016 more than four out of five fixed broadband lines were faster than 10 Mbps.[21] The greatest relative gains in download speed have come in the mobile market. Remember how painfully slow accessing the Internet was on your mobile phone ten years ago? The technologies available in 2007 typically allowed download speeds of no more than about 0.5 Mbps under laboratory conditions,[22] whereas by 2015 the median actual LTE download speeds of all four nationwide mobile network operators were in the range of 6 to 15 Mbps. All this while the price of Internet services fell by roughly 11 percent in official indexes (which do not even adequately account for quality improvements) compared to the overall Consumer Price Index from 2010 to 2017.[23]

Make no mistake: any critic faces a daunting task when arguing that somehow the lack of strict public utility-style net neutrality regulations has led to a less-than-robust broadband ecosystem and high-quality Internet experience for Americans. It is easy to come up with a wish list of how the situation could be improved. One could wish rural broadband were always just as fast and ubiquitous as in urban areas or one could wish that prices were always even lower and quality even higher. However, it is difficult – if not impossible – to see how saddling the Internet service providers with more regulation would have encouraged the additional investment necessary to move those margins.

Looking Across: The International Experience with Net Neutrality

At times the debate about net neutrality regulation appears to be a war of competing claims about investment and innovation. The literature discussed above clearly points out the potential for ill-conceived regulation to hamper investment in the network by ISPs and other network providers. What about innovation "on the edge" of the network, however? Some supporters of net neutrality regimes claim that without such regulation app developers and content providers would not innovate as copiously. Given the great success of the Internet to date, largely in the absence of codified, much less public utility-style net neutrality regulation, this seems like an unpromising case to advance. Nevertheless, let's consider whether the evidence backs it up. As I discussed in a previous FSF Perspectives,[24] the theoretical evidence on this point in the economics literature is mixed. When theory does not indicate clearly which of two possible outcomes is expected, it becomes doubly important to consider empirical evidence – i.e., actual outcomes.

While the relatively recent nature of formalized net neutrality regimes means that empirical studies are just beginning to be performed, evidence is starting to be gathered and assessed. Dr. Roslyn Layton has placed net neutrality regulatory regimes around the world into three categories: hard regimes, in which net neutrality practices are regulated or legislated; soft net neutrality, where self-regulation is the main approach; and places where there are no net neutrality policies or practices. She then compared the experiences of Denmark, with its relatively soft net neutrality rules, and the Netherlands, which has a hard regime.[25] In Denmark, the ISPs and mobile network operators largely regulate themselves regarding net neutrality, which means that while operators do not discriminate based on (for example) the intellectual or political content of the Internet traffic, they are able to offer free data plans that target particular services such as Facebook (i.e., so-called "zero rating" plans). In the Netherlands, on the other hand, net neutrality rules were legislated during the period studied.

Dr. Layton first examined the 250 most used mobile apps within each of these two countries at two points in time (for a total of 1000 apps), and examined which were developed locally (i.e., within the country). This allows her to address the question of which set of practices around net neutrality actually stimulated more innovation around the edge of the network. She found that during 2011-2016, Denmark produced 13% more of the top apps in these countries than did the Netherlands (115 apps were from the former while 102 were from the latter). Furthermore, during this time Denmark was increasing its local share of top apps while that share was falling in the Netherlands. Thus, the differential impact on edge innovation was rising the longer hard net neutrality rules were in place in the latter country.

Dr. Layton also looked at other countries of origin of the top mobile apps used in Denmark and the Netherlands. Strikingly, almost all top apps from outside the U.S.[26] came from countries with either no net neutrality rules or those with soft rules such as self-regulation. Only 20 of the top apps across both these countries – a mere 3.9% of top non-American apps for which the country of origin could be determined – came from countries with hard net neutrality regimes.

While there may be other factors involved in this comparison – after all, this was not a randomized experiment performed in a sterile laboratory setting – it is striking how poorly fares the claim that hardline net neutrality regulation will unleash innovation at the edge of the network. On the other hand, the "permissionless innovation" that mobile network operators and ISPs enjoyed in Denmark meant that they could entice many more users onto next-generation mobile networks with innovative plans involving zero rating. Rather than demonizing zero rating, as net neutrality advocates are wont to do, it appears better to view it as offering something that consumers want at a price they like (free), which increases the size of the network, and which in turn makes the market more attractive for app developers (both those included and those not part of the zero rating).

Looking Ahead: The Costs of Delayed or Deterred Investment

Each dollar of forgone investment destroys valuable economic activity, and not just from the large ISPs.[27] Users of broadband are harmed, as well as the economy generally from lost economic activity. Let's begin with the potential impacts on broadband users. From the literature discussed above, it is clear that by restricting which business arrangements are allowed with an ISP's subscribers and edge developers, ISPs' incentives to invest in next-generation networks can be harmed. Lower quality or less-available broadband access and capacity hurts current and potential broadband users.

Consider business users for the moment. If local businesses have less access to high quality, reliable broadband, or fewer possibilities to adopt services enabled by next-generation networks, their productivity will be harmed. The links between businesses' productivity and their usage of broadband and other forms of information and communications technology (ICT) are well established in the economic literature.

One study found that when businesses invest an additional 10% in ICT, their average labor productivity growth goes up by 0.6%.[28] Broadband adoption in particular is known to increase firms' productivity by 7-10%.[29] Advanced broadband applications of the kind that benefit highly from high-speed broadband networks, such as video communication, virtual private networks, and supply chain management, increase productivity the most.[30] These forgone productivity enhancements for firms can aggregate to significant negative economic impacts in the economy at large, since the positive links between investment in ICT and broadband and economic growth are well attested.[31]

There are other negative economic impacts from reduced investment by Internet service providers. Any investment not undertaken due to overly strict net neutrality regulation will have a multiplied negative impact on the economy. The reason is straightforward: every dollar not invested in communications infrastructure destroys more than a dollar of economic activity in the aggregate. As with any form of investment, spending on broadband infrastructure contributes to economic performance through direct and indirect channels. The direct impacts are obvious, as money is spent on the infrastructure and jobs are created or sustained to deploy and maintain the infrastructure.

However, there are also several indirect negative impacts on the economy, because the lost spending on infrastructure and employment creates ripple effects. When ISPs purchase additional network equipment, the suppliers of the inputs need more inputs themselves to produce their goods. Similarly, those input purchases stimulate demand for inputs in the supporting upstream industries, and so on. Thus, the investment expenditure by ISPs and network operators results in many rounds of new spending because the inputs used by the intermediate and final industries are the outputs of the supplying industries. Similarly, the extra earnings going to workers involved with deploying or maintaining infrastructure stimulate consumption in the broader economy.

Putting all the pieces together, researchers have calculated that each dollar invested in network infrastructure creates about three dollars' worth of economic activity overall.[32] There is also a multiplier for employment: each job created for broadband network construction or maintenance leads to total job creation of between 1.4 and 3.6 jobs after accounting for the supporting industries.[33] And for those predisposed to downplay economic activity by "big business," it is important to note that about half of these jobs come from small businesses.[34]

Conclusion

This guided tour through the economic research, recent history of the Internet market, exploration of the differential impacts of net neutrality on innovation at the edge, and the economic costs of discouraging investment through poor policy now concludes. Against the hypothetical argument that strict net neutrality regulation would spur innovation, investment, or job creation, we have a solid case, based on empirical analysis, showing that the more strict forms of regulation typically lead to worse outcomes, not better. Against the wishful thinking of the "how good it could be" pro-regulatory advocates, which is divorced from marketplace reality, we have actual evidence in varied U.S. regulatory settings of "how good it has been" in the absence of heavy-handed regulation.

The FCC should come down on the side of the evidence and return its oversight of ISPs to light-touch regulation.

* James E. Prieger is Professor of Economics and Public Policy at the Pepperdine University School of Public Policy and a member of the Free State Foundation's Board of Academic Advisors. The Free State Foundation, an independent, nonpartisan free market-oriented think tank located in Rockville, Maryland.

Endnotes

1   See, for one example, the regulatory comments of Free Press summarized at https://www.savetheInternet.com/press-release/76056/free-press-clear-net-neutrality-rules-will-promote-investment-innovation-and

2   John W. Mayo, Michelle Connolly, Ev Ehrlich, Gerald R. Faulhaber, Robert Hahn, Robert Litan, Jeffrey T. Macher, Michael Mandel, James E. Prieger, Robert J. Shapiro, Hal J. Singer, Scott Wallsten, Lawrence J. White, and Glenn A. Woroch, "An Economic Perspective of Title II Regulation of the Internet," Georgetown University McDonough School of Business Economic Policy Vignette, July 2017 (hereafter An Economic Perspective). In this article I review some of the arguments made in An Economic Perspective but I do not claim to speak for any of the other authors.

3   For the specific studies and references of the research mentioned in the remainder of this summary, see the discussion and footnotes in the subsequent sections.

4   James E. Prieger, "Investment in Business Broadband in Rural Areas: The Impacts of Price Regulation and the FCC's Blind Spot," filed by Invest in Broadband for America to the FCC in the matter of Investigation of Certain Price Cap Local Exchange Carrier Business Data Services Tariff Pricing Plans, Special Access Rates for Price Cap Local Exchange Carriers, and Business Data Services in an Internet Protocol Environment, August 2016, (https://ecfsapi.fcc.gov/file/10809108333211/160808%20Invest%20in%20Broadband%20for%20America%20Letter%20FINAL.pdf).

5   James E. Prieger, "Regulation, Innovation, and the Introduction of New Telecommunications Services," Review of Economics and Statistics, November 2002, pp. 704-715.

6   James E. Prieger (2001). Telecommunications regulation and new services: A case study at the state level. Journal of Regulatory Economics, 20(3), 285-305.

7   Prieger, J.E., & Lee, S. (2008). Regulation and the deployment of broadband. In Y.K. Dwivedi, et al. (Eds.), Handbook of Research on Global Diffusion of Broadband Data Transmission (pp. 241-259). Hershey, PA: IGI Global.

8   See Theodore R. Bolema, "Too Much Unnecessary Regulation Is Impeding Telecom Investment," Perspectives from FSF Scholars, Vol. 12, No. 13, Free State Foundation, April 17, 2017, for a good discussion of how communications regulation is linked to investment, with citations to the large literature on this subject.

9   See OECD, Communications Outlook 1995, OECD Publishing.

10 Alberto Alesina, Silvia Ardagna, Giuseppe Nicoletti, and Fabio Schiantarelli, "Regulation and Investment," Journal of the European Economic Association, June 2005, pp. 791-825.

11 See Hal J. Singer, "Three Ways the FCC's Open Internet Order Will Harm Innovation," Progressive Policy Institute, May 2015, available at: http://www.progressivepolicy.org/issues/economy/three-ways-the-fccs-open-Internet-order-will-harm-innovation/.

12 See Jerry A. Hausman." Internet-related services: the results of asymmetric regulation." In Broadband–Should We Regulate High-Speed Internet Access, (2002),129-156, AEI-Brookings Joint Center for Regulatory Studies; and Jerry A. Hausman, J. Gregory Sidak and Hal J. Singer, "Cable Modems and DSL: Broadband Internet Access for Residential Customers," The American Economic Review, Vol. 91, No. 2, (May, 2001), pp. 302-307.

13 Theodore R. Bolema, "Allow Paid Prioritization on the Internet for More, Not Less, Capital Investment," Perspectives from FSF Scholars, Vol. 12, No. 16, Free State Foundation, May 1, 2017.

14 See https://haljsinger.wordpress.com/2017/03/01/2016-broadband-capex-survey-tracking-investment-in-the-title-ii-era/.

15   See Organization for Economic Co-operation and Development
      (OECD), Gross Domestic Product by Expenditure in Constant
      Prices: Gross Fixed Capital Formation for the United States
      [NAEXKP04USA652S], retrieved from FRED, Federal
      Reserve Bank of St. Louis; https://fred.stlouisfed.org/series/
      NAEXKP04USA652S, October 15, 2017.

16   The statistics cited here are from James E. Prieger, "The
      Growth of the Broadband Internet Access Market in California:
      Deployment, Competition, Adoption, and Challenges for Policy"
      (2016), Pepperdine University, School of Public Policy Working
      Papers, Paper 63 (http://digitalcommons.pepperdine.edu/
      sppworkingpapers/63), updated as necessary. See that publication
      for sources of the statistics.

17   See http://www.Internetworldstats.com/stats14.htm.

18   See Jeffrey T. Macher, John W. Mayo, Olga Ukhaneva, and Glenn
      Woroch, "From Universal Service to Universal Connectivity,"
      Journal of Regulatory Economics, August 2017, Volume 52, Issue
      1, pp 77–104.

19   FCC, Internet Access Services: Status as of June 30, 2016 and
      FCC, Internet Access Services: Status as of June 30, 2009.

20   Ibid., Figure 4.

21   See Federal Communications Commission, Industry Analysis
      and Technology Division Wireline Competition Bureau, Internet
      Access Services: Status as of June 30, 2016, April 2017; and
      Internet Access Services: Status as of December 31, 2013, October
      2014.

22   See FCC, Annual Report and Analysis of Competitive Market
      Conditions With Respect to Commercial Mobile Services (12th
      CMRS Competition Report), January 28, 2008.

23   See U.S. Bureau of Labor Statistics, Consumer Price Index, Series
      IDs: CUUR0000SA0, CUUS0000SA0, and CUUR0000SEEE03.
      This statistic is cited in An Economic Perspective, op. cit.

24   James E. Prieger, "What Do Economists Know About Net Neutrality Regulation? Quite a Lot, and the FCC Should Pay Attention," *Perspectives from FSF Scholars*, Vol. 12, No. 29, Free State Foundation, Sept. 6, 2017.

25   Roslyn Layton, "Does Net Neutrality Spur Internet Innovation," American Enterprise Institute publication, August 2017 (http://www.aei.org/publication/does-net-neutrality-spur-internet-innovation/).

26   Dr. Layton analyzes apps from the U.S. separately, given the unique dominance that the U.S. has always had in the market for mobile apps.

27   This section draws heavily from a similar discussion in another work of mine: James E. Prieger, Investment in Business Broadband in Rural Areas, op. cit.

28   See M. Cardona, T. Kretschmer, and T. Strobel, "ICT and productivity: conclusions from the empirical literature," Information Economics and Policy, vol. 25 (2013), pp. 109–125.

29   See A. Grimes, C. Ren, and P. Stevens, "The need for speed: impacts of Internet connectivity on firm productivity," Journal of Productivity Analysis, vol. 37 (2012), pp. 187–201.

30   See M.G. Colombo, A. Croce, and L. Grilli, "ICT services and small businesses' productivity gains: An analysis of the adoption of broadband Internet technology," Information Economics and Policy, vol. 25 (2013), pp. 171–189.

31   See L. Holt and M. Jamison, "Broadband and contributions to economic growth: Lessons from the U.S. experience," Telecommunications Policy, vol. 33 (2009), pp. 575–581; N. Bloom, M. Draca, T. Kretschmer, et al., "The economic impact of ICT: Final report," Centre for Economic Performance, London School of Economics, 2010; F. Biagi, "ICT and Productivity: A Review of the Literature," European Commission Joint Research Centre, Institute for Prospective Technological Studies, Digital Economy Working Paper 2013/09; and M. Cardona, T. Kretschmer, and T. Strobel, op. cit., for reviews of the sizeable

literature on the positive links between economic growth and ICT, broadband investment, and Internet usage.

32   J.A. Eisenach, H. Singer, and J.D. West ("Economic effects of tax incentives for broadband infrastructure deployment," Fiber-To-The-Home Council, 2009) calculate output multipliers of 2.8–3.1 for fixed broadband investment. See also Theodore R. Bolema ("An Assessment of the FCC's Proposal to Conduct a Cost-Benefit Analysis," *Perspectives from FSF Scholars*, Vol. 12, No. 23, Free State Foundation, July 14, 2017), who suggests that a multiplier in the range of 1.25 to 1.75 as a conservative estimate based on current research.

33   See R. Katz and S. Suter, "Estimating the economic impact of the broadband stimulus plan," Columbia Institute for Tele-Information Working Paper 7.

34   See R.D. Atkinson, D. Castro, and S.J. Ezell, "The digital road to recovery: a stimulus plan to create jobs, boost productivity and revitalize America," The Information Technology and Innovation Foundation, Washington, DC, 2009.

Part IV – Alternatives for Restoring Internet Freedom

15.
Free Market Orientation Spurs Reestablished Unlimited Data Plans

Michael J. Horney

FSF Blog, March 23, 2017

Unlimited data plans are back with all four major mobile providers in the United States. In my view, it is no coincidence that announcements regarding such unlimited plans were made shortly after FCC Chairman Ajit Pai indicated his disposition for relying on free market-oriented communications policy approaches.

On February 3, 2017, Chairman Pai announced that the FCC would close its investigation into mobile providers' free data offerings. On February 12, 2017, Verizon announced that it was launching a number of unlimited data plans. A day later, T-Mobile updated its existing unlimited plan to include high-definition video streaming. A day after T-Mobile's announcement, Sprint announced very similar updates to its existing unlimited plan. And then two days after Sprint's updates, AT&T expanded the reach of its unlimited data plan to all consumers, which was previously available to only U-Verse and DirecTV subscribers.

During his keynote speech at the Mobile World Congress on February 28, 2017, Chairman Pai summed up the mobile market's response to his decision to end the FCC's investigation:

Earlier this month, for example, we ended the
FCC's investigation into so-called "zero-rating," or
free data offerings. Free data plans have proven to
be popular among consumers, particularly those
with low incomes, because they allow consumers
to enjoy content without data limits or charges.
They have also enhanced competition. Nonetheless,
the FCC had put these plans under the regulatory
microscope. It claimed that they were anticompetitive, would lead to the end of unlimited
data plans, or otherwise limit online access. But
the truth is that consumers like getting something
for free, and they want their providers to compete
by introducing innovative offerings. Our recent
decision simply respected consumers' preference.

The best evidence of the wisdom of our new
approach is what happened afterward. In the days
following our decision, all four national wireless
providers in the United States announced new
unlimited data plans or expanded their existing
ones. Consumers are now benefiting from these
offers—offers made possible by a competitive
marketplace. And remember: Preemptive
government regulation did not produce that result.
The free market did.

Some critics of Chairman Pai's policies say that the recent
announcements regarding unlimited data plans are not related to
the FCC's decision to end the investigation of free data programs.
Instead, they claim that competition is responsible for the emergence of these plans. But I think it is both.

In this instance, the emergence of free data programs and
unlimited data plans are direct results of dynamic competition

and permissionless innovation. Unlimited data plans are only profitable when mobile providers are able to effectively manage their networks and efficiently deliver data to consumers. The reestablishment of unlimited data plans over the last month is an indication that mobile providers recognize that the FCC, under Chairman Pai's leadership, will not be monitoring and second-guessing every decision they make experimenting with new business models as they seek to be responsive to consumer demands.

The use of unlimited data plans will increase significantly the amount of data consumers use. And while mobile providers are updating their networks constantly to improve the speeds and quality of connections, the emergence of these plans does not improve automatically the capacity of mobile networks. So as long as there is a shortage between the amount of data consumers demand and the amount of spectrum allocated for private use, mobile providers will need to engage in network management techniques in order to allocate data efficiently to all consumers. (See this February 2017 blog regarding the projected growth in consumer demand and mobile data traffic.)

Unfortunately, network management practices could violate the Network Neutrality rules established in the *Open Internet* Order. Before the adoption of the *Open Internet* Order and soon thereafter when the Order was under appeal, the uncertainty of its imposition discouraged broadband providers from making major network investments. Chairman Pai opposed the adoption of the *Open Internet* Order while he was Commissioner in February 2015 and recently reiterated that the Order had a direct negative impact on broadband capital investment. Preemptive regulations often have unintended consequences that increase the costs of performing day-to-day business practices, like network man-agement. While the *Open Internet* Order includes an allowance of "reasonable network management," if the FCC construes the scope of its review for reasonableness too broadly, and divorces from marketplace realities, then innovative business models like unlimited data plans will be chilled.

But despite that the *Open Internet* Order is still in effect, Chairman Pai's statements and actions have created more certainty among broadband providers that the new Commission will not burden ISPs unnecessarily with more costly regulations. As a result, providers are willing to bear the costs of network management that come with offering unlimited data plans because they are less concerned about being hit with enforcement actions for performing such day-to-day business practices.

Free data offerings and unlimited data plans give consumers multiple cost-effective options for accessing more mobile data and online content. But these innovative offerings would not have emerged if not for permissionless innovation and dynamic competition in the mobile broadband market. Of course, the *Open Internet* Order still needs to be curtailed substantially to avoid further uncertainty and to lessen the regulatory costs that may discourage providers from creating new and innovative services. Also, regulatory barriers at the state and local levels should be reduced or eliminated to encourage additional broadband investment.

All that said, in my view, it is no coincidence that mobile broadband providers now are willing to offer consumers unlimited data plans as Chairman Pai leads the new FCC toward a free market-oriented approach to communications policy.

16.
The Right Way to Protect Privacy Throughout the Internet Ecosystem

Daniel A. Lyons [*]

Perspectives from FSF Scholars, March 24, 2017, Vol. 12, No. 10

I. Introduction and Summary

Yesterday the Senate passed a joint resolution pursuant to the Congressional Review Act that disapproved the Federal Communications Commission's privacy rules.[1] These rules, passed during the waning days of the Obama administration, restrict the ability of Internet service providers to collect and use consumer information.[2] Congressional action comes on the heels of the agency's decision to stay a portion of the rules pending resolution of several motions for reconsideration currently before the agency.[3] Along with the stay, Chairman Ajit Pai released a rare joint statement with Federal Trade Commission Acting Chairman Maureen Ohlhausen,[4] which criticized the FCC for applying a different privacy regime to ISPs than the FTC applies to the rest of the entities throughout Internet ecosystem—themes echoed in the floor debate in Congress.[5] If the House of Representatives concurs with the joint resolution and the president signs it, the rules will be nullified.

The privacy rules are precisely the type of agency overreach that the Congressional Review Act was designed to rein in. Born as an unintended consequence of the FCC's ill-advised reclassification order, the privacy order unnecessarily disadvantages ISPs in the competition for the digital advertising dollars that drive the Internet economy. ISPs are singled out for a greater regulatory burden not because they pose a greater threat to consumer privacy, but rather because they happen to be subject to FCC regulation while edge providers such as Google and Facebook are not. This disparate treatment is doubly problematic given that edge providers, not ISPs, dominate the digital advertising space, and the burden placed on ISPs achieves little, if any, measurable benefit to consumer privacy. Whether the joint resolution succeeds or fails, the FCC should, as an interim step, level the playing field by following Chairman Pai's plan to mirror the FTC's rules. Then, as soon as feasible, the agency should remove the root problem by repealing its reclassification decision and working with Congress to restore the FTC's complete jurisdiction over American privacy law.

II. The FCC's Problematic Privacy Rules

If successful, the joint resolution would mark only the fifth time ever that an agency rule was revoked under the Congressional Review Act.[6] While this debacle is embarrassing for the agency, it is largely a self-inflicted wound. The FCC privacy saga began as an unintended consequence of the agency's 2015 capitulation to the demand by pro-regulatory forces for "strong" net neutrality rules. In its *Open Internet* order, the FCC reclassified broadband providers as common carriers under Title II of the Communications Act, as a vehicle by which to secure the ban on paid prioritization that President Obama and various interest groups sought.[7] In doing so, the agency eschewed the less intrusive roadmap proposed by the D.C. Circuit[8] and ignored an eleventh-hour statutory compromise offered by congressional Republicans that would have accomplished the agency's goals without reclassification.[9] Undiscussed in the order is the effect reclassification would have on the FTC, whose regulatory authority under Section 5 of the Federal Trade Commission Act does not extend to common carriers.[10] The FTC had long used its Section 5 authority to build a robust and comprehensive regime to protect consumer privacy, both offline and online. The FCC's rash reclassification decision stripped the FTC of jurisdiction to enforce the law against broadband providers, leaving a legal gap.

The agency compounded this mistake by the way it chose to fill that gap. Broadband providers recognized that some agency action was appropriate to eliminate this legal vacuum, and comments filed before the agency showed broad support for FCC rules that would mirror the FTC's "opt-out" approach to consumer privacy. Under this approach, companies must provide consumers notice of what data is collected and how it is to be used, and the option to opt out of data collection if the consumer so chooses.[11] But the FCC eschewed this traditional model in favor of a more stringent "opt-in" model. Specifically, broadband Internet providers were prohibited from collecting and using information about a consumer's browsing history, app usage, or geolocation data without permission—all of which edge providers such as Google or Facebook are free to collect under FTC policies.[12]

As Michael Horney noted in an earlier Free State Foundation Perspectives release,[13] these restrictions create barriers for ISPs to compete in digital advertising markets. With access to consumer information, companies can provide more targeted advertising, ads that are more likely to be relevant to the consumer and therefore more valuable to the advertiser. The opt-in requirement means that ISPs will have access to less information about customers than Google, Facebook, and other edge providers that fall under the FTC's purview—meaning ISPs cannot serve advertisers as effectively as the edge providers with whom they compete. This disadvantage is doubly problematic when one realizes that edge providers, not ISPs, currently dominate the digital advertising market. A recent study estimates that Google collected over half of all U.S. digital advertising in the first half of 2016, and Facebook represented another 17 percent.[14] ISPs such as AT&T and Verizon are relative latecomers to this market. By restricting their access to consumer information, the FCC is making it harder for these insurgents to challenge incumbents, and is therefore reinforcing the dominance of a duopoly that commands over two-thirds of the market.

Some including the FCC have suggested that a higher privacy standard for ISPs is appropriate because ISPs "sit at a privileged place in the network" and can collect "an unprecedented breadth of electronic personal information."[15] But this argument rings hollow. First, it is not clear that ISPs are in a position to learn more about a consumer than leading edge providers. Google not only processes roughly two-thirds of all U.S. Internet searches,[16] it also runs the operating system on over half of all U.S. smartphones.[17] Both Google and Facebook permit other content providers to use their logins for identity verification, allowing these titans to build a consumer profile across platforms and locations. My broadband provider may know my online behavior while at home, but Google and Facebook can build a more complete profile of my activity while at home, at work, and on mobile networks as well. Moreover, as Professor Christopher Yoo (who is also a member of the Free State Foundation Board of Academic Advisors) has observed, there is very little an ISP can determine from its allegedly "privileged position" on the network. Whereas edge providers can see all content the consumer accesses, ISPs can only see metadata and traffic flow (unless they engage in deep packet inspection, which is legally suspect under the Electronic Communications Privacy Act).[18]

For these reasons, Chairman Pai is correct to call for a revisiting of the privacy rules. The Commission should level the playing field by making sure all players are governed by the same rules. This would avoid the prospect of the government picking winners and losers in the digital advertising market.

III. The Difficulties with an Opt-In Rule

Of course, the argument that the playing field should be level does not answer the question whether to level down or level up. Although the FCC's rules focused primarily on ISPs, at times the order seemed to endorse an opt-in model as the preferable standard throughout the Internet ecosystem. This is the position recently taken by Gigi Sohn, who served as special assistant to then-Chairman Tom Wheeler during the FCC privacy debate.[19] From this perspective, the FCC adopted opt-in rules in part as a way for the agency to nudge the FTC to adopt similar opt-in rules generally, including in markets where the FCC has no expertise or authority to regulate.

As an initial matter, it's worth noting that a shift to opt-in rules does little, if anything, to empower consumers. It's not as if the FTC opt-out regime allows companies to use consumer data surreptitiously or against the consumer's will. Both approaches require companies to notify consumers of what information is being collected about them and how it could potentially be used. Both approaches give consumers a choice about whether the company can use their personal data. Under either model, the consumer has ultimate decisionmaking authority over whether and how his or her information will be used. The primary difference is the default rule: if the consumer fails express a preference, is the company free to collect and use information or not? Thus, the additional burden to consumers of an opt-out rule is minimal. If a consumer does not wish his or her information to be collected, that consumer simply must notify the company.

But while the difference between opt-out and opt-in rules is not especially significant for consumers, it can potentially be devastating to the companies that comprise the Internet economy, depending on how the consent is secured. To understand why, one must recognize that Internet privacy cannot be considered in a vacuum. Rather, choosing the proper privacy rule requires an appreciation of the role that consumer information plays online.

Simply put, consumer information is the lifeblood of the Internet. It is the packaging of consumer information into advertising bundles that allows companies like Google to offer the "free" services that consumers have come to expect from the Internet experience, such as search results, email use and storage, and YouTube access. Shifting from opt-out to opt-in dries up the pool of information available for monetization, by removing any information from a consumer that does not make his or her consent known. With less information available, these companies will have fewer advertising dollars with which to subsidize their consumer-facing services. At the margin, this could lead companies to charge for services like gmail that they currently offer for free. And, importantly, a shift to a fee-based access model risks widening the digital divide, by putting Internet-based services beyond the reach of those who cannot or will not pay for them.

Moreover, contrary to the FCC's findings, an opt-out regime may be more efficient than opt-in. Michael Horney cites a 2000 paper by Fred Cate and Michael Staten, in which the authors argue that "opt-in is more costly precisely because it fails to harness the efficiency of having customers reveal their own preference as opposed to having to explicitly ask them."[20] Opt-in requires companies to expend effort asking each and every customer for permission, and then maintain a record of each consent in case of a future dispute. An opt-out rule shifts the burden onto consumers, meaning the company needs only communicate with and document those consumers who object—thus freeing resources for other endeavors. Moreover, by setting the default rule to "no permission," an opt-in regime risks barring advertisers from using information from those consumers who in fact do not object to its use, but who for whatever reason fail to make that known to the company, which creates inefficiency.

IV. Short-Term and Long-Term Solutions

Having laid bare the problems with the FCC's current unlevel playing field and with the opt-in model generally, the question becomes how to solve the current dilemma. If the joint resolution passes the House and is signed by the president, the existing rules will be revoked.[21] Should the resolution fail, the FCC nonetheless may repeal the rules by granting the various motions for reconsideration currently pending before the agency. Either decision will expose anew the privacy gap created by the reclassification decision that initially prompted the rules.

But this temporary circumstance is not as problematic as it may seem. First, that gap existed for well over a year after the March 2015 reclassification decision took effect – yet there were no major complaints about ISP treatment of consumer information during this period, largely because most ISPs have adopted voluntary data management practices even in the absence of administrative oversight. Second, repeal is the necessary first step for the agency to restore regulatory symmetry in this area. In their joint statement, Chairmen Pai and Ohlhausen endorsed a "comprehensive and consistent" framework for privacy issues.[22] Specifically, they committed to "harmonizing the FCC's privacy rules for broadband providers with the FTC's standards for other companies in the digital economy." While some critics have asserted that the joint resolution would prohibit the FCC from considering a new privacy order, that is incorrect. The Congressional Review Act prohibits the agency from reissuing a rule "in substantially the same form" as the rejected rule or issuing "a new rule that is substantially the same as such a rule."[23] A new, different order that ties FCC enforcement to existing FTC standards would not be "substantially the same" as the current rule, as it would adopt an opt-out rather than an opt-in rule and would unify rather than bifurcate privacy law. Thus assuming the joint resolution passes, the FCC remains free to enact interim measures that could fill the prospective legal gap without creating regulatory asymmetry.

As soon as feasible, the FCC should move toward restoring the FTC's jurisdiction over broadband providers. This must start with a repeal of its ill-advised decision to reclassify broadband providers as Title II common carriers. To the extent there is a claimed privacy gap, it is only one of many unintended consequences of the reclassification decision. These difficulties are unsurprising: as Free State Foundation scholars often have noted, much of Title II was written in the 1930s to discipline the Bell Telephone monopoly. Trying to adapt it to today's competitive Internet marketplace is like trying to fit a square peg in a round hole (with only the tool of forbearance to try to shave off the sharp corners). Repeal of Title II reclassification would strip broadband providers of the "common carrier" designation and would thus restore the authority the FTC had to regulate broadband privacy prior to 2015.

There is, however, one potential wrinkle in this repeal-and-restore plan. Late last year, the Ninth Circuit Court of Appeals decided *FTC v. AT&T Mobility*, which found a somewhat surprising additional limitation on the FTC's Section 5 authority.[24] That case involved AT&T's challenge to a fine leveled by the FTC pursuant to its Section 5 authority for the company's failure to disclose its data-throttling practices during the period before Title II reclassification. The FTC argued that the fine was appropriate because before reclassification, data services were not common carrier services and so the limitation on Section 5 was inapposite. The Court, however, sided with AT&T, holding that the Section 5 "common carrier" exemption was status-based, not activity-based. In other words, if a company acts as a common carrier in some capacity, it is exempt from Section 5 authority even if the activity giving rise to liability is not itself a common carrier activity. Because AT&T

operated a traditional telephone company (which unquestionably offered Title II common carriage service), the court said the company was exempt even though the conduct at issue had little to do with the company's common carrier activities.

FTC v. AT&T Mobility therefore suggests that if Title II reclassification were to be repealed, this would still leave a gap because the FTC would be unable to use Section 5 to regulate the privacy practices of any broadband provider (such as AT&T Mobility) that also operates a different common carriage business. But this is not as significant a challenge as it appears at first glance, for several reasons:

> *First*, the Ninth Circuit decision has not yet become final. The FTC has filed a petition for rehearing *en banc*. The court ordered AT&T to file a response to the petition, and also granted leave for numerous parties to file *amicus curiae* briefs in the case, many of which urged reversal. The court may take the case *en banc* and reverse it, and even if it does not, the FTC can still seek Supreme Court review. (I will admit that I was skeptical when I first heard of the panel's decision, but upon reading the opinion in full, there are surprisingly strong arguments in favor of the panel's conclusion that Congress intended the exemption to be status-based rather than activity-based.)

> *Second*, even if the decision is affirmed, that does not mean that repeal of reclassification will leave all broadband providers free of privacy regulation. The only companies that would escape FTC authority would be those that also happen to operate a common carrier business—to wit, landline and wireless telephone companies. Cable companies,

which comprise America's two largest broadband providers and 60% of the market nationwide,[25] would fall squarely under the FTC's umbrella, as would standalone broadband providers. Thus, while repeal might not bring all broadband providers within the FTC's jurisdiction, it will restore FTC authority over most.

Third, it is unclear how future courts will limit this status-based exemption. As Public Knowledge's Harold Feld notes, it cannot be correct that any company, no matter how large, can add a small rural telephone company to its portfolio and thus escape the FTC's Section 5 authority entirely.[26] I agree with Feld that Google cannot credibly argue that its $89.5 billion empire is completely exempt from FTC Section 5 regulation because it owns Google Fiber with about 50,000 subscribers within its portfolio of businesses.[27] Future courts will likely determine that at least some companies are subject to Section 5 regulation despite also operating a common carrier business—though just they will define the line separating exempt from non-exempt entities is not yet clear.

More generally, the potential for a gap in FTC jurisdiction is not sufficient to justify continuing to classify broadband providers as common carriers. This argument, that the FCC should classify broadband providers under Title II to correct a problem with the FTC Act, commits the same error that underlay the net neutrality proceeding. The question of how to classify broadband providers under the Communications Act should start—and end—by asking what Congress intended. It is not a goal-seeking exercise to see which classification yields one's preferred policy result. The consequences should flow from the classification decision, not the other way around.

If the FTC Act's common carrier exemption creates a regulatory gap, as the Ninth Circuit decision suggests, then it is up to Congress, not the FCC, to fix it. Congress can act to limit or repeal Section 5's common carrier exemption. As Feld notes, the exemption was created at a time when most common carriers had an agency that comprehensively regulated their operations, and therefore FTC oversight was at best redundant and potentially harmful to industry-specific regulatory schemes. Following the advent of competition and deregulation of those industries (at least to some extent in some instances), that rationale is somewhat suspect. If the Ninth Circuit is right that Section 5 exempts common carriers generally, the gap thus exposed goes far beyond privacy law to include all actions the FTC takes under Section 5. And it similarly goes beyond telecommunications providers, to encompass other common carriers such as airlines, railroads, bus services, and several other industries. No matter how much the FCC twists the language of Title II, it cannot stretch it enough to close the Section 5 gap completely. That problem can only be solved by Congress—but the FCC can help by signaling its support for this change and assuring the Congress that it is unconcerned about the potential interagency rivalry that initially spawned the common carrier exemption.

V. Conclusion

The privacy rules reflect some of the worst agency tendencies toward administrative overreach. Having manufactured a "gap" in privacy law as an unintended consequence of its quixotic pursuit of rigid net neutrality regulation, the FCC then took advantage of the "opportunity" thus presented to call into question the FTC's expertise and to try to influence privacy norms throughout the Internet ecosystem. In doing so, the FCC went far beyond its statutory mandate. By doing so it entrenched incumbent edge providers and hobbled the efforts of insurgent ISPs to compete against them, without improving consumer privacy in any significant way.

I applaud the Senate's effort to repeal these rules and urge the House and the president to follow suit. Repeal would rein in this overreach and mark an important first step toward restoring the competitive balance between ISPs and edge providers. As an interim measure, the FCC should enact new rules that mirror existing FTC practices. Then, as soon as feasible, the Commission should repeal its ill-advised Title II reclassification decision and return privacy jurisdiction back to the FTC, where it belongs. Consumer privacy rules should apply equally to all companies regardless of the role they play in the Internet ecosystem, and they should be subject to oversight by a regulator with a clear view of how privacy interests affect that ecosystem as a whole.

* Daniel A. Lyons, an Associate Professor of Law at Boston College Law School, is a Member of the Free State Foundation's Board of Academic Advisors. The Free State Foundation is an independent, nonpartisan free market-oriented think tank located in Rockville, Maryland.

Endnotes

1   S.J. Res. 34, 115th Congress (2017).

2   Protecting the Privacy of Consumers of Broadband and other Telecommunications Services, Report and Order, FCC No. 16-148 (Nov. 2, 2016), available at https://apps.fcc.gov/edocs_public/attachmatch/FCC-16-148A1.pdf.

3   Protecting the Privacy of Consumers of Broadband and other Telecommunications Services, Order Granting Stay in Part, WC Docket No. 16-106 (Mar. 1, 2017), available at https://transition.fcc.gov/Daily_Releases/Daily_Business/2017/db0301/FCC-17-19A1.pdf.

4   Joint Statement of FCC Chairman Ajit Pai and Acting FTC Chairman Maureen K. Ohlhausen on Protecting Americans' Online Privacy, March 1, 2017, available at http://transition.fcc.gov/Daily_Releases/Daily_Business/2017/db0301/DOC-343702A1.pdf.

5   FCC Commissioner Mignon Clyburn and FTC Commissioner Terrell McSweeney issued a similar joint statement criticizing the stay. See Joint Statement of FCC Commissioner Mignon Clyburn and FTC Commissioner Terrell McSweeney on Indefinite Suspension of Data Security Rules, Feb. 24, 2017, available at http://transition.fcc.gov/Daily_Releases/Daily_Business/2017/db0224/DOC-343629A1.pdf.

6   Importantly, all but one of those have come in the last two months as the Trump administration has targeted last-minute Obama administration rules. As of today's date, there are seven other joint resolutions that have passed both houses and are awaiting the president's approval or veto.

7   Protecting and Promoting the Open Internet, GN Docket No. 14-28 (Mar. 12, 2015).

8   Verizon v. FCC, 740 F.3d 623 (D.C. Cir. 2014).

9   See Larry Downes, Eight Reasons to Support Congress's
     Net Neutrality Bill, Washington Post, Jan. 20, 2015, available
     at https://www.washingtonpost.com/news/innovations/
     wp/2015/01/20/eight-reasons-to-support-congresss-net-
     neutrality-bill/?utm_term=.a34f5c42222c.

10   15 U.S.C. § 45(a)(2).

11   Congress has adopted a stricter opt-in model for certain sensitive
     categories of data, most notably health information (via HIPPA),
     financial information (via the Gramm-Leach-Bliley Act), and
     information about children (via COPPA).

12   See Report and Order, supra note 2, at ¶167. Consistent with
     FTC practice, the FCC also required opt-in treatment for use
     of health, financial, and children's records, which were less
     controversial.

13   See Michael J. Horney, FCC Privacy Rules Would Harm
     Consumers by Creating Barriers for ISP Advertising, 11 FSF
     Perspectives 28 (2016).

14   See Peter Kafka, Google and Facebook are booming. Is the
     rest of the digital ad business shrinking? Recode, Nov. 2, 2016,
     available at http://www.recode.net/2016/11/2/13497376/
     google-facebook-advertising-shrinking-iab-dcn.

15   See Report and Order, supra note 2, at ¶28.

16   See comScore Explicit Core Search Share Report, February
     2016, available at https://www.comscore.com/Insights/Rankings/
     comScore-Releases-February-2016-US-Desktop-Search-Engine-
     Rankings.

17   comScore Reports January 2016 U.S. Smartphone Subscriber
     Market Share, available at https://www.comscore.com/Insights/
     Rankings/comScore-Reports-January-2016-US-Smartphone-
     Subscriber-Market-Share.

18 See The Fate of the FCC's Privacy Rule: A Chat with Professor Christopher Yoo, Forbes Washington Bytes Blog, Feb. 9, 2017, available at https://www.forbes.com/sites/washingtonbytes/2017/02/09/the-fate-of-the-fccs-privacy-rule-a-chat-with-law-professor-christopher-yoo/#634fb5433180.

19 Gigi Sohn, FCC, FTC Are Playing a Shell Game with Online Privacy, The Hill, Mar. 18, 2017, available at http://thehill.com/blogs/pundits-blog/technology/324520-fcc-ftc-are-playing-a-shell-game-with-online-privacy.

20 Fred Cate and Michael Staten, Protecting Privacy in the New Millennium: The Fallacy of 'Opt-In', available at http://home.uchicago.edu/~mferzige/fallacyofoptin.pdf.

21 See 5 U.S.C. § 801.

22 See Joint Statement, supra note 4.

23 5 U.S.C. § 801.

24 FTC v. AT&T Mobility, Inc., 835 F.3d 993 (9th Cir. 2016).

25 See Press Release, 27 Million Added Broadband from Top Providers in 2016, Leichtman Research Group, Mar. 17, 2017, available at http://www.leichtmanresearch.com/press/031717release.html.

26 Harold Feld, Ninth Circuit Knee-Caps Federal Trade Commission. Or, "You Know Nothing, Josh Wright." Tales of the Sausage Factory Blog, Aug. 31, 2016, available at http://www.wetmachine.com/tales-of-the-sausage-factory/ninth-circuit-knee-caps-federal-trade-commission-or-you-know-nothing-josh-wright/.

27 Id.

17.
Restoring Internet Freedom: Rolling Back "Net Neutrality" Will Restore Innovation to Broadband Transmission

Randolph J. May *

Perspectives from FSF Scholars, May 4, 2017, Vol. 12, No. 17

The Washington Times
May 2, 2017

Thankfully, on April 26, Federal Communications Commission Chairman Ajit Pai formally announced a proposal to curtail the overweening internet regulation regime adopted in February 2015 under the leadership of his predecessor, Tom Wheeler. The Obama administration's FCC's rules went overboard in restricting the freedom of internet service providers to innovate and to invest in extending and modernizing their high-speed broadband networks.

Consumers, of course, were the real losers.

At bottom, running under the guise of ensuring "net neutrality," in order to assert much greater government control over internet providers, the FCC reversed the previous light-touch internet regulatory regime that generally had prevailed since the Clinton administration.

And worst of all, the FCC did this while conceding there was no real evidence of a market failure justifying heavy-handed government intervention. Rather, the FCC's internet power grab was based on reams of rhetorical conjecture about "possible" harms that "might" occur in the future if internet service providers adopted practices that possibly "could" harm consumers or competitors.

Let me be clear: I am not opposed to government oversight, or even more active regulation, in cases where there is convincing evidence of market failure resulting in harm to consumers. But basing government regulation on conjectured possible harms that may never materialize usually has negative consequences. And it is especially wrong when such government intervention occurs in a marketplace as technologically dynamic as the internet.

There are many troublesome aspects to the Wheeler FCC's net neutrality rules that Chairman Pai now seeks to revise. To his credit, Mr. Pai is attacking, frontally, the two most harmful rules, the two that place internet service providers in a regulatory straitjacket that limits their freedom and, consequently, their incentive to innovate and invest.

The first objective of the new rule making proceeding is to reverse the classification of internet providers as Title II common carriers, so called because they are subject to Title II of the Communications Act of 1934. In effect, under Title II, the internet service providers are regulated like public utilities. This form of strict government regulation, with controlled rates and non-discrimination prohibitions at its core, was conceived in the 1800s to regulate railroads, and applied in the 1900s to the Ma Bell telephone monopoly. It is ill-suited for the 21st century's dynamic internet, with competitive providers offering services over different broadband platforms in nearly all areas of the country.

Predictably, adoption of the public utility regulatory regime has slowed the rate of investment by internet service providers. According to a Free State Foundation analysis, which was cited by

Mr. Pai in announcing his proposal, the Obama administration's net neutrality order has already cost our country $5.1 billion in broadband capital investment. Other estimates are higher.

It's worthwhile noting that the decline in the rate of investment has occurred even though the most stringent forms of public utility regulatory controls haven't yet been implemented, though they could be. It's likely that just the overhanging threat of even more stringent regulation in the future has contributed to the decline in investment.

The second objective of the proposed rule making is to eliminate the amorphous "good conduct" rule adopted by the Wheeler FCC. This rule prohibits internet providers from engaging in "unreasonable" discrimination or anti-competitive conduct, but provides little guidance as to what practices actually would be subject to sanctions. Don't take my word for it. The commission itself called the "good conduct" rule a "catch all" provision. Mr. Pai had it right when he said the good conduct regulation "gives the FCC a roving mandate to micromanage the internet."

Indeed, soon after the good conduct rule was adopted, the agency invoked its new roving mandate to begin investigating wireless internet providers' consumer-friendly free data plans like T-Mobile's "Music Freedom" and "Binge" programs for music and TV streaming. Without any evidence that these popular free data programs caused any anti-competitive harm, the FCC put them into a legal never-never land. One of Mr. Pai's first acts as chairman was to halt the free data investigations.

Aside from public utility and good conduct regulation, there are other unnecessary burdensome regulatory mandates that will be re-examined in the FCC's new proceeding. For example, the absolute ban on so-called paid prioritization, which requires that even Amber alerts and medical imaging data be accorded the very same priority as ordinary emails, needs to be revised in a way that provides internet service providers with some degree of flexibility to differentiate their services without harming consumers.

Restoring internet providers' freedom will incentivize more investment and more innovation. This will create more jobs and grow the economy. Above all, it will ensure that the internet continues to evolve, dynamically, in a way that meets consumers' expectations and demands.

---

* Randolph J. May is President of the Free State Foundation, an independent, nonpartisan free market-oriented think tank located in Rockville, Maryland. *Restoring Internet Freedom: Rolling Back "Net Neutrality" Will Restore Innovation to Broadband Transmission* was published in *The Washington Times* on May 2, 2017.

18.
Antitrust Provides a More Reasonable Framework for Net Neutrality Regulation

Joshua D. Wright *

Perspectives from FSF Scholars, **August 16, 2017, Vol. 12, No. 27**

Introduction and Summary

In 2015, the FCC departed from almost 20 years of precedent and reclassified the framework for regulating the Internet under Title II of the Telecommunications Act. This departure, done at the behest of President Obama, meant that Internet access is regulated as a "telecommunications service" under Title II rather than as an "information service" regulated under Title I. The effect of the 2015 Order is to classify Internet service providers (ISPs) as common carriers, regulating them like a public utility.

After classifying Internet service providers as common carriers, the FCC found it necessary to forbear from enforcing "30 statutory provisions" and rendered "over 700 codified rules inapplicable."[1] Further, the FCC adopted no-blocking, no-throttling, and no-paid prioritization rules, as well as a general Internet conduct standard and "enhancements" to the transparency rule. In 2016, the D.C. Circuit affirmed the validity of the Title II classification in a divided decision.[2]

In April 2017, the FCC issued a Notice of Proposed Rulemaking (NPRM) to end the Title II regulatory approach, and return to the lighter-touch Title I approach, which would again regulate Internet access as an "information service." The explicit rationale was to "reverse the decline in infrastructure investment, innovation, and options for consumers put into motion by the FCC in 2015."[3] The NPRM proposes to eliminate the Internet conduct standard, and seeks comment on blocking, throttling, and paid prioritization. Finally, the NPRM proposes to return jurisdiction to the FTC to police ISPs, thereby shifting the regulatory approach from an aggressive *ex ante* regime to a more reasonable *ex post* framework.

One primary point of contention has been whether the 2017 NPRM will increase capital expenditures in the Internet ecosystem. Prior to the 2017 NPRM, the FCC claimed ISPs continued to invest at the same or even higher rates despite the imposition of a heavy-handed regulatory scheme. However, data indicate that between 2014 (the year before the 2015 Order) and 2016 (the year after) capital expenditures by broadband ISPs decreased by $3.6 billion, or 5.6%.[4]

Another point of contention in the net neutrality debate concerns the reversion to the FTC of jurisdiction to police claims that ISPs unfairly or unreasonably discriminate against content providers and thereby harm competition. While there is no apparent dispute that the FTC's authority to prohibit deceptive practices can be deployed to reach broadband providers,[5] there appears to be greater confusion about the appropriate role of antitrust and its domain in broadband markets. Some even go so far as to claim relying upon antitrust law amounts to no regulation at all.[6] A useful comparison of antitrust law to alternative regulatory schemes, such as Title II, requires first an accurate description of what the former entails. A careful comparison makes clear that claims that antitrust amounts to "doing nothing" are a combination of overzealous advocacy and deception. But the more interesting issue is which regulatory framework – each with its own strengths and weaknesses – best protects competition and consumers.

Antitrust law has developed a sophisticated "rule of reason" framework to determine whether vertical agreements are procompetitive or anticompetitive. The rule of reason approach examines vertical agreements on a case-by-case basis by weighing costs and benefits and recognizing possible losses from enforcement errors that go in either direction. Despite the 2015 Order ban on vertical agreements by Internet service providers, rule of reason analysis would not similarly result in a total ban on vertical agreements because economics literature clearly indicates that while vertical agreements are capable of harming competition in the manner contemplated by net neutrality proponents, more often than not they are beneficial to consumers. Furthermore, with few exceptions, the literature does not support the view that these practices are used for anticompetitive reasons. In short, the vertical agreements at the heart of the net neutrality debate are generally procompetitive.

Economic analysis predicted the 2015 Open Internet Order ban on vertical agreements would likely harm consumers and depress investment. Now, empirical evidence is consistent with those predictions. Reclassifying Internet service providers under Title I would restore incentives to invest in broadband markets. A less obvious benefit is that it replaces the 2015 Order's categorical ban on contract arrangements that benefit consumers – including paid prioritization and other vertical arrangements – with antitrust jurisprudence's rule of reason. A close look at the antitrust approach shows not only that it can reach the harms envisioned by net neutrality proponents, but also that it is superior to alternatives that would condemn vertical arrangements in broadband markets without proof of harm to competition.

The Antitrust Framework

The crux of the net neutrality debate is the fear that via paid prioritization, ISPs will enter vertical business agreements that will prove to be anticompetitive, and ultimately harm consumers. Vertical agreements are agreements between firms at different levels of a supply chain; in this context, they are between an ISP and a content provider. Even though there was no evidence of a single harmful agreement during the fourteen years of Title I coverage, the Title II Order chose to prohibit all vertical agreements. The net neutrality debate is marked by a dearth of economic perspective – framing consumer harm without consideration of the promotion of consumer welfare. These ephemeral hypothetical harms do not provide regulatory clarity and do not allow the FCC to create precedent in the appropriate cases. Instead, net neutrality categorically banned vertical agreements.

There seems to be a consensus that some regulation of vertical agreements is necessary to protect consumers. One option is *ex ante* regulation that is effectively a categorical prohibition on vertical agreements. In the 2015 Order, the FCC adopted this *ex ante* approach, which is now known generally as "net neutrality." The second option is *ex post* regulation that seeks to permit procompetitive vertical agreements, while preventing anticompetitive ones. The *ex post* approach aims to maximize consumer welfare wherever possible by applying the tenets of antitrust law.

Antitrust law has developed a sophisticated "rule of reason" approach to determine whether vertical agreements are procompetitive or anticompetitive. The rule of reason approach examines vertical agreements on a case-by-case basis by "weighing costs and benefits, and recogniz[ing] possible losses from enforcement errors that go in either direction."[7] According to FTC staff, rule of reason "weigh[s] potential anticompetitive effects against the procompetitive effects and efficiencies that drive business practices in fast-growing industries."[8] The rule of reason analysis would not result in a categorical ban on vertical agreements. Instead, by applying rule of reason, vertical agreements would be analyzed on a case-by-case basis, and be rejected only if careful economic analysis concluded there are anticompetitive effects greater than any procompetitive effects or efficiencies.

The regulatory framework must also minimize the social costs of regulatory errors and the costs of administering the regulatory system. The inputs required to apply the "error cost framework" are: (1) the probability that the agreements at issue (in this case vertical restraints) are anticompetitive; (2) the magnitude of errors associated with erroneous enforcement; and (3) the administrative costs of implementing the system. The errors can either be false positives, in which agreements that benefit consumers are prohibited, or false negatives, in which agreements that harm consumers are allowed.[9] Overall, consumers are best protected by an *ex ante* categorical ban if all vertical agreements are anticompetitive, or if there are an abundance of false negatives. And consumers are best protected by an *ex post* approach if there are even a few procompetitive vertical agreements, or an abundance of false positives.

The economics literature on vertical agreements is consistent and very clear: while vertical agreements are capable of harming competition in the manner contemplated by net neutrality proponents, vertical agreements are more often beneficial to consumers.[10] Furthermore, "with few exceptions, the literature does not support the view that these practices are used for anticompetitive reasons," which supports "a fairly strong prior belief that these practices are unlikely to be anticompetitive in most cases."[11] Thus, the vertical agreements at the heart of the net neutrality debate are generally procompetitive. Indeed, vertical agreements are often observed between firms without any plausible market power. Vertical agreements can reduce double marginalization, prevent free riding on manufacturer-supplied investments, and align incentives of manufacturers and distributors. Consumers benefit from these efficiencies "in the form of lower prices, increased output, higher quality, and greater innovation."[12] In short, vertical contracts can improve consumer outcomes by creating demand or lowering costs.

Despite this literature, the FCC's 2015 Order proposed a categorical ban on vertical agreements without any plausible economic justification or evidence to support it. Indeed, the 2010 Order offered up only a frail attempt to justify its proposal on economics grounds – citing to a single paper, later omitted from the 2015 Order after substantial criticism.[13]

Any regulatory regime somewhat reflecting the state of economic knowledge on vertical restraints would accept the premise that these contracts can generate both pro- and anticompetitive results. The 2015 Order did not implement a regime that attempted to differentiate between the two – sacrificing for broadband consumers the benefits from the many "good" vertical restraints, in the name of prohibiting the few "bad" ones. Such a regulatory regime is easily outperformed by one that is capable of distinguishing between the two with even a mundane level of accuracy. This is where antitrust comes into play.

The 2017 Restoring Internet Freedom NPRM proposes to shift the regulatory scheme back to Title I. With that shift, the 2017 rulemaking proposal contemplates that antitrust and its "rule of reason" framework will provide the competitive rules of the road for vertical agreements between broadband providers and content providers.

Over the last 125 years, antitrust jurisprudence has developed a method to analyze vertical arrangements: rule of reason.[14] Under a rule of reason approach, every vertical arrangement is analyzed individually to determine if the agreement is anticompetitive.[15] The main function of rule of reason analysis is to condemn vertical restraints that harm consumers and allow those that are either not anticompetitive or beneficial.[16] It seems clear that antitrust's rule of reason framework is a superior regulatory framework than the categorical ban on vertical agreements that was proffered in the 2015 Order.[17]

What Harms Can the Antitrust Framework Reach?

Some critics acknowledge the role a rule of reason framework can play in regulating ISPs' vertical agreements, but claim that it might not work in all instances, or reach all possible types of harms.[18] These critics contend that antitrust's consumer welfare framework allows it to reach anticompetitive conduct that manifests in the form of a reduction in output or an increase in price, but not reductions in quality or incentives to innovate.[19] Some critics have argued that the possibility of harms existing "outside" the antitrust framework justify a blanket prohibition on vertical contracts and paid prioritization, as laid out by the 2015 Order. Others argue this alleged "gap" in the antitrust laws calls for a "new" framework that substitutes a focus on consumer welfare with an analysis of whether discrimination is "unreasonable," regardless of its effects on consumers.

Both groups of critics reveal a profound and fundamental lack of understanding of the rule of reason framework. The rule of reason, and antitrust jurisprudence generally, has evolved to reach all forms of competitive harms – including innovation and quality. One need not go beyond the *Horizontal Merger Guidelines* to see evidence of this evolution. Neither the original 1968 Merger Guidelines, nor the 1982 Merger Guidelines, mentioned potential harm to innovation. The 1992 Guidelines and their 1997 revision only loosely allude to the subject as a potential merger efficiency.[20] However, two decades later, the 2010 *Guidelines* prominently include an entire section on potential harm to innovation, suggesting that the FTC believes such harms are clearly actionable and within their purview.[21] Importantly, the 2010 HMGs, like all Merger Guidelines, do not initiate new policies, but describe what is already happening inside the agencies.

Furthermore, the FTC has acted on numerous mergers that in either strong or weak terms reference "innovation" or "research and development" harms. Between 2004 and 2014 the FTC challenged 164 mergers, and 54 of them alleged harm to innovation. Clearly, there were other mergers that alleged conduct amounting to harm to innovation without specifically using those phrases.[22] These developments clearly show that harms to innovation are cognizable within antitrust; but net neutrality proponents skeptical of the antitrust approach will be quick to point out that these are mergers and not potentially exclusionary or discriminatory conduct such as vertical restraints.

Antitrust can reach innovation concerns in those cases too. The FTC has pursued several conduct cases where the theory of harm was decreased innovation. For example, consider the FTC's allegations against Intel.[23] The FTC alleged Intel's conduct would likely result in the monopolization of the GPU market in violation of Section 2 of the Sherman Act. Intel manipulated CPU industry standards to advance their own products and prevented competitors from introducing a competing product – in short harming CPU innovation. The FTC alleged that "the loss of price and innovation competition in the relevant markets will continue to have an adverse effect on competition and hence consumers."[24] Further, the FTC alleged that there were no offsetting procompetitive efficiencies and sought to enjoin Intel.[25] This case is a clear example that under existing antitrust laws the FTC alleged harm to innovation based upon vertical agreements.[26]

The FTC has also been active in alleging harm to innovation in the pharmaceutical industry.[27] For example, in the case *Grifols, S.A./Talecris Biotherapeutics Holdings Corp.*, the FTC alleged that the proposed merger between two manufacturers of plasma-derived drugs would "increase the likelihood that consumers experience lower levels of innovation and service" in the relevant product markets.[28] The FTC's concerns could not be remedied by further investigation, but rather through a consent decree. The

FTC required the merging firms to divest a significant number of production facilities as well as manufacture three plasma-derived products for another firm in the industry for several years.[29]

In *Mylan Pharmaceuticals, Inc. v. Warner Chilcott plc, et al.*, the FTC filed an *amicus* brief urging the Third Circuit to reverse the district court's ruling.[30] Mylan alleged that the Defendants intentionally circumvented generic competition for their acne drug by engaging in anticompetitive product hopping.[31] Invoking the rule of reason analysis in support of Mylan, the FTC asserted that "policies favoring innovation do not categorically preclude antitrust liability for product-hopping."[32]

The Antitrust Division at the Department of Justice has brought similar cases. Such was the case in the landmark antitrust case, *United States v. Microsoft*, where Microsoft's long-term market dominance, "browser wars," and pattern of penalizing companies that were offering consumer efficiencies led Judge Jackson to clearly note that Microsoft's conduct was harmful to innovation.[33]

Since *Microsoft*, the Antitrust Division has brought similar cases such as a lawsuit to prevent H&R Block Inc. from purchasing TaxACT.[34] The Antitrust Division alleged that the proposed merger would have an effect on competition "resulting in less innovation and higher prices for consumers."[35] The Antitrust Division alleged that H&R Block's acquisition of TaxACT would eliminate a firm that substantially "disrupted" the market for do-it-yourself tax preparation products and lessened the incentives to innovate.[36]

The Antitrust Division has alleged harm to innovation in several mergers, including those in high-technology markets.[37] Like the FTC, harm to innovation is a consideration that the Antitrust Division consistently considers in merger enforcement.[38] Thus, claims that the antitrust laws cannot reach harm to innovation either because such harms are not cognizable under antitrust law or because the agencies are unwilling to bring cases are each incorrect.

Conclusion

Economic analysis predicted the 2015 Open Internet Order ban on vertical agreements would likely harm consumers and depress investment. Empirical evidence is consistent with those predictions. Reclassifying Internet service providers under Title I restores incentives to invest in broadband markets. A less obvious benefit is that it replaces the 2015 Order's categorical ban on contract arrangements that benefit consumers – including paid prioritization and other vertical arrangements – with antitrust's rule of reason. A close look at the antitrust approach shows not only that it can reach the harms envisioned by net neutrality proponents, but also that it is superior to alternatives that would condemn vertical arrangements in broadband markets without proof of harm to competition.

* Joshua D. Wright is a University Professor and Executive Director of the Global Antitrust Institute, Scalia Law School at George Mason University, a former Member of the Federal Trade Commission, and a Member of the Free State Foundation's Board of Academic Advisors. The valuable research assistance of Jay Kaplan and Thomas Rucker is gratefully acknowledged.

Endnotes

1   In the Matter of Protecting and Promoting the Open Internet, WC Docket No. 14-28, Report and Order on Remand, Declaratory Ruling, and Order, 30 FCC Rcd 5616 (2015).

2   United States Telecom Ass'n v. FCC, 825 F.3d 674 (D.C.C. 2016), *reh'g en banc denied*, No. 15-1063, 2017 WL 1541517, at *1 (D.C.C. May 1, 2017) (stating that "[e]n banc review would be particularly unwarranted at this point in light of the uncertainty surrounding the fate of the FCC's Order").

3   In the Matter of Restoring Internet Freedom. Federal Communications Commission, WC Docket No. 17-108, April 27, 2017.

4   *See* Hal Singer, *2016 Broadband Capex Survey: Tracking Investment in the Title II Era* (Mar. 1, 2017), *available at* https://haljsinger.wordpress.com/2017/03/01/2016-broadband-capex-survey-tracking-investment-in-the-title-ii-era. Investment decreased for eight of the twelve major ISPs in Singer's study. The largest decrease was $3.4 billion or 16.2% by AT&T and $2.4 billion or 62.7% by Sprint. *See generally* Thomas W. Hazlett & Joshua D. Wright, *The Effect of Regulation on Broadband Markets: Evaluating the Empirical Evidence in the FCC's 2015 "Open Internet" Order*, 50 Rev. of Indus. Org. 487, 489 (2017).

5   *See* Joint Statement of Acting FTC Chairman Maureen K. Ohlhausen and FCC Chairman Ajit Pai on Protecting Americans' Online Privacy, (Mar. 1, 2017) ("We still believe that jurisdiction over broadband providers' privacy and data security practices should be returned to the FTC, the nation's expert agency with respect to these important subjects.") *available at* https://www.ftc.gov/news-events/press-releases/2017/03/joint-statement-acting-ftc-chairman-maureen-k-ohlhausen-fcc; Alden Abbott, *You Don't Need the FCC: How the FTC Can Successfully Police Broadband-Related Internet Abuses*, (May 20, 2015) ("The…FTC has ample authority under Section 5 of the …FTC Act…to challenge any

harmful conduct by entities involved in Internet broadband services markets when such conduct undermines competition or harms consumers.") *available at* http://www.heritage.org/government-regulation/report/you-dont-need-the-fcc-how-the-ftc-can-successfully-police-broadband.

6   Brandon Sasso, *Forget the FCC – Should the FTC Enforce Net Neutrality?*, (June 20, 2014) ("I have the highest admiration for the antitrust laws," [Tim] Wu testified. "But I simply don't think they're equipped to handle the broad range of values and policies that are implicated by net neutrality and the open Internet.") *available at* https://www.theatlantic.com/politics/archive/2014/06/forget-the-fcc-should-the-ftc-enforce-net-neutrality/456918/; Hal Singer, *A New Path Forward For Net Neutrality*, (Jan. 10, 2017) ("Unfortunately, antitrust laws are not up to the task of policing discrimination on the Internet."), *available at* https://www.forbes.com/sites/washingtonbytes/2017/01/10/a-new-path-forward-for-net-neutrality/#2bb207ce79c2.

7   *See* Hazlett & Wright, *supra* note 4, at 489.

8   Letter from the Staff of the Fed. Trade Comm'n, to Marlene H. Dortch, Secretary, Fed. Comm. Comm'n (July 17, 2017) *available at* https://www.ftc.gov/system/files/documents/advocacy_documents/comment-staff-bureau-consumer-protection-bureau-competition-bureau-economics-federal-trade/ftc_staff_comment_to_fcc_wc_docket_no17-108_7-17-17.pdf [hereinafter Letter from FTC Staff].

9   *See* Joshua D. Wright, Comm'r, Fed. Trade Comm'n, Net Neutrality Meets Regulatory Economics 101, Remarks at the Federalist Society Media and Telecommunications Practice Group Event: *The Future of Media – Is Government Regulation in Today's Media Landscape "Over-The-Top"?* (Feb. 25, 2015), *available at* https://www.ftc.gov/system/files/documents/

public_statements/626591/150225wrightfedsoc.pdf.

10 *See* Francine LaFontaine and Margaret Slade, *Vertical Integration and Firm Boundaries: The Evidence*, 45 J. Econ. Lit. Vol. 629, 680 (2007) ("Under most circumstances, profit maximizing vertical-integration decisions are efficient, not just from the firms' but also from the consumers' points of view…we have found clear evidence that restrictions on vertical integration…are usually detrimental to consumers. Given the weight of the evidence, it behooves government agencies to reconsider the validity of such restrictions."); *see also* Letter from FTC Staff, *supra* note 8, at 28 ("Most forms of vertical integration can generate procompetitive efficiencies, thus antitrust analysis generally regards them as harmless or even beneficial to consumer welfare.").

11 Daniel O'Brien, *The Antitrust Treatment of Vertical Restraints: Beyond the Possibility Theorems*, Report: The Pros and Cons of Vertical Restraints 40, 72-73 (2008). There is a consensus among empirical economists that vertical agreements are procompetitive.

12 Wright Remarks, *supra* note 9.

13 *See* Austan Goolsbee, *Vertical Integration and the Market for Broadcast and Cable Television Programming*. (Apr. 2007), *available at* https://apps.fcc.gov/edocs_public/attachmatch/DA-07-3470A10.pdf. The 2010 Order claims "the Goolsbee Study provides empirical evidence that cable providers have acted in the past on anticompetitive incentives to foreclose rivals, supporting our concern that these and other broadband providers would act on analogous incentives in the future."; *but see* Thomas W. Hazlett & Joshua D. Wright, *The Law and Economics of Network Neutrality*, 45 Ind. L. Rev. 767, 813-34 (2012). Hazlett & Wright point out that in Goolsbee's actual findings "operators have discriminated against the programming services that they owned—the opposite of [harms stemming from] vertical foreclosure," certainly do not support the economic logic underlying the 2010 or 2015 Orders.

14   *See* Wright Remarks, *supra* note 9.

15   *Id.* ("The rule of reason requires that each vertical arrangement be assessed on a case-by-case basis by marshaling the available economic literature and empirical evidence to evaluate the evidence of actual competitive harm under the specific circumstances of the case.").

16   *See generally* Hazlett & Wright, *supra* note 4.

17   *See* Letter from FTC Staff, *supra* note 8, at 29 ("The FTC's activities in Internet-related markets demonstrate its ability to protect the competitive process, promote the innovation that such competition fosters, and preserve the resulting benefits to consumers.").

18   See e.g., Hal Singer, *Why Antitrust Cannot Reach the Part of Net Neutrality That Everyone Is Concerned About* (Apr. 29, 2017), https://haljsinger.wordpress.com/2017/04/29/why-antitrust-cannot-reach-the-part-of-net-neutrality-that-everyone-is-concerned-about/; Washington Bytes, *The Future Of Antitrust Enforcement: Innovation, Wage Inequality And Democracy*, (June 15, 2017), https://www.forbes.com/sites/washingtonbytes/2017/06/15/the-future-of-antitrust-enforcement-innovation-wage-inequality-and-democracy/#70114556145d; Washington Bytes, *Is Antitrust The Right Framework For Net Neutrality?* (Mar. 15, 2017), https://www.forbes.com/sites/washingtonbytes/2017/03/15/is-antitrust-the-right-framework-for-net-neutrality/#17c9d5e28b53.

19   *Id.*

20   U.S. Dep't of Justice & Fed. Trade Comm'n, Horizontal Merger Guidelines § 4 (rev. 1997), *available at* https://www.justice.gov/atr/horizontal-merger-guidelines-0. The 1992 *Horizontal Merger Guidelines* do not explicitly refer to harm to innovation, but only that "[e]fficiencies also may result in benefits in the form of new or improved products, and efficiencies may result in benefits even when price is not immediately and directly affected."

21   Richard J. Gilbert & Hillary Greene, *Merging Innovation into Antitrust Agency Enforcement of the Clayton Act*, 83 Geo. Wash. L. Rev. 1919, 1931-32 (2015).

22   *Id.* at 1933.

23   *See* Complaint, Intel Corp., Docket No. 9341 (F.T.C. Dec. 16, 2009) *available at* https://www.ftc.gov/sites/default/files/documents/cases/091216intelcmpt.pdf.

24   *Id.* at ¶ 27.

25   *Id.* at ¶ 91 ("Intel's conduct has no legitimate or sufficient business justification and has and will continue to harm competition, innovation, and consumers, unless it is enjoined.").

26   *See generally* Joshua D. Wright, *An Antitrust Analysis of the Federal Trade Commission's Complaint Against Intel*, 38 Rev. Ind. Org. 387 (June 2011).

27   *See, e.g.,* Novartis AG/GlaxoSmithKline, PLC, FTC File No. 141-0141 (Filed Feb. 23, 2015) (alleging harmful effects on the future development of cancer treatment products), *available at https://www.ftc.gov/system/files/documents/cases/complaint_0.pdf*; Pfizer Inc./Wyeth, FTC File No. 0910053 (Filed Jan. 29, 2010) (alleging a reduction in incentives to innovate in the markets for animal pharmaceuticals and vaccines), *available at* https://www.ftc.gov/sites/default/files/documents/cases/2010/01/091014pwyethcmpt.pdf; Genzyme Corp./Novazyme Pharms., Inc., FTC File No. 021-0026 (investigating potential harm to innovation in the development of treatments for Pompe disease); Pfizer Inc./Warner-Lambert Co., FTC File No. 001-0059 (Filed July 28, 2000) (alleging reduction of innovation in the markets for OTC pediculicides and drugs for the treatment of Alzheimer's disease), *available at https://www.ftc.gov/sites/default/files/documents/cases/2000/07/pfizercmp.htm*; Ciba-Geigy, Ltd./Sandoz, FTC File No. 961-0055 (Filed Apr. 8, 1997) (alleging a harmful impact on innovation in the market for gene therapies and flea control products), *available at https://www.ftc.gov/sites/default/files/documents/cases/1997/04/c3725cmp.pdf.*

28   Grifols, S.A./Talecris Biotherapeutics Holdings Corp., FTC File No. 1010153 (Filed Jul. 22, 2011), *available at* https://www.ftc.gov/sites/default/files/documents/cases/2011/07/110601grifolsacmpt.pdf.

29   *Id.*

30   838 F.3d 421 (3rd Cir. 2016). The district court held that Warner Chilcott lacked monopoly power and that product hopping almost never constitutes exclusionary conduct. *Mylan Pharms. Inc. v. Warner Chilcott Pub. Co.*, No. 12-3824, 2015 WL 1736957 (E.D. Pa. 2015).

31   *Mylan*, 838 F.3d at 426.

32   Brief for Amicus Curiae Fed. Trade Comm'n Supporting Plaintiff-Appellant at 14, *Mylan Pharms. Inc. v. Warner Chilcott Pub. Co.*, 883 F.3d 421 (3rd Cir. 2016) (filed Oct. 19, 2016).

33   United States v. Microsoft Corp., 253 F.3d 34, 60 (D.C.C. 2001).

34   United States v. H&R Block, Inc., 833 F. Supp. 2d 36, (D.C.C. 2011).

35   Complaint ¶ 2, H&R Block, Inc., 833 F. Supp. 2d 36 (D.D.C. 2011) (filed May 23, 2011) *available at* https://www.justice.gov/atr/case-document/complaint-119. Speaking about the potential harm to innovation resulting from the merger, Christine Varney, then Assistant Attorney General, asserted that "TaxACT has aggressively competed in the digital do-it-yourself tax preparation market with innovation such as free federal filing. If this merger is allowed to proceed, that type of innovation will be lost." *Justice Department Files Antitrust Lawsuit to Stop H&R Block Inc. From Buying TaxACT*, Department of Justice (May 23, 2011) *available at* https://www.justice.gov/opa/pr/justice-department-files-antitrust-lawsuit-stop-hr-block-inc-buying-taxact.

36   Complaint, *supra* note 35, at ¶ 28.

37   *See* Complaint ¶ 50, *United States v. Bazaarvoice*, No. 3:13-cv-00133 (N.D. Cal. 2014) (filed Jan. 10, 2013) ("Quality and innovation for PRR platforms will likely be less than the levels that would have prevailed absent the transaction."), *available at* http://www.justice.gov/atr/cases/f291100/291187.pdf; Second Amended Complaint, ¶ 48, *United States v. AT&T et al.*, No. 11-01560 (D.D.C.) (filed Sept. 30, 2011) ("[I[nnovation and product variety likely will be reduced"), *available at* https://www.justice.gov/atr/case-document/second-amended-complaint.

38   *See* Renata B. Hesse, Deputy Assistant Att'y Gen., Antitrust Div., Dep't of Justice, Remarks at the Conference on Competition and IP Policy in High-Technology Industries (Jan. 22, 2014) ("While competitive prices are…a key objective, the division fully appreciate the importance of innovation.").

19.
The FTC Has the Authority, Expertise, and Capability to Protect Broadband Consumers

Theodore R. Bolema [*]

Perspectives from FSF Scholars, October 19, 2017, Vol. 12, No. 35

I. Introduction and Summary

As part of its *Restoring Internet Freedom* Notice of Proposed Rulemaking (NPRM), the Federal Communications Commission is reevaluating its regulatory authority over consumer protection matters involving Internet service providers (ISPs).[1] If the FCC decides it lacks authority to regulate ISPs as telecommunications carriers under Title II of the Communications Act, the effect of this decision should be to restore the Federal Trade Commission to the role it held until 2015. In essence, this means the FTC would be the lead federal agency with responsibility for safeguarding online privacy and for protecting consumers against other ISP practices that allegedly are anticompetitive or cause consumer harm.

Consumers will be well served if the FTC takes the lead in fulfilling these important consumer protection functions. The FTC's capabilities, expertise, and analytical approach toward privacy enforcement make it the preferred agency for addressing online privacy practices across all digital platforms. The FTC has gained extensive experience protecting privacy from several decades of investigating and bringing cases in many industries, including cases involving online privacy and ISPs.

By reclassifying ISPs as Title II telecommunications service providers, the 2015 *Open Internet Order* ("*Title II Order*") effectively stripped the FTC of its jurisdiction over broadband ISP practices that are potentially harmful to consumers, including practices involving online privacy.[2] After assuming this newly-derived Title II regulatory authority, the FCC adopted stringent, prescriptive privacy restrictions on ISPs, including opt-in requirements, which were not applicable to non-ISPs like Google, Facebook, and Amazon that collect far more personal data over the Internet than ISPs. Under the FTC's privacy regime, these non-ISPs remained subject to less stringent privacy protecting regulation, including opt-out requirements.[3]

The resulting asymmetric and confusing privacy enforcement approach has been criticized by current and former consumer protection officials from both political parties. When the FCC's overreaching privacy order was blocked by a joint resolution from the U.S. Congress, the Internet privacy protection regime was further complicated.[4] The FCC now has an opportunity to help end the current uncertainty about Internet consumer protection policy and enforcement by restoring the primary authority to the agency best suited to the task – the Federal Trade Commission.

If its authority is restored, the FTC will be re-empowered to use Section 5 of the Federal Trade Commission Act of 1914 to investigate and bring enforcement actions to stop law violations and require ISPs to take affirmative steps to remediate any unlawful behavior. If a company violates an FTC order, the FTC can seek civil monetary penalties for the violations. The FTC can also obtain civil monetary penalties for violations of certain privacy statutes and rules. Using this authority, the FTC says that to date it has brought hundreds of privacy and data security cases protecting billions of consumers.[5]

The FTC's Bureau of Consumer Protection already includes a dedicated Division of Privacy and Identity Protection, a staff of economists, and investigative staff in field offices around the country.[6] Even though the FTC has been precluded from privacy enforcement regarding ISPs' practices recently, it has continued its privacy protection activities in all of the other Internet ecosystem market segments subject to its jurisdiction. And it still has staff with experience in privacy enforcement with regard to telecommunications. In contrast, the FCC staff has limited experience that is specific to ISP privacy protection.

Federal antitrust enforcement, by the FTC and by the Antitrust Division of the Department of Justice, can also address consumer protection concerns related to Internet providers. The Antitrust Division and the FTC both have authority to investigate and pursue legal action in instances where broadband ISPs engage in anticompetitive practices that could be considered potential antitrust violations. The Antitrust Division already has an established Telecommunications and Media Enforcement Section that "is responsible for civil antitrust enforcement, competition advocacy, and competition policy in the areas of the Internet, including the services infrastructure and hardware that comprise the Internet."[7]

One of the main arguments that has been asserted for retaining Title II classification of ISPs is that only public utility-style prescriptive regulations are sufficient to address broadband privacy and consumer protection concerns. Pro-regulation groups have asserted that the *ex post* enforcement approach of the FTC is not up to the task, and only prescriptive regulation imposed *ex ante* can protect consumers.

This argument fails to appreciate how the case-by-case enforcement of the FTC has a strong deterrent effect as companies look at past enforcement instances to guide their conduct. It also ignores the considerable problems with *ex ante* prescriptive regulation in a technologically dynamic, rapidly changing market. Rulemaking imposes standards based on regulators' predictions about the future conduct and incentives impacting regulated firms. Prescriptive regulations often do more harm than good as markets evolve in ways regulators cannot predict. Case-by-case enforcement, by contrast, involves no such predictions because it challenges and remedies conduct that has already occurred. The *ex ante* approach also requires frequent revision through a notice-and-comment process, which generally will be even more time-consuming than the *ex post* investigative and enforcement approach long used by the FTC. As such, *ex ante* privacy regulation by the FCC inevitably would fail to anticipate and keep up with rapid changes in Internet technology and market practices. For these reasons, the arguments for *ex ante* prescriptive regulation over *ex post* case-by-case regulation provide no support for retaining Title II regulation of broadband providers.

The Federal Trade Commission has been the primary agency for privacy protection enforcement in the United States for several decades. Its expertise in this field exceeds that of any other federal or state agency and makes the FTC the better choice over the FCC to be the primary federal regulatory agency in charge of addressing privacy and other allegedly harmful ISP practices, such as throttling or paid prioritization. The reasons the FTC is better suited for this role include the FTC's established institutional structures and expertise gained from its enforcement experience, the FTC's established protocols and precedents from its enforcement activities, and the uncertainty added to the market from having an agency without such attributes take over this important regulatory function.

II. Broadband Consumer Protection Before and Since the *Open Internet Order*

The Telecommunications Act of 1996 draws a distinction between Title I "information services" and Title II "telecommunications services." Title I information services are lightly regulated, if at all, while Title II telecommunications services are considered common carriers and may be subject to public utility-style regulation.[8] Before 2015, ISPs were classified as Title I information services, which allowed broadband services to develop and thrive with relatively light touch regulation. During this time, the Federal Trade Commission, as well as other state and federal enforcement agencies, had the same authority over broadband that they have over other market participants under their general enforcement statutes.

By reclassifying broadband providers as Title II telecommunications services, the 2015 *Title II Order* effectively stripped the FTC of jurisdiction over broadband ISP practices that are potentially harmful to consumers, including practices involving online privacy.[9] After assuming this regulatory authority, the FCC adopted its 2016 *Broadband Privacy Order*.[10] This *Order* imposed stringent privacy restrictions on ISPs, including opt-in consent requirements. The *Order* also, in effect, left non-ISPs like Google, Facebook, and Amazon that collect far more personal data over the Internet than ISPs do, with less stringent requirements, including in most instances only opt-out consent requirements. Therefore, the effect of the *Broadband Privacy Order* was to unfairly disadvantage broadband ISPs and confuse consumers with its uneven application.[11]

Thomas Pahl, Acting Director of the FTC's Bureau of Consumer Protection, speaking this year at the Free State Foundation's Ninth Annual Telecom Policy Conference, critiqued the FCC's approach and contrasted it with the long-standing privacy policy of the FTC:

The FCC's *Open Internet Order* therefore effectively prevented the FTC from engaging in enforcement, rulemaking, and other consumer protection activities concerning ISPs' online data security and privacy. In 2016, as many of you know, the FCC followed its *Open Internet Order* with the issuance of rules restricting and limiting ISPs' data security and practices. In doing so, the FCC chose a more rigid and prescriptive approach to broadband data security and privacy issues than the FTC's traditional case-by-case approach to these topics. The FCC's rules also set standards for broadband providers separate and apart from standards applicable to others in the online space, eschewing the FTC's more comprehensive approach.[12]

The FCC's *Broadband Privacy Order* attracted strong bipartisan criticism, as former FTC Chairman Jon Leibowitz explained:

> As the former Democratic chairman of the Federal Trade Commission, the nation's leading privacy enforcement agency, which has brought more than 500 privacy cases, including more than 50 cases against companies for misusing or failing to reasonably protect customer data, let me assure you: the FCC's rules are deeply flawed.
>
> By creating a separate set of regulations that bind only internet service providers — but not other companies that collect as much or more consumer data — with heightened restrictions on the use and sharing of data that are out of sync with consumer expectations, the FCC rejected the bedrock principle of technology-neutral privacy rules

recognized by the FTC, the Obama administration, and consumer advocates alike. Protecting privacy is about putting limits on what data is collected and how it is being used, not who is doing the collecting, and for that reason, a unanimous FTC — that is, both Democratic and Republican commissioners — actually criticized the FCC's proposed rule in a bipartisan and unanimous comment letter as "not optimal," among 27 other specific criticisms of the rule.[13]

The implementation of the *Broadband Privacy Order* was later blocked by a joint resolution from the U.S. Congress pursuant to the Congressional Review Act.[14] Thus, as the FCC considers its current NPRM and whether to return ISPs to their former Title I classification, consumer protection regarding Internet ecosystem players has been in flux. The FCC now has an opportunity to end the current uncertainty about consumer protection policy and enforcement by restoring authority over this field to the agency best suited to the task – the Federal Trade Commission.

III. The FTC Possesses the Authority, Expertise, and Capability to Protect Broadband Consumers

The FCC should recognize that the FTC's capabilities, expertise, and analytical approach toward privacy issues make it the preferred agency for addressing online privacy practices across all digital platforms. The FTC has gained extensive experience in protecting privacy from investigating and bringing cases in many industries, including cases involving online privacy and ISPs.

Institutional Capabilities of the FTC

The FTC has considerable authority to implement, investigate, and enforce privacy and consumer protection under Section 5 of the Federal Trade Commission Act of 1914, as well as from other federal statutes that further enhance its regulatory authority. The FTC describes the source of its consumer protection authority as follows:

> The Federal Trade Commission . . . is an independent U.S. law enforcement agency charged with protecting consumers and enhancing competition across broad sectors of the economy. The FTC's primary legal authority comes from Section 5 of the Federal Trade Commission Act, which prohibits unfair or deceptive practices in the marketplace. The FTC also has authority to enforce a variety of sector specific laws, including the Truth in Lending Act, the CAN-SPAM Act, the Children's Online Privacy Protection Act, the Equal Credit Opportunity Act, the Fair Credit Reporting Act, the Fair Debt Collection Practices Act, and the Telemarketing and Consumer Fraud and Abuse Prevention Act. This broad authority allows the Commission to address a wide array of practices affecting consumers, including those that emerge with the development of new technologies and business models.[15]

In carrying out this regulatory mission, the FTC can draw on an extensive toolbox that it uses to protect privacy and enforce other consumer protections:

> The FTC uses a variety of tools to protect consumers' privacy and personal information. The FTC's principal tool is to bring enforcement actions to stop law violations and require

companies to take affirmative steps to remediate the unlawful behavior. This includes, when appropriate, implementation of comprehensive privacy and security programs, biennial assessments by independent experts, monetary redress to consumers, disgorgement of ill-gotten gains, deletion of illegally obtained consumer information, and provision of robust notice and choice mechanisms to consumers. If a company violates an FTC order, the FTC can seek civil monetary penalties for the violations. The FTC can also obtain civil monetary penalties for violations of certain privacy statutes and rules, including the Children's Online Privacy Protection Act, the Fair Credit Reporting Act, and the Telemarketing Sales Rule. To date, the Commission has brought hundreds of privacy and data security cases protecting billions of consumers.

The FTC's other tools include conducting studies and issuing reports, hosting public workshops, developing educational materials for consumers and businesses, testifying before the U.S. Congress and commenting on legislative and regulatory proposals that affect consumer privacy, and working with international partners on global privacy and accountability issues.[16]

The FTC's Bureau of Consumer Protection already includes a dedicated Division of Privacy and Identity Protection. This Division works closely with the FTC's other divisions, including the economists in its Bureau of Economics and the investigative staff in field offices across the country, which also have developed their own expertise in consumer protection matters. The FTC currently has field offices in Atlanta, Chicago, Cleveland, Dallas, Los Angeles, New York, San Francisco, and Seattle which "help to amplify our national impact and local presence, and allow us to respond better to the diversity of the U.S. marketplace."[17]

Expertise of the FTC

Pro-regulation groups seeking to have the FTC retain its Title II regulation of ISP have claimed that the FTC does not have sufficient expertise to protect consumer privacy on the Internet. For example, Public Knowledge and Common Cause have claimed:

> [A]lthough the FTC does have experience and expertise protecting consumer privacy, it is not the expert agency on communications networks. . . . By giving the FTC exclusive jurisdiction to protect consumer broadband privacy, the FCC would not only turn a blind eye to its own expertise on communications networks but would also rob consumers of the sole privacy cop on the beat with that expertise (citations omitted).[18]

This claim significantly mischaracterizes the experience and expertise of the FTC. Maureen K. Ohlhausen, Acting Chairman of the Federal Trade Commission, speaking at the Free State Foundation's Eighth Annual Telecom Policy Conference in 2016, explained the FTC's expertise over privacy issues as follows:

> Despite rumors to the contrary, the FTC is the primary privacy and data protection agency in the U.S., and probably the most active enforcer of privacy laws in the world. We have brought more than 150 privacy and data security enforcement actions, including actions against ISPs and against

some of the biggest companies in the Internet ecosystem. (For our purposes here I consider data security to be a subset of privacy. So when I say "privacy" today I also mean data security.) The FTC has gained this expertise because of - not in spite of - our prudent privacy approach, which maximizes consumer self-determination.[19]

In contrast, the FCC has not claimed regulatory authority over privacy matters relating to ISP offerings until recently, so it is behind the curve vis-à-vis the FTC. While the FCC has a strong staff of economists and other experts, as well as its own offices throughout the country, the FCC's personnel have limited experience that is specific to Internet service provider privacy protection.

Even though the FTC has been precluded from privacy enforcement relating to Internet service providers recently as a result of the FCC's Title II classification, it has continued its privacy protection activities in all of the other industries subject to its jurisdiction. And it still has staff with experience in privacy enforcement in telecommunications. Acting Director Pahl of the FTC described what the public could expect if jurisdiction over broadband ISP privacy practices is returned to the FTC:

> The FTC is ready, willing, and able to protect the data security and privacy of broadband subscribers . . . .We have a wealth of consumer protection and competition experience and expertise, which we will bring to bear on online data security and privacy laws. We will apply data security and privacy standards to all companies that compete in the online space regardless of whether the companies provide broadband services, data analysis, social media, or other services.

Our approach would ensure the standards the
government applies are comprehensive, consistent,
and pro-competitive.[20]

The FTC Has Established Protocols and Precedents

The FTC website describes the balance the agency must strike in
its privacy protection enforcement:

> In all of its privacy work, the FTC's goals have
> remained constant: to protect consumers' personal
> information and ensure that consumers have the
> confidence to take advantage of the many benefits
> offered in the marketplace.[21]

Acting Chairman Maureen Ohlhausen further explained the
FTC's approach to privacy protection:

Specifically, our unfairness authority prohibits practices that
cause substantial harm that is unavoidable by consumers and
which is not outweighed by benefits to consumers or competition.
Practices that the FTC has found unfair consistently match practices that consumers generally reject. For example, we brought
an unfairness case against a data broker that sold highly sensitive
financial information to individuals whom the data broker knew
or should have known were identity thieves.

> Thus, unfairness establishes a baseline prohibition
> on practices that the overwhelming majority
> of consumers would never knowingly approve.
> Above that baseline, consumers remain free to find
> providers that match their preferences, and our
> deception authority governs those arrangements.

Establishing the baseline at the proper level
is important. Too low, and we would not stop
harmful practices that most consumers oppose.
Too high, and we would prohibit services many
consumers would prefer. If we set the privacy
baseline too high, the privacy preferences of the
few are imposed on the many. Our unfairness test's
emphasis on real consumer harm and cost-benefit
analysis helps ensure that the baseline is in the
right place. And the FTC's procedural protections,
such as review by our Bureau of Economics and
mandatory Commission votes on settlements,
create consensus and force changes to be
incremental. Thus, privacy practices found by the
FTC to be unfair are those that reflect consumer
consensus (footnotes omitted).[22]

The FTC's record on privacy regulation is hardly immune
from criticism, but it has the advantage of being performed by
an agency with a long history of applying economic analysis to its
enforcement actions. Professor Joshua Wright, a member of the
Free State Foundation's Board of Academic Advisors and former
FTC Commissioner, in a speech in which he criticized some FTC
analysis in privacy cases for a lack of rigor and transparency, nonetheless argues that the FTC still can and should be the intellectual
leader in creating economically coherent privacy regulation:

The FTC is at its best when it combines its unique
combination of institutional features. Perhaps the
most unique is that the FTC's statutory mandate
includes a research and reporting function
that distinguishes it from many agencies. The
Commission has a long and well-regarded history
of conducting its own research and using its

authority to produce public reports that examine
novel, emerging or otherwise important issues.
Privacy should be no exception. The case for
strengthening the incentives within the agency for
FTC economists to produce their own research,
and to be active and engaged scholars in the field of
privacy economics, is quite clear.[23]

IV. Federal Antitrust Enforcement Can Also Address Many Consumer Protection Concerns

If the FCC rescinds its Title II public utility regulation of broadband Internet access services and declines to impose new regulations, there are other avenues available to protect consumers
and market competition. With the FTC's jurisdiction restored by
Title I reclassification, allegedly harmful blocking, degrading, and
throttling practices, which are the subject of current prohibitions
contained in the *Title II Order*, might be considered violations of
the terms of service by broadband ISPs and could be investigated
by the FTC as deceptive trade practices that are subject to enforcement actions.[24]

The Department of Justice and the FTC both have authority to
investigate and pursue legal action in instances where broadband
ISPs engage in anticompetitive practices that could be considered
potential antitrust violations. The DOJ Antitrust Division already
has an established Telecommunications and Media Enforcement
Section that "is responsible for civil antitrust enforcement, competition advocacy, and competition policy in the areas of the
Internet, including the services infrastructure and hardware that
comprise the Internet."[25]

Professor Wright explains why antitrust is superior to the
Open Internet Order approach that banned paid prioritization and
other vertical arrangements involving ISPs without proof of harm
to competition:

Despite the 2015 Order ban on vertical agreements by Internet service providers, rule of reason analysis would not similarly result in a total ban on vertical agreements because economics literature clearly indicates that while vertical agreements are capable of harming competition in the manner contemplated by net neutrality proponents, more often than not they are beneficial to consumers. Furthermore, with few exceptions, the [economics] literature does not support the view that these practices are used for anticompetitive reasons. . . . Reclassifying Internet service providers under Title I would restore incentives to invest in broadband markets. A less obvious benefit is that it replaces the 2015 Order's categorical ban on contract arrangements that benefit consumers – including paid prioritization and other vertical arrangements – with antitrust jurisprudence's rule of reason. A close look at the antitrust approach shows not only that it can reach the harms envisioned by net neutrality proponents, but also that it is superior to alternatives that would condemn vertical arrangements in broadband markets without proof of harm to competition.[26]

V. *Ex Post* Regulation Is Generally Superior to *Ex Ante* Regulation in Dynamic Markets

One of the main arguments that had been asserted for retaining Title II classification of ISPs is that only public utility-style prescriptive regulations are sufficient to address broadband privacy and consumer protection concerns. Pro-regulation groups have asserted that the *ex post* enforcement approach of the FTC is too weak, and only prescriptive regulation imposed *ex ante* will protect consumers.

For example, Public Knowledge and Common Cause have argued:

> The FTC protects consumer privacy pursuant to its general consumer protection authority under section 5 of the Federal Trade Commission Act to bar unfair and deceptive acts or practices. Because the FTC lacks both effective rulemaking authority and specific power from Congress to develop standards to protect consumer privacy specifically, the agency is constrained by the limits of section 5 to apply the same, general "unfair and deceptive" standard to online privacy issues. Consequently, the FTC's enforcement actions usually involve broken privacy promises or determining whether companies are adhering to general industry practices rather than what practices would best protect consumers. Consumers expect adequate privacy protections when accessing broadband networks. Unfortunately, enforcement actions without the ability to adopt bright line rules are not enough to protect consumer broadband privacy (citations omitted).[27]

> Similarly, the Open Technology Institute has claimed:
> For broadband customers to retain genuine choice over how companies use their data, there should be *ex ante* rules in place, and a regulatory agency tasked with enforcing those rules. It is crucial for Americans to retain an expert agency in charge of protecting their privacy from broadband

companies in such a consolidated marketplace. That privacy protection, however, is contingent on the Commission retaining its Title II classification of broadband (citations omitted).[28]

The Open Technology Institute adds:

Shifting jurisdiction to the FTC would shift consumer privacy to an agency with less authority and more roadblocks to clear, bright-line protections. The FTC's effectiveness is undermined by a lengthy review process and limited enforcement of consent orders (citations omitted).[29]

Acting Director of the FTC's Consumer Protection Division Pahl recently explained the flaws in claims that *ex ante* privacy regulation would be superior:

Some have argued it would be better for the government to address online data security and privacy through regulation rather than proceeding case by case. Rulemaking imposes standards based on a prediction that they will be necessary and appropriate to address future conduct. Case-by-case enforcement, by contrast, involves no such prediction because it challenges and remedies conduct that has already occurred. Of course, such enforcement also has a prophylactic effect as companies look at past enforcement to guide their conduct. The Internet has evolved in ways that we could not have predicted, and is likely to continue to do so. Given the challenges of making predictions about the Internet's future, we need case-by-case enforcement which is strong, yet flexible, like steel guardrails. We do not need prescriptive regulation, which would be an iron cage.[30]

The *ex ante* prescriptive approach has other serious drawbacks, which are especially problematic in a dynamic market with ongoing technological change. Contrary to the claim by the Open Technology Institute, the *ex ante* approach would require constant revision through a notice-and-comment process, which generally will be even more time-consuming than the *ex post* investigative approach long used by the FTC. As such, *ex ante* privacy regulation by the FCC would inevitably fail to anticipate and keep up with rapid changes in Internet technology and practices. As Mr. Pahl explains:

> The call for rules to provide guidance on online data security and privacy also overestimates the guidance provided by prescriptive regulation. Prescriptive regulation, of course, can provide some certainty in the short term. But in fast-changing areas like online data security and privacy, regulations would need to be amended very often to remain current. Amending regulations is cumbersome and time consuming, even where agencies can use APA notice and comment rulemaking procedures. And so such amendments by agencies are very unlikely to keep up with the pace of change. Out-of-date rules can be very unclear in their application to new technologies and cause confusion and unintended consequences in the marketplace. [31]

Professor Daniel Lyons, a member of FSF's Board of Academic Advisers, speaking on the same panel as Mr. Pahl, stated:

> The FTC is well equipped to evaluate on a case-by-case basis whether a particular agreement is one that might harm consumers. Using robust law that's been developed from a number of different cases elsewhere in the economy... they have a broader scope informed by a lot more history than the Federal Communications Commission. I agree that the *ex post* review and flexibility the FTC brings is a lot better in a dynamic marketplace than the more rigid FCC *ex ante* rulemaking.[32]

These arguments by pro-regulation groups for *ex ante* privacy regulation by the FCC describe a false choice between an idealized version of *ex post* regulation and a version of *ex post* regulation that ignores some of its more important benefits. Besides failing to appreciate the tremendous institutional advantage of the established FTC Consumer Protection Division over a Federal Communications Commission that has only recently asserted its authority in this area, pro-regulation groups' arguments fail to appreciate the deterrence benefits that are achieved from *ex post* privacy regulation. They also completely fail to consider the impossibility of effectively tailoring *ex ante* regulation to future conduct that has not occurred, as well as to changing market realities. For these reasons, the arguments for *ex ante* regulation over *ex post* regulation provide no support for retaining Title II regulation of broadband providers.

VI. Conclusion

The Federal Trade Commission has been the primary agency for privacy and consumer protection enforcement in the United

States for several decades. Its expertise in this field exceeds that of any other federal or state agency and makes the FTC the better choice over the FCC to be the primary federal regulatory agency in charge of addressing privacy and other ISP practices. The reasons the FTC is better suited for this role include the FTC's established institutional structures and expertise gained from its enforcement experience, the FTC's established protocols and precedents from its enforcement activities, and the uncertainty added to the market from having an agency without such attributes assume primary responsibility for this important regulatory function. Broadband consumers will be well served if the FTC takes the lead in fulfilling these important consumer protection functions.

* Theodore R. Bolema is a Senior Fellow at the Free State Foundation, an independent, nonpartisan free market-oriented think tank located in Rockville, Maryland

Endnotes

1   Federal Communications Commission, "Protecting and Promoting the Open Internet Notice of Proposed Rulemaking" ("NPRM"), WC Docket No. 17-108; FCC 17-60, at ¶66, adopted May 18, 2017, available at: https://www.fcc.gov/document/restoring-internet-freedom-notice-proposed-rulemaking.

2   NPRM, at ¶66; Federal Communications Commission, "Protecting and Promoting the Open Internet Notice of Proposed Rulemaking," GN Docket No. 14-28 (February 26, 2015), at ¶462, available at: https://apps.fcc.gov/edocs_public/attachmatch/FCC-15-24A1.pdf.

3   Federal Communications Commission, "Protecting the Privacy of Customers of Broadband and Other Telecommunications Services," WC Docket No. 16-106 (October 27, 2016), available at: https://apps.fcc.gov/edocs_public/attachmatch/FCC-16-148A1.pdf.

4   U.S. Congress. Senate. A joint resolution providing for congressional disapproval under chapter 8 of title 5, United States Code, of the rule submitted by the Federal Communications Commission relating to "Protecting the Privacy of Customers of Broadband and Other Telecommunications Services," 115th Cong. 1st sess. S.J.R. 34.

5   U.S. Federal Trade Commission, "Privacy & Data Security Update" (January 2016), available at: https://www.ftc.gov/reports/privacy-data-security-update-2015#privacy.

6   U.S. Federal Trade Commission, "About the Bureau of Consumer Protection Update" (visited October 12, 2017), available at: https://www.ftc.gov/about-ftc/bureaus-offices/bureau-consumer-protection/about-bureau-consumer-protection.

7   U.S. Department of Justice, "Telecommunications and Media Enforcement Section," available at: https://www.justice.gov/atr/about-division/telecommunications-and-media-enforcement-section.

8   For a more complete discussion of the legal and jurisdictional issues raised by the Title II Order, see Comments of Free State Foundation, WC Docket No. 17-108 (July 17, 2017), available at: http://www.freestatefoundation.org/images/FSF_Initial_Comments_-_Restoring_Internet_Freedom_-_071717.pdf.

9   NPRM, at ¶66; Federal Communications Commission, "Protecting and Promoting the Open Internet Notice of Proposed Rulemaking," GN Docket No. 14-28 (February 26, 2015), at ¶462, available at: https://apps.fcc.gov/edocs_public/attachmatch/FCC-15-24A1.pdf.

10   Federal Communications Commission, "Protecting the Privacy of Customers of Broadband and Other Telecommunications Services," WC Docket No. 16-106 (October 27, 2016), available at: https://apps.fcc.gov/edocs_public/attachmatch/FCC-16-148A1.pdf.

11   For a more complete discussion of the flaws in 2016 Broadband Privacy Order, see Free State Foundation, Reply Comments to Oppositions for Petitions for Reconsideration, Protecting the Privacy of Customers of Broadband and Other Telecommunications Services, WC Docket No. 16-106 (March 16, 2017), available at: https://ecfsapi.fcc.gov/file/1031625753193/FSF%20Reply%20Comments%20Re%20Protecting%20the%20Privacy%20of%20Customers%20of%20Broadband%20and%20Other%20Telecommunications%20Services%20031617.pdf.

12   Thomas B. Pahl, "The View from the FTC: Overseeing Internet Practices in the Digital Age," panel discussion at the Free State Foundation's Ninth Annual Telecom Policy Conference (May 31, 2017), available at: http://www.freestatefoundation.org/images/May_31_2017_FTC_Panel_Transcript_072017.pdf.

13   Jon Leibowitz, Letter to the Editor, *Kennebec Journal* (April 13, 2017), available at: http://www.centralmaine.com/2017/04/13/former-ftc-chairman-collins-right-on-privacy/.

14   U.S. Congress. Senate. A joint resolution providing for congressional disapproval under Chapter 8 of Title 5, United States Code, of the rule submitted by the Federal Communications Commission relating to "Protecting the Privacy of Customers of Broadband and Other Telecommunications Services," 115th Cong. 1st sess. S.J.R. 34.

15   U.S. Federal Trade Commission, "Privacy & Data Security Update" (January 2016), available at: https://www.ftc.gov/reports/privacy-data-security-update-2015#privacy.

16   *Id.*

17   U.S. Federal Trade Commission, "About the Bureau of Consumer Protection Update" (visited June 25, 2017), available at: https://www.ftc.gov/about-ftc/bureaus-offices/bureau-consumer-protection/about-bureau-consumer-protection.

18   Comments of Public Knowledge and Common Cause, WC Docket No. 17-108 (July 17, 2017), at 91-92, available at: https://ecfsapi.fcc.gov/file/1071932385942/PK%20CC%20Updated%20Comments%20with%20Appendices%20FINAL.pdf.

19   Maureen K. Ohlhausen, Commissioner, U.S. Federal Trade Commission, "Privacy Regulation in the Internet Ecosystem," Free State Foundation Eighth Annual Telecom Policy Conference (March 23, 2016), available at: https://www.ftc.gov/system/files/documents/public_statements/941643/160323fsf1.pdf.

20   Thomas B. Pahl, "The View from the FTC: Overseeing Internet Practices in the Digital Age," panel discussion at the Free State Foundation's Ninth Annual Telecom Policy Conference (May 31, 2017), available at: http://www.freestatefoundation.org/images/May_31_2017_FTC_Panel_Transcript_072017.pdf.

21 U.S. Federal Trade Commission, "Privacy & Data Security Update" (January 2016), available at: https://www.ftc.gov/reports/privacy-data-security-update-2015#privacy.

22 Maureen K. Ohlhausen, Commissioner, U.S. Federal Trade Commission, "Privacy Regulation in the Internet Ecosystem," Free State Foundation Eighth Annual Telecom Policy Conference (March 23, 2016), available at: https://www.ftc.gov/system/files/documents/public_statements/941643/160323fsf1.pdf.

23 Joshua D. Wright, "The FTC and Privacy Regulation: The Missing Role of Economics" (speech, George Mason University Law and Economics Center, November 12, 2015), available at: http://masonlec.org/site/rte_uploads/files/Wright_PRIVACYSPEECH_FINALv2_PRINT.pdf.

24 This is not to suggest that these practices necessarily should be prohibited as per se unlawful or under the antitrust rule of reason, but rather that if ISPs do include them in their terms of service as a matter of business judgment that the FTC would enforce them like any other terms of service.

25 U.S. Department of Justice, "Telecommunications and Media Enforcement Section," available at: https://www.justice.gov/atr/about-division/telecommunications-and-media-enforcement-section.

26 Joshua D. Wright, "Antitrust Provides a More Reasonable Framework for Net Neutrality," Free State Foundation (August 16, 2017), at 3, available at: http://www.freestatefoundation.org/images/Antitrust_Provides_a_More_Reasonable_Framework_for_Net_ Neutrality_Regulation_081617.pdf.

27 Comments of Public Knowledge and Common Cause, WC Docket No. 17-108 (July 17, 2017), at 92-93, available at: https://ecfsapi.fcc.gov/file/1071932385942/PK%20CC%20Updated%20Comments%20with%20Appendices%20FINAL.pdf.

28   Comments of the Open Technology Institute at New America,
      WC Docket No. 17-108 (July 17, 2017), at 39-40, available
      at: https://na-production.s3.amazonaws.com/documents/
      OTI_NN_COMMENTS_JULY17_FINAL.pdf.

29   *Id.*, at 38.

30   Thomas B. Pahl, "The View from the FTC: Overseeing Internet
      Practices in the Digital Age," panel discussion at the Free State
      Foundation's Ninth Annual Telecom Policy Conference (May 31,
      2017), available at: http://www.freestatefoundation.org/images/
      May_31_2017_FTC_Panel_Transcript_072017.pdf.

31   *Id.*

32   Daniel Lyons, "The View from the FTC: Overseeing Internet
      Practices in the Digital Age," panel discussion at the Free State
      Foundation's Ninth Annual Telecom Policy Conference (May 31,
      2017), available at http://www.freestatefoundation.org/images/
      May_31_2017_FTC_Panel_Transcript_072017.pdf.

Part V – Defending the *Restoring Internet Freedom Order*

20.
Revisiting Net Neutrality

Daniel A. Lyons [*]

Perspectives from FSF Scholars, November 10, 2017, Vol. 12, No. 40

I. Introduction

The Federal Communications Commission is poised to repeal its 2015 Title II reclassification order (*Title II Order*).[1] That decision subjected cutting-edge broadband providers to a common carrier regime originally designed to discipline the old Bell Telephone monopoly, as a means of satisfying President Obama's request for "strong net neutrality rules" to govern the telecommunications network of the future. This past May, the agency circulated a Notice of Proposed Rulemaking that seeks to reverse that decision and restore the "light touch" regulatory regime that governed most broadband providers since the Internet's inception.[2]

On the eve of that action, which could occur as early as next month, it is worth revisiting the arguments offered in support of the 2015 *Title II Order*. At base, net neutrality seeks to prevent Internet service providers from interfering in upstream markets for Internet-based content and applications. But this harm was both largely conjectural and adequately addressed by existing antitrust law. The order's prophylactic rules thus provide little additional protection, while barring potentially consumer-beneficial innovation and implicating broadband providers' First Amendment rights. Moreover, the Title II reclassification required to support the rules was both bad law and bad policy.

II. The Specious Case for Net Neutrality

Although "net neutrality" is a somewhat amorphous term, most would agree that, at its core, it represents the idea that broadband providers should allow customers to access all lawful Internet content and should treat all traffic the same regardless of source or content. The movement focuses on broadband providers because of their allegedly privileged place in the Internet ecosystem: in the words of former FCC Chairman Julius Genachowski, broadband companies control the "onramps to the Internet" and thus are supposedly in a unique position to shape the flow of information online.

Initially, net neutrality seemed driven by the concern that a broadband provider would suppress Internet content that was critical of the company or with which the company disagreed. But this was a spurious concern, as no Internet services provider ever did so, and any company that would attempt such a move would be pilloried in the press. Perhaps surprisingly, the first significant instance of a company suppressing Internet speech with which it disagreed came this year, with the silencing of the neo-Nazi news site *Daily Stormer* following the Charlottesville Unite the Right Rally. But the culprit was not a broadband provider; it was instead GoDaddy and Google (which refused hosting services)[3] and Cloudflare (which refused to protect the site from denial-of-service attacks).[4] The *Daily Stormer* incident illustrates that there are multiple pressure points in the Internet ecosystem, which calls into question the assumption by net neutrality advocates that broadband providers pose a unique threat to Internet content.

Net neutrality proponents also feared that broadband providers would engage in anticompetitive conduct. One concern is that broadband providers would exploit their positions in broadband markets to give affiliated companies (such as cable services) an unfair advantage against Internet-based rivals (like Netflix). And even without anticompetitive intent, the 2015 order found that broadband providers have "powerful incentives to accept fees from edge providers" to exclude competitors or secure priority delivery.[5] The order feared that such offerings would distort competition among edge providers by giving advantages to well-funded companies that can afford priority delivery over those who lack the resources to do so.

Antitrust scholars recognize this as a classic example of vertical foreclosure. They also recognize that vertical agreements rarely have negative effects on consumer welfare.[6] One significant empirical study explains that according to the data, "efficiency considerations overwhelm anticompetitive motives in most contexts" and even in natural monopolies or oligopolistic markets, "the evidence of anticompetitive harm is not strong."[7] Therefore "under most circumstances, profit-maximizing vertical-integration decisions are efficient, not just from the firms' but also from the consumers' point of view."[8] As law professor and former FTC Commissioner Joshua Wright explains, "the *economic theory* literature establishes that vertical restraints may be anticompetitive, but the *empirical* literature clearly demonstrates that they most often are not, and are instead generally procompetitive."[9]

Experience in the broadband industry supports Commissioner Wright's observation. For all the *strum und drang* about net neutrality, one can identify only two instances of arguably anticompetitive behavior by Internet access providers. In 2005, Madison River Communications paid a $15,000 fine to settle FCC charges that it blocked third-party VOIP services from operating on its broadband network, allegedly because these VOIP providers competed against the company's traditional telephone service.[10] Three years later, the FCC fined Comcast for throttling BitTorrent traffic on its broadband network. While Comcast claimed throttling was necessary to prevent a BitTorrent user from overwhelming the limited upload bandwidth shared within a local area, critics argued that the company sought to limit traffic in copyrighted movies (which comprised the bulk of BitTorrent traffic at the time) to protect the company's video-on-demand products.[11] One could argue that, with net neutrality never far from the Commission's mind, the threat of potential regulation may have deterred other anticompetitive abuses.[12] But the fact remains that two complaints in twenty years reflects a healthy industry, not one in need of regulatory intervention. As critics often claimed, net neutrality was always a solution in search of a problem.

Moreover, it is easy to imagine instances wherein paid prioritization might be helpful to consumers. Different Internet applications have different sensitivities to congestion. A consumer is unlikely to notice trivial congestion-related delays when loading an email or a webpage. But such delays can significantly erode the quality of a video stream or videoconferencing service. Allowing such applications to insulate themselves from congestion would improve the user experience for these consumers without adversely affecting consumers of congestion-insensitive services. In this way, paid prioritization could improve the overall Internet experience: the price mechanism signals which applications are most susceptible to congestion and allocates them greater bandwidth during congested times – just as prices allocate scarce resources in most other parts of a capitalist economy.

One of the *Title II Order's* biggest flaws is its failure to appreciate the possibility that some – perhaps many – forms of prioritization may in fact benefit consumers. Though the 2015 order acknowledges that "some forms of paid prioritization could be beneficial," it nonetheless finds that "the threat of harm is overwhelming" and "simply too great" to allow experimentation.[13] The order's *per se* prohibition on paid prioritization is thus a policy choice to block potentially consumer-welfare-enhancing business models because of an overwhelming fear of anticompetitive abuse. In this way, the net neutrality rules are even more stringent than the requirements that Title II placed on the old Bell Telephone monopoly, which could offer different tiers of service as long as each tier was available at tariffed rates.[14]

Indeed, even the post office – America's quintessential "common carrier" – can offer paid prioritization: first class mail is available to everyone, but those who need their packages delivered faster can pay a premium for priority or next-day delivery. Net neutrality's refusal to offer similar flexibility to broadband providers because of a paranoid risk of anticompetitive abuse is somewhat bizarre, especially since antitrust law already exists to protect consumers from the harm that proponents most fear. In essence, the law prohibits a potentially significant amount of pro-consumer behavior in the interest of securing some (undefined) marginal consumer protection above and beyond that already afforded by antitrust.

III. The *Title II Order* and First Amendment Rights of Broadband Providers

Broadband providers can – and have – argued that strong net neutrality rules violate the First Amendment. The Supreme Court has long recognized that speech conduits such as newspapers and cable providers have a First Amendment right of editorial control that limits the government's ability to force them to deliver speech against their will.[15] Some commentators have argued that because broadband providers simply transmit messages requested by consumers, they do not make editorial decisions and therefore are not analogous to these other entities.[16] But when presented with this argument, the D.C. Circuit court reviewing the 2015 order curiously sidestepped the question. It held that because, by definition, broadband providers covered by the 2015 order held themselves out as offering access to all or virtually all Internet endpoints, it does not violate the First Amendment to hold them to that commitment.[17] Interestingly, the court explained that "insofar as a broadband provider might offer its own content… separate from its internet access service, the provider would receive the same protection under the First Amendment as other producers of internet content."[18]

In his opinion concurring in the denial of rehearing *en banc*, panel judge Sri Srinivasan reiterated that "an ISP that offers subscribers a curated experience by blocking websites lying beyond a specified field of content" or otherwise "making sufficiently clear to potential customers that it provides a filtered service" would exercise editorial discretion and would lie outside the scope of the FCC's rules.[19] This consumer protection-focused view of net neutrality suggests that an ISP can behave in a non-net-neutral fashion as long as it makes clear to consumers that it is doing so. While this understanding is somewhat at odds with the beliefs of the FCC and most net neutrality advocates, it might have been necessary to avoid a more serious First Amendment question. But the court's discussion of the First Amendment issue begs the question what work the rules are doing if a company can opt out of the legal regime merely by stating clearly that it does not offer indiscriminate service to all or nearly all Internet content.

IV. The Harm of Title II Reclassification

Perhaps the most controversial portion of the 2015 order was the Commission's decision to reclassify broadband providers as Title II common carriers. The Commission had previously gone all the way to the Supreme Court to defend its determination that broadband Internet access providers were not Title II common carriers, but were instead information service providers under Title I and were, at most, lightly regulated.[20] This was the regime that governed most Internet service providers from broadband's infancy. But in *Verizon v. FCC*, the D.C. Circuit held that the Commission could not prohibit all paid prioritization under Title I, because this would effectively impose common carriage obligations on non-common carriage companies in violation of a different portion of the Communications Act.[21] The court explained that a prohibition that left room for individual companies to bargain would have been permissible, and on remand the FCC Notice of Proposed Rulemaking favored this path. But then-President Obama declared his support for "strong net neutrality rules" and recommended the agency avoid the problem identified by the *Verizon* court by reclassifying broadband Internet service providers as Title II common carriers – a decision that the D.C. Circuit ultimately upheld in *United States Telecom Association v. FCC*.

It was this reclassification decision, more than the net neutrality rules themselves, that the reconstituted Commission has taken issue with in the 2017 Notice of Proposed Rulemaking. And with good reason. Although the D.C. Circuit properly followed the Supreme Court's earlier holding that the statute was ambiguous about the proper classification of broadband Internet access, broadband does not fit well within the Act's definition of a Title II service. The Act explains that "telecommunications," providers of which are governed by Title II, is "the transmission, between or among points specified by the user, of information of the user's choosing, without change in form or content of the information as sent and received."[22] By comparison, an "information service," which falls under Title I, is "the offering of a capability for generating, acquiring, storing, transforming, processing, retrieving, utilizing, or making available information via telecommunications."[23] As the 2017 NPRM explains, broadband access more closely fits the latter category. Consumers use broadband access to engage in activities such as "generating" and "making available" blog posts or status updates, "storing" and "utilizing" an address book or grocery list, or "transforming" and "processing" filtered photographs.[24] Information transmitted via a broadband connection is not "between or among points specified by the user." Routing decisions are instead chosen by network architecture, with the user having little to no knowledge of where the information is stored and instead dependent upon functions such as DNS lookup and local caching to retrieve desired content.[25] In short, broadband service is "the offering of a capability" to manipulate information stored online, which falls much more comfortably into Title I.

Moreover, the Commission notes that the imposition of a complex and onerous regulatory regime is likely to deter investment in broadband networks. The Commission cited, among other studies, an analysis by Free State Foundation Research Associate Michael Horney showing that broadband investment slowed by $5.6 billion since the imposition of the Title II regime in the 2015 order.[26] Other analysts have reached similar conclusions.[27] Free Press, an ardent net neutrality supporter, has challenged these findings and produced its own report showing an increase in spending,[28] though as critics note, this study improperly includes non-broadband spending such as AT&T's capital investments in Mexico and costs associated with its purchase of DirecTV.[29]

- But the broader harm of reclassification is the damage done to innovation in the broadband space. The public utility regime contemplated by Title II works best in stodgy, unchanging industries like water delivery that uneventfully fulfill the same service to consumers each year. These rigid rules are ill-suited to an industry as dynamic as the Internet ecosystem. Title II regulation exhibits a status quo bias, a belief that the way the Internet currently runs is the way it should always run, and for all people. Perhaps in the early days of the Internet, when consumers were mostly using their network connections for the same basic activities of email and web surfing, a one-size-fits-all, static access model posed less of a risk to innovation. But as more of our daily activities move online, the broadband user base has grown both more heterogeneous, meaning the same old one-size-fits-all model may not be optimal for all users.

- As a real-world example, many countries feature wireless providers that offer unlimited talk, text, and Facebook or Twitter access for a lower rate than a plan incorporating all Internet content. I would love such a phone for my teenage daughter, who routinely exceeds the monthly data allowance of our shared plan and spends 95% of her time online using Instagram. So when Sprint teased a similar plan in the United States, I was interested. But the plan immediately came under fire by net neutrality advocates for offering only certain social media applications rather than all lawful Internet content, and ultimately Sprint dropped its plans. Similar criticism faced T-Mobile's decision to zero-rate music and later to zero-rate low-resolution video. Yet these plans were critical to T-Mobile's successful effort to gain market share and lure away customers whose needs were imperfectly satisfied by a traditional mobile broadband plan.

- By biasing the status quo, Title II classification discourages this type of experimentation by broadband Internet access providers. And the amount of regulatory authority afforded the FCC by Title II could stifle a dynamic market for broadband access. Though the Commission has forborne from applying several parts of Title II, these forbearances are a notice-and-comment exercise away from repeal. Title II thus hangs like a Sword of Damocles over broadband providers, and the Commission is absolutely right to propose freeing them from this ongoing threat.

V. Conclusion

Ultimately, the ongoing seesaw battle over net neutrality is a problem that Congress created. As the late Justice Antonin Scalia wrote, "[i]t would be gross understatement to say that the…Act is not a model of clarity. It is in many important respects a model of ambiguity or indeed even self-contradiction."[30] The Communications Act's unnecessarily obtuse language and vague definitions, coupled with its relative lack of reference of broadband networks, opens the door for successive agencies to interpret and reinterpret Congress's meaning. As Justice Scalia noted, this "is most unfortunate for a piece of legislation that profoundly affects a crucial segment of the economy worth tens of billions of dollars."[31]

But if the problem ultimately lies with Congress, so too does the solution. For the last two decades, the Act has led the FCC to develop a makeshift "law of the Internet" from the detritus of the "law of the telephone" regime. Rather than forcing the agency to continue hammering square pegs into round holes, Congress should settle definitively the scope of the Federal Communications Commission's authority to regulate the primary communications network of the early 21st century.

The Commission's 2017 NPRM is a positive step toward this final goal. It represents the next phase of an ongoing dialogue between the agency and the D.C. Circuit about the shortcomings of the current statute. By continuing this dialogue, the Commission is continuing to highlight this issue to Congress in the hope of prompting it to action. In the meantime, the proposed repeal of Title II reclassification will restore the light-touch regulatory framework that historically has governed Internet service providers, and which provides room for innovation and growth while the gears of the congressional machinery slowly begin to turn.

Although the NPRM left open the ultimate fate of the agency's net neutrality rules, I hope the final order will repeal the rules and again permit broadband providers to pursue innovative new business models for consumers, protected from anticompetitive harm and abusive practices by the same antitrust and consumer protection laws that govern consumers throughout the rest of the American economy.

* Daniel A. Lyons, an Associate Professor of Law at Boston College Law School, is a Member of the Free State Foundation's Board of Academic Advisors. The Free State Foundation is an independent, nonpartisan free market-oriented think tank located in Rockville, Maryland.

Endnotes

1   Protecting and Promoting the Open Internet, Report and Order on Remand, Declaratory Ruling, and Order, 30 FCC Rcd. 5601 (2015) (hereafter "2015 Order").

2   Restoring Internet Freedom, Notice of Proposed Rulemaking, 32 FCC Rcd. 4434 (2017) (hereafter "2017 NPRM").

3   "Google cancels Neo-Nazi site registration soon after it was dumped by GoDaddy". CNBC. Reuters. August 14, 2017, available at https://www.cnbc.com/2017/08/14/godaddy-boots-the-daily-stormer-because-of-what-it-wrote-about-charlottesville-victim.html.

4   "Daily Stormer: Cloudflare drops neo-Nazi site". BBC News. August 17, 2017, available at http://www.bbc.com/news/technology-40960053.

5   2015 Order ¶19 (quoting *Verizon v. FCC*, 740 F.3d 623, 645-646 (D.C. Cir. 2014).

6   *See* James C. Cooper et al., *Vertical Antitrust Policy as a Problem of Inference*, 23 Int'l J. Indus. Org. 639, 643–47 (2005).

7   Francine Lafontaine & Margaret Slade, *Vertical Integration and Firm Boundaries: The Evidence*, 45 J. Econ. Literature 629, 677 (2007).

8   *Id.* at 680.

9   Lindsey M. Edwards & Joshua D. Wright, The Death of Antitrust Safe Harbors: Causes and Consequences, 23 Geo. Mason L. Rev. 1205, 1243 (2016) (emphasis added); see also Phillip E. Areeda & Herbert Hovenkamp, 3B Antitrust Law: An Analysis of Antitrust Principles and Their Application ¶ 756a, at 9 (3d ed. 2008).

10 Madison River Commc'ns, LLC and Affiliated Companies, 20 FCC Rcd. 4295, 4297 (2005).

11 Comcast Corp. v. FCC, 579 F.3d 1 (D.C. Cir. 2009). The fine was vacated on appeal for lack of jurisdiction. See id.

12   For this observation I am indebted to Blake Reid, who made this point in a Twitter conversation with me.

13   2015 Order ¶ 19.

14   See Daniel A. Lyons, *Net Neutrality and Nondiscrimination Norms in Telecommunications*, 54 Ariz. L. Rev. 1029 (2012).

15   See Miami Herald Pub. Co. v. Tornillo, 418 U.S. 241 (1974); Turner Broadcasting Sys. Inc. v. FCC, 512 U.S. 622 (1994); Denver Area Ed. Telecomm. Consortium, Inc. v. FCC, 518 U.S. 727, 812 (Thomas, J., concurring in the judgment in part and dissenting in part).

16   See, e.g., Stuart Benjamin, *Transmitting, Editing, and Communicating: Determining What "The Freedom of Speech" Encompasses*, 60 Duke L.J. 1673 (2011).

17   United States Telecom Ass'n v. FCC, 825 F.3d 674, 741 (D.C. Cir. 2016).

18   *Id.* at 741-742.

19   United States Telecom Ass'n v. FCC, 855 F.3d 381 (Srinivasan, J., concurring).

20   See Nat'l Cable & Telecomm. Ass'n v. Brand X Internet Servs., 545 U.S. 967 (2005).

21   Verizon v. FCC, 740 F.3d 623 (D.C. Cir. 2014).

22   47 U.S.C. § 153(50).

23   Id. § 153(24).

24   2017 NPRM ¶ 27.

25   Id. ¶29.

26   Michael Horney, Free State Foundation, Broadband Investment Slowed by $5.6 Billion Since Open Internet Order (May 5, 2017), available at http://freestatefoundation.blogspot.com/2017/05/broadband-investment-slowed-by-56.html.

27   See, e.g., Hal Singer, 2016 Broadband Capex Survey: Tracking
     Investment in the Title II Era (Mar. 1, 2016), available at https://
     haljsinger.wordpress.com/2017/03/01/2016-broadband-capex-
     survey-tracking-investment-in-the-title-ii-era; George S. Ford,
     Net Neutrality, Reclassification and Investment: A Counterfactual
     Analysis, Phoenix Center for Advanced Legal & Economic Public
     Policy Studies, Perspectives 17-02, at 2, available at http://www.
     phoenixcenter.org/perspectives/Perspective17-02Final.pdf.

28   Free Press, Internet Service Providers' Capital Expenditures
     (Feb. 28, 2017), available at https://www.freepress.net/sites/
     default/files/resources/internet_service_providers_capital_
     expenditures_2013- 2016_reported_as_of_2_27_17.pdf (noting
     a decrease in investment from 2015 to 2016, but claiming an
     increase in investment in the 2-year period of 2015–16 compared
     to 2013–14).

29   See Hal Singer, Tracing AT&T's Capital Expenditures Over
     Time, https://haljsinger.wordpress.com/2017/02/10/tracing-
     atts-capital-expenditure-over-time/. The Free Press model also
     does not adjust for Sprint's changed accounting treatment of
     leased handset devices from an operating expense to a capital
     expense. See Hal Singer, 2016 Broadband Capex Survey: Tracking
     Investment in the Title II Era, https://haljsinger.wordpress.
     com/2017/03/01/2016-broadband-capex-survey-tracking-
     investment-in-the-title-ii-era/.

30   AT&T v. Iowa Utilities Board, 525 U.S. 366, 397 (1999).

31   *Id.*

21.
The Sunshine Act and Transparency at the FCC

Randolph J. May *

Perspectives from FSF Scholars, December 12, 2017,
Vol. 12, No. 47

The Regulatory Review
December 12, 2017

On Thursday, the Federal Communications Commission (FCC) will consider whether to repeal regulations adopted in 2015 by the Obama Administration's FCC that imposed public utility-style mandates on Internet service providers. I happen to think the FCC should repeal the 2015 regulations, but this piece is not about the merits of the heated "net neutrality" controversy over those utility-like mandates.

Rather, it is about a process issue that, surprisingly, has attracted little attention from administrative law scholars: the new practice at the FCC of releasing to the public, prior to Commission meetings, drafts of the proposed actions the commissioners will consider at their meetings.

The FCC will be voting Thursday on its repeal proposal at a so-called Sunshine meeting, a meeting open to the public as required by the 1976 Government in the Sunshine Act. Yet until earlier this year, the drafts of the items upon which the agency's five commissioners were voting would generally not be released to the public. In other words, prior to the newly reconstituted FCC under the Trump Administration, the public has been more or less in the dark at the Sunshine meeting about the details of proposed action before the commissioners.

I say "more or less" because, to be sure, once the draft orders were circulated by the chairman to the other commissioners three weeks in advance of the Sunshine meeting, it was not uncommon for there to be leaks concerning selective aspects of the proposed draft text. And often the agency's chairman would publish a blog purporting to summarize key points in the draft item, or even release a "fact sheet" purporting to recite the key elements. Of course, the leaks, blogs, and fact sheets were susceptible to spin.

A principal rationale offered historically for not publicly releasing draft texts was that such releases might interfere with the commissioners' deliberative process. The theory was that late lobbying for changes might make it less likely that the commissioners—or their staffs—would be able to consider thoughtfully their own positions or to engage in deliberations with their fellow commissioners.

Now, I have a long record – including chairing a special committee of the Administrative Conference of the United States (ACUS) that proposed Sunshine Act reforms – of supporting changes to the Sunshine Act that would allow a majority of the commissioners, under certain circumstances, to deliberate among themselves in private and then to summarize such meetings for the public record. I still favor changes to the law, even if limited to a trial basis, as a way to foster greater collegiality and collaboration among commissioners and, thereby, to improve the quality of agency decisions.

Nevertheless, given the Sunshine Act as it stands, not releasing the draft text on which the agency's commissioners are voting runs against fundamental notions of transparency and openness upon which the law supposedly rests. Of course, the draft text might be changed before the vote, perhaps even in material ways. Indeed, in a longstanding practice, FCC chairs routinely grant the staff "editorial privileges" before each vote. So, even after the vote, the item's language might be changed before the official text is released to the public, sometimes a week or more later. At least if the draft text has been made public in advance of the Sunshine meeting, members of the public will know which changes were made when the official text is released.

It is worth taking note of ACUS recommendations on the Government in the Sunshine Act, adopted in 2014, which are intended to highlight a number of "best practices" undertaken by agencies covered by the Sunshine Act. One of ACUS's recommendations is especially relevant:

For open meetings, covered agencies should post a meeting agenda on their websites as far in advance of the meeting as possible. Except for documents that may be exempt from disclosure under the Freedom of Information Act, agencies should also post in advance all documents to be considered during the meeting.

The research report accompanying the ACUS recommendations states that many independent agency officials pointed to the electronic posting of agency documents relevant to open meetings as worthwhile. With respect to matters to be considered at a Sunshine meeting, the report states:

Documents that agencies post in connection with open meetings include the following: meeting notices (including *Federal Register* notices announcing upcoming meetings), press releases, meeting agendas, staff memoranda to be considered at meetings, meeting transcripts and/or minutes, public comments received by the agency, and background documents needed to comprehend the meeting discussions.

Shortly after President Donald Trump appointed him FCC Chairman in January, Ajit Pai announced that, on a trial basis, he would begin releasing the draft items to the public at the same time he circulated them to his fellow commissioners. Then, a few months ago, he announced he was making the change permanent because none of the supposed ill effects from public disclosure had materialized.

In Commissioner Michael O'Rielly's view, the ability to talk in specifics about a proposed item increases the usefulness of exchanges with the public and produces more informed decisions. Indeed, although the agency's Republican and Democratic commissioners are deeply divided on the merits of "net neutrality" and many other substantive communications policy issues, they appear to agree that the new practice Pai instituted is worthwhile.

It was not that long ago that the idea of releasing draft texts on which the FCC commissioners would be voting was characterized by many as radical. But think about it. What is so radical about increasing transparency and disclosure to enhance the public's ability to understand what is taking place at a Sunshine meeting?

* Randolph J. May is President of the Free State Foundation, an independent, nonpartisan free market-oriented think tank located in Rockville, Maryland. *The Sunshine Act and Transparency at the FCC* was published in *The Regulatory Review* on December 12, 2017.

22.
The FCC's Defining Case for Repealing Internet Regulations

Seth L. Cooper *

Perspectives from FSF Scholars, December 13, 2017, Vol. 12, No. 48

The Hill
December 12, 2017

The expected blizzard of social media and online commentary has followed the FCC's announced proposal to repeal public utility regulation it imposed on broadband Internet access back in 2015. Yet much of the online chatter ignores the legal issue upon which the FCC's proposed Restoring Internet Freedom Order will stand or fall. The fate of the agency's repeal proposal, if adopted at its Dec. 14 meeting, will come down to definitions of statutory terms.

If broadband Internet access service fits the definition of an "information service" under Title I of Communications Act, then the FCC has no lawful authority to impose public utility regulation on the service. Information services may only be lightly regulated — if at all — under the act, whereas "telecommunications services" under Title II of the act are subject to an arsenal of public utility-like restrictions. "Network neutrality" sloganeering by companies like Netflix and Google, by celebrities, or by millions of robo-spam comments to the FCC cannot substitute for lack of agency authority. Repeal of public utility regulation is the only proper agency response if broadband Internet access service meets the definition of an information service.

Based on a plain reading of the Communications Act, the FCC's draft Restoring Internet Freedom Order presents a convincing, straightforward explanation for why broadband Internet access service is an information service. Title I of the act defines an "information service" as "the offering of a capability for generating, acquiring, storing, transforming, processing, retrieving, utilizing, or making available information via telecommunications." The FCC's proposal rightly finds that broadband Internet service providers routinely offer consumers the capability of engaging in all these functions in connection with third-party websites and applications. For instance, by enabling end users to upload photos to websites or create documents on web-hosted platforms, broadband service providers offer capabilities for "generating" information. And by enabling streaming video or file downloads, such providers offer information "acquiring" capabilities.

Also, the FCC's proposal finds that broadband internet service "provides information processing functionalities itself, such as DNS and caching, which satisfy the capabilities set forth in the information service definition." For end users to surf the Web, DNS or "domain name service" functionality provided by broadband service providers translates domain names typed by end users in their browsers into numerical IP addresses that computers can process. Additionally, caching "enables end users to obtain more rapid retrieval of information through networks" based on "complex algorithms to determine what information to store where and in what format."

These "information service" definitions and descriptions may be mind numbing to casual readers. And they hardly make for exciting policy debates or public relations campaigns about Internet freedom or net neutrality. But the extent of the FCC's regulatory authority over broadband Internet access services hinges on the definitions of those terms.

The 2015 Title II Order manufactured new and significantly narrower interpretations of information service-related definitions in the course of redefining broadband Internet service as a telecommunications service. The Title II Order never sufficiently explained those sudden interpretive shifts. The draft Restoring Internet Freedom Order rightfully calls out the Title II Order for "its seemingly end — results driven effort to justify a telecommunications service classification of broadband Internet access service."

Importantly, the Restoring Internet Freedom Order's conclusion that broadband Internet access service meets the definition of an "information service" is strongly backed by earlier agency and court precedents. The Supreme Court's decision in NCTA v. Brand X (2005) appears to have upheld the classification of cable modem Internet access service as an information service based on straightforward statutory interpretation.

Proponents of public utility regulation have pledged support for lawsuits challenging the draft Restoring Internet Freedom Order once it is adopted. But given the FCC proposal's straightforward reading of the Communications Act as well as the Supreme Court's reasoning in Brand X, the agency's conclusion that broadband Internet service meets the statutory definition of an "information service" will almost certainly be upheld in court.

Moreover, if an appellate court applies the deferential Chevron standard of review for agency interpretations of federal statutes, the Restoring Internet Freedom Order's legal validity should be a foregone conclusion. Under the "Chevron doctrine," an agency's interpretation of a statutory provision will be upheld unless it is unreasonable or impermissible. In practice, Chevron poses a near-insurmountable barrier to challenging federal agencies. Even the Title II Order's imposition of public utility regulation based on far-fetched reinterpretation of statutory definitions received extraordinary deference from the D.C. Circuit Court of Appeals in USTelecom v. FCC (2016). Needless to say, if a future appellate court employs a similarly deferential approach, the Restoring Internet Freedom order passes in a cakewalk.

The significant economic and policy issues surrounding repeal of public utility regulation of broadband Internet services makes it easy to overlook the legal issue upon which the entire matter ultimately will turn. But in the end, the FCC's draft Restoring Internet Freedom Order presents a clearly defined case for repeal that should stand on appeal.

* Seth L. Cooper is a Senior Fellow of the Free State Foundation, an independent, nonpartisan free market-oriented think tank located in Rockville, Maryland. *The FCC's Defining Case for Repealing Internet Regulations* was published in *The Hill* on December 12, 2017.

23.
Why Consumers Won't Be Left Unprotected

Randolph J. May and Seth L. Cooper *

Perspectives from FSF Scholars, January 5, 2018, Vol. 13, No. 2

The Washington Times
January 4, 2018

On Dec. 14, the Federal Communications Commission adopted its Restoring internet Freedom Order (RIF Order) repealing public utility-like regulations imposed on internet service providers in 2015 by the Obama administration FCC.

All too predictably, the FCC's order has been subjected to a seemingly endless stream of groundless attacks by pro-regulation advocates who claim consumers will be left unprotected by the Commission's action. These attacks, under the guise of preserving a supposedly sacrosanct version of "net neutrality," ignore two inconvenient truths.

Inconvenient Truth No. 1. The RIF Order did not give internet service providers (ISPs) any new power to block or throttle subscribers' access to internet content of their choice, or to prioritize internet traffic. This is because the now-repealed 2015 FCC regulations already permitted blocking, throttling, or prioritizing traffic by any ISPs that informed subscribers of their intent to do so.

Inconvenient Truth No. 2. By repealing the classification of ISPs as public utilities, or "common carriers" in Communications Act parlance, the RIF Order restores the Federal Trade Commission's legal authority to hold ISPs accountable for their promises to refrain from blocking, throttling, or prioritizing internet traffic.

The FTC had been divested of this authority by the FCC's 2015 regulations because the FTC lacks jurisdiction over common carriers.

Only by ignoring these two inconvenient truths are pro-regulatory advocates able to falsely claim that the FCC has left consumers in danger of being denied any remedy for abusive or anti-competitive practices by internet service providers.

It's clear that the FCC's 2015 "net neutrality" order, which the pro-regulatory advocates now insist is gospel, actually allowed ISPs to engage in the very practices that they loudly proclaim the Commission has just now authorized. In May 2017, in USTelecom v. FCC, the full D.C. Circuit declined to rehear the June 2016 three-judge panel decision which had affirmed the FCC's 2015 order.

Judges Sri Srinivasan and David Tatel, the two judges who comprised the panel majority, issued a concurring opinion to clarify the import of the court's decision. In a key passage, Judge Srinivasan stated:

> While the net neutrality rule applies to those ISPs that hold themselves out as neutral, indiscriminate conduits to internet content, the converse is also true: the rule does not apply to an ISP holding itself out as providing something other than a neutral, indiscriminate pathway — i.e., an ISP making sufficiently clear to potential customers that it provides a filtered service involving the ISP's exercise of "editorial discretion."

> Quoting the FCC's 2015 order, Judge Srinivasan observed that an ISP remains free to offer "edited" services without running afoul of the net neutrality requirements. Moreover, no party before the D.C. Circuit disputed that ISPs could exercise editorial discretion, thus taking themselves out of the purview of the "net neutrality" restrictions.

"In that sense," declared Judge Srinivasan, "the rule could be characterized as 'voluntary.'" This understanding that ISPs became subject to the FCC's 2015 neutrality requirements only by voluntarily choosing to hold themselves out as "neutral" was key to refuting a claim that the mandates violated the First Amendment.

In other words, repealing the FCC's 2015 public utility-like mandates did not give ISPs any new power they didn't already possess to block or throttle internet content. What the order did is establish a different — and preferable — institutional mechanism for holding accountable ISPs that represent themselves as neutral conduits.

By repealing the public utility-like common carrier classification of ISPs, the order restored the FTC as the primary enforcement agency responsible for preventing unfair and deceptive trade practices involving broadband internet services.

Now, pursuant to the Restoring internet Freedom Order and a memorandum of understanding between the FCC and the FTC, the FTC will enforce ISPs' representations. All of the major ISPs, and almost all the others, presently promise not to block or throttle access to internet content of their subscribers' choosing, or to prioritize internet traffic in ways that are anticompetitive, and they have pledged to maintain those representations.

Going forward, ISPs that fail to follow their own terms of service regarding such practices will be subject to enforcement actions by the FTC under its authority to prohibit unfair and deceptive trade practices. Moreover, FTC enforcement will be aided by strong transparency requirements promulgated by the FCC that require ISPs to clearly disclose their practices.

These two inconvenient truths bear repeating: The FCC's Restoring internet Freedom Order does not actually give ISPs any new power to block or throttle access to internet content or to unfairly prioritize traffic. And the order restores the FTC's authority to hold ISPs to their promises to refrain from these practices if they make such representations.

So, in reality, the Restoring internet Freedom Order does not leave consumers unprotected. By repealing the Obama administration FCC's public utility regulatory regime, what the FCC has done is provide internet service providers with a measure of freedom to innovate and to invest in ways that will satisfy the always evolving consumer demands for the internet services of the future.

* Randolph J. May is President and Seth L. Cooper is a Senior Fellow of the Free State Foundation, an independent, nonpartisan free market-oriented think tank located in Rockville, Maryland. *Why Consumers Won't Be Left Unprotected* was published in *The Washington Times* on January 4, 2018.

24.
State Executive Orders Reimposing Net Neutrality Regulations Are Preempted by the *Restoring Internet Freedom Order*

Seth L. Cooper *

Perspectives from FSF Scholars, February 2, 2018, Vol. 13, No. 5

Introduction and Summary

The *Restoring Internet Freedom Order* (2017) repealed public utility regulation of broadband Internet services and reclassified those services as information services largely unregulated by the Federal Communications Commission. The FCC thereby established a free market-oriented national framework based on the deregulatory goals of the 1996 Telecommunications Act. Relying on Congressional policy, agency precedent, and Supreme Court jurisprudence, the Order expressly preempted any measure that effectively would reimpose the repealed rules at the state level.

Governors in Montana and New York have issued executive orders regarding state contracting as a roundabout way of reimposing repealed public utility-like regulation. Both attempts to establish statewide "net neutrality" regulatory regimes run afoul of the FCC's order and federal preemption principles. The New York and Montana executive orders are not narrowly confined to proprietary interests of their governments but instead are "tantamount to regulating" on a statewide basis broadband Internet service providers' (ISPs) conduct. Because both executive orders are inherently regulatory and seek to advance the repealed net neutrality restrictions as general policy ends, they fail to qualify for immunity from preemption under the Supreme Court's market-participant doctrine. In short, federal law provides the FCC with ample authority to preempt both state executive orders.

Although ostensibly based on state procurement authority and proprietary roles, the Montana and New York executive orders expressly apply to broadband ISP conduct regarding all end user consumers within their states. Specifically, to be eligible to enter into public contracts with their state governments, ISPs in Montana and New York must agree to adhere to net neutrality restrictions identical to those that were repealed in the *Restoring Internet Freedom Order*. Those include no-blocking, no-throttling, and no paid prioritization rules. The Montana executive order adds the no-unreasonable discrimination rule as well as repealed transparency requirements, and it charges the Montana Department of Administration with interpreting and enforcing those rules. Unmistakably, the New York and Montana executive orders seek to reimpose net neutrality restrictions as statewide policy despite the FCC order's expressly stated intent to "preempt any state or local measure that would effectively impose rules or requirements that we have repealed or decided to refrain from imposing."

Further, both executive orders fail to satisfy the market-participant doctrine recognized by the Supreme Court in cases such as *Building & Construction Trades Council v. Associated Builders & Contractors of Massachusetts/Rhode Island, Inc.* (1993) and *Wisconsin Department of Industry v. Gould Inc.* (1986). The market-participant doctrine is rooted in a concern that state governments may attempt to conduct proprietary functions in ways unrelated to their proprietary interests and thereby alter the conduct of private actors in the market. Such conduct by state governments can result in *de facto* regulation and thwart congressional policies.

The market-participant doctrine immunizes from federal preemption state government actions in the marketplace that are narrow and consistent with the actions of ordinary private actors in the market. But broadband Internet access services are mass-market retail services. Broadband ISPs do not make their network management practices and engineering decisions subject to arms-length negotiation with end user consumers. The net neutrality requirements contained in the New York and Montana executive orders amount to a demand that broadband ISPs must alter or restrict the network and business-wide practices for their mass-marketed retail service.

Further, it is obvious that ordinary end user consumers in the broadband Internet access services market do not negotiate how their broadband ISP treats other end-user consumers. However, that is what the New York and Montana executive orders do by requiring that broadband ISPs seeking to enter into contracts with those states must agree to adhere to net neutrality restrictions regarding all of their end user subscribers in their states.

On their face, both the New York and Montana executive orders reveal their primary goal to be promoting net neutrality regulation as a general policy. Unmistakably, both executive orders are "tantamount to regulation," as they are clearly and specifically intended to impose net neutrality regulation. Allegedly proprietary actions by state governments that are regulatory in nature and aimed at promoting broad social policy goals do not receive immunity from preemption under the market-participant doctrine.

The *Restoring Internet Freedom Order* stressed that allowing state governments to adopt their own separate requirements could "impose far greater burdens than the federal regulatory regime," "significantly disrupt the balance" struck by the federal regime, and "impair the provision of such service by requiring each ISP to comply with a patchwork of separate and potentially conflicting requirements across all of the different jurisdictions in which it operates." The New York and Montana executive orders undoubtedly would impose greater regulatory burdens than the *Restoring Internet Freedom Order*'s balanced approach consisting of FCC transparency requirements and Federal Trade Commission enforcement against unfair and deceptive trade practices by broadband ISPs. Indeed, the New York and Montana executive orders would impose the same heavy regulatory burdens that the FCC's order sought to remove in favor of a deregulatory policy.

The restrictions on broadband ISPs contained in the New York and Montana executive orders conflict with the *Restoring Internet Freedom Order*'s reliance on the congressionally approved "preemptive federal policy of nonregulation for information services." The FCC's order concluded that "it is impossible or impracticable for ISPs to distinguish between intrastate and interstate communications over the Internet or to apply different rules in each circumstance" and that "any effort by states to regulate intrastate traffic would interfere with the Commission's treatment of interstate traffic." Both state executive orders also clash with those FCC policy pronouncements. Statewide reimposition of net neutrality restrictions on broadband ISPs would affect network engineering and other aspects of their services in a manner that would conflict with and unavoidably affect service in other states, all the while posing serious technological and other practical obstacles for broadband ISPs.

Given the solid preemptive authority behind the *Restoring Internet Freedom Order* and given the clash with federal deregulatory policy for interstate broadband Internet access services like the interstate broadband Internet access services that are the subject of the New York and Montana executive orders, the FCC should be in a position to preempt them.

Finally, it should be noted that, aside from the FCC's authority to preempt, there is a whole separate line of authority not discussed here under the Dormant Commerce Clause jurisprudence that, as a constitutional matter, likely would invalidate the state executive orders and similar state actions.

The *Restoring Internet Freedom Order* Has Preemptive Authority

In the *Restoring Internet Freedom Order* the FCC reclassified broadband information access services as largely nonregulated Title I information services. To that end, the Order expressly states the FCC's intent to "preempt any state or local measure that would effectively impose rules or requirements that we have repealed or decided to refrain from imposing." Among other things, this precludes states from requiring broadband Internet access service providers to adhere to the no-blocking, no-throttling, no-paid prioritization, and no-unreasonable discrimination rules that were repealed.

As paragraph 194 of the *Restoring Internet Freedom Order* correctly points out: "Federal courts uniformly have held that an affirmative federal policy of *de*regulation is entitled to the same preemptive effect as a federal policy of regulation." The FCC's order cites, for instance, the Supreme Court's holding in *Arkansas Electric Cooperative Corp. v. Arkansas Public Service Commission* (1983): "[A] federal decision to forgo regulation in a given area may imply an authoritative federal determination that the area is best left *un*regulated, and in that event would have as much pre-emptive force as a decision *to* regulate." The order also cites *Minnesota Public Utilities Commission v. FCC* (8th Cir. 2007), which concluded that "deregulation" is a "valid federal interest[] the FCC may protect through preemption of state regulation."

The FCC based the preemptive authority of its order primarily on the "impossibility exception to state jurisdiction."

The Supreme Court recognized that exception in *Louisiana Public Service Commission v. FCC* (1986), where it ruled: "FCC pre-emption of state regulation [has been] upheld where it was *not* possible to separate the interstate and intrastate components of the asserted FCC regulation." Lower courts have applied the impossibility exception in many relevant circumstances since then. Accordingly, the *Restoring Internet Freedom Order* concluded that "it is impossible or impracticable for ISPs to distinguish between intrastate and interstate communications over the Internet or to apply different rules in each circumstance" and that "any effort by states to regulate intrastate traffic would interfere with the Commission's treatment of interstate traffic."

Additionally, the FCC based its preemptive authority on the Congressionally approved "preemptive federal policy of nonregulation for information services." In bolstering that separate source of preemptive authority, the order cited provisions such as Section 230(b) of the Communications Act – adopted in 1996 – which established the policy of the United States "to preserve the vibrant and competitive free market that presently exists for the Internet . . . unfettered by Federal or State regulation." The FCC's order also cited Section 153(51)'s provision that service providers "shall be treated as a common carrier under [this Act] only to the extent that it is engaged in providing telecommunications services," as forbidding federal or state common carriage regulation of information services.

Given its strong basis in federal preemptive authority, the *Restoring Internet Freedom Order* clearly would preempt any state law that attempts to reimpose the repealed "net neutrality" or public utility-like regulation within that state's borders. In a strange twist, however, governors in New York and Montana have sought effectively to reimpose the FCC's repealed rules by restricting state contracting eligibility – as opposed to signing laws passed by their legislatures. Nonetheless, as will be discussed below, the governors' unusual approach is legally flawed and both the New York and Montana executive orders are subject to federal preemption.

The New York and Montana Executive Orders Are Preempted by the *Restoring Internet Freedom Order*'s Terms and Legal Authority

In late January New York Governor Cuomo and Montana Governor Bullock each issued executive orders ostensibly regarding private party eligibility for state contracting as means of reimposing the FCC's repealed rules on broadband ISPs within their states. Although ostensibly based on state procurement authority and proprietary roles, the Montana and New York executive orders expressly apply to ISP conduct regarding *all* end user consumers within their states. Specifically, in order to be eligible to enter into public contracts with their state governments, broadband Internet service providers in Montana and New York would have to adhere to "net neutrality" or public utility-like rules identical to those repealed by the *Restoring Internet Freedom Order*.

By executive order, New York Governor Andrew Cuomo "order[ed] and direct[ed] New York State's government…not to enter into any contracts for internet service unless the ISPs agree to adhere to net neutrality principles." That is, beginning March 1, 2018, "all agencies and departments over which the Governor has Executive Authority" as well as many other state government entities, may only enter into or renew contracts with ISPs that agree they "will not block, throttle, or prioritize internet content or applications or require that end users pay different or higher rates to access specific types of content or applications."

Montana Governor Steve Bullock's executive order states: "After July 1, 2018, to receive a contract from the State of Montana for the provision of telecommunications services [which includes internet and data services], a service provider must not, with respect to any consumer in the State of Montana (including but not limited to the State itself)" engage in conduct that violates the no-blocking, no-throttling, no-paid prioritization, and no-unreasonable discrimination rules mirroring those contained in the repealed FCC *Title II Order* (2015). Additionally, to receive a contract from the State of Montana, broadband service providers "must publicly disclose to all of its customers in the State of Montana (including but not limited to the State itself)" network management information identical to disclosures required in the repealed *Title II Order*'s transparency rules.

In other words, the Montana executive order essentially copies the repealed *Title II Order* rules and requires broadband ISPs to adhere to them with respect to all end users within the state in order to be eligible to enter into procurement contracts with the state government and its agencies. The Montana executive order then sets up the Montana Department of Administration as the State's net neutrality police "to monitor its enforcement" and "resolve any dispute over the definition of terminology used in this Executive Order."

Given their mirroring of the repealed public utility-like regulation as well as their applicability to all end users within their states, both the New York and Montana executive orders are contrary to the *Restoring Internet Freedom Order*'s express preemption of "any state or local measure that would effectively impose rules or requirements that we have repealed or decided to refrain from imposing." Although executive orders regarding state contracting issued by governors are obviously different from generally applicable laws passed by state legislatures, both executive orders are "measures" applicable to all in-state broadband ISPs that become parties to public contracts with their states, and those measures "effectively impose" no-blocking, no-throttling, no-paid prioritization, no-unreasonable discrimination, and transparency rules that the FCC repealed.

The FCC's order stressed that allowing state governments to adopt their own separate requirements could "impose far greater burdens than the federal regulatory regime," "significantly disrupt the balance" struck by the federal deregulatory approach, and "impair the provision of such service by requiring each ISP to comply with a patchwork of separate and potentially conflicting requirements across all of the different jurisdictions in which it operates." The New York and Montana executive order-based net neutrality restrictions undoubtedly would impose far greater regulatory burdens than the *Restoring Internet Freedom Order*'s balanced policy consisting of FCC transparency requirements and Federal Trade Commission enforcement against unfair and deceptive trade practices by broadband ISPs. Indeed, the purpose of the New York and Montana executive orders is to reimpose the exact same type of heavy regulatory burdens that the FCC's order sought to remove. The resulting restrictions on broadband ISPs would affect network engineering and other aspects of their services in a manner that would conflict with and unavoidably affect service in other states, all the while posing serious technological and other practical obstacles for broadband ISPs.

Both executive orders therefore are preempted under the "impossibility exception to state jurisdiction" because, as the FCC concluded in its order, it is impossible or impractical to regulate the intrastate aspects of broadband Internet access service without affecting interstate aspects of that service. Moreover, both state executive orders interfere with the federal government's nationwide deregulatory objective of not regulating information services in a public utility-like manner.

The New York and Montana Executive Orders Are Not Shielded from Preemption by Market-Participant Doctrine

In seeking to reimpose net neutrality requirements in their states, resort by Governors Cuomo and Bullock to executive orders concerning state contracting appears designed to achieve immunity from federal preemption under the market-participant doctrine.

Despite the ostensibly proprietary purposes asserted in the New York or Montana executive orders, both such orders clearly attempt to impose statewide regulatory policy goals and fall outside the scope of that doctrine.

The Supreme Court's market-participant doctrine immunizes from federal preemption state governments actions in the marketplace that are narrow and consistent with other market participants. As the Supreme Court explained in *Building & Construction Trades Council v. Associated Builders & Contractors of Massachusetts/Rhode Island, Inc.* (1993), often referred to as the "*Boston Harbor*" case: "Our decisions in this area support the distinction between government as regulator and government as proprietor," and a state's proprietary acts are immune from preemption when those acts are "not tantamount to regulation or policymaking." Although state government proprietary acts serve important purposes and are not typically subject to preemption, in *Wisconsin Department of Industry v. Gould Inc.* (1986), the Supreme Court pointed out that "government occupies a unique position of power in our society, and its conduct, regardless of form, is rightly subject to special restraints." The market-participant doctrine is rooted in a concern that state governments may conduct proprietary functions in ways unrelated to their actual proprietary interests and thereby alter the conduct of private actors in the market or alter the markets itself. Such conduct by state governments can result in *de facto* regulation and unduly disturb or thwart congressional policies.

Under the market-participant doctrine, the Supreme Court and lower courts have immunized state proprietary acts from preemption when a state acts in the same manner that a private company might have acted in similar situations. In *Boston Harbor*, the Supreme Court upheld a state agency's pre-hire agreement with a union workforce that included a no-strike guarantee because the agency was only "attempting to ensure an efficient project that would be completed as quickly and effectively as possible at the lowest cost." The state agency's action was narrowly limited to one particular contract job and was not a prohibition regarding all future contract bidders. Nor did it penalize bidders for practices on different projects for other clients. As the Fifth Circuit stated in *Cardinal Towing & Auto Repair v. City of Bedford* (5th Cir. 1999): "Courts have similarly shielded contract specifications from preemption when they applied to a single discreet contract and were designed to insure efficient performance rather than advance abstract policy goals."

In *Gould*, the Supreme Court struck down a statute that barred the state from contracting with employers who had repeatedly been sanctioned by the National Labor Relations Board (NLRB). The statute's prohibitions could be triggered by conduct unrelated to the state as a contracting party, and its prohibitions applied to all of the state's future contracting decisions. The Supreme Court observed: "[O]n its face the debarment statute serves plainly as a means of enforcing the NLRA." And because the statute "assumes for the State of Wisconsin a role Congress reserved exclusively for the Board," it was preempted. According to the Fifth Circuit in *Cardinal Towing*: "Following the logic of *Gould*, courts have found preemption when government entities seek to advance general societal goals rather than narrow proprietary interests through the use of their contracting power."

The market-participant doctrine is ably summed up in an oft-quoted paragraph from the Fifth Circuit's decision in *Cardinal Towing*:

> The Supreme Court has found that when a state or municipality acts as a participant in the market and does so in a narrow and focused manner consistent with the behavior of other market participants, such action does not constitute regulation subject to preemption… When, however, a state attempts to use its spending power in a manner "tantamount

to regulation," such behavior is still subject to preemption.

Although issued under the guise of state procurement authority, the analysis that follows shows that both the New York and Montana executive orders are regulatory in nature, not proprietary, and therefore outside the scope of the market-participant doctrine.

A Market-Participant Doctrinal Analysis of the New York and Montana Executive Orders

As an initial matter, the net neutrality or public utility-like restrictions contained in both executive orders are not narrowly focused interactions with the market or characteristic of private party conduct in the market. Significantly, broadband ISPs do not make their network management practices subject to arms-length negotiation with end user consumers. According to FCC regulations and the *Restoring Internet Freedom Order*, "broadband Internet access services" is defined as "a mass-market retail service by wire or radio that provides the capability to transmit data to and receive data from all or substantially all Internet endpoints." As the FCC's order notes: "By mass market, we mean services marketed and sold on a standardized basis to residential customers, small businesses, and other end-user customers such as schools and libraries." But that definition "does not include enterprise service offerings or special access services, which are typically offered to larger organizations through customized or individually negotiated arrangements." Although broadband ISPs routinely offer pricing discounts, service tier options, and bundling choices, such providers do not make network-wide engineering and related business-wide operational decisions for their mass-market retail offerings the basis of individualized contracts. Yet the net neutrality requirements contained in the New York and Montana executive orders amount to demands that broadband ISPs must alter or restrict the network management practices for their mass-marketed retail service.

Further, it is obvious that ordinary end user consumers in the broadband Internet access services market do not negotiate how their broadband ISP treats other end-user consumers. But as previously indicated, the New York and Montana executive orders do so. Both executive orders require that broadband ISP eligibility for state contracts must agree to adhere to net neutrality restrictions regarding all of their end user subscribers in their states. New York's executive order is titled "Ensuring Net Neutrality for New Yorkers," and its "whereas" clauses are directed to "all New Yorkers," "New York businesses," "New York Students," and "New Yorkers" generally. Similarly, the whereas clauses in the Montana executive order refer broadly to "Montanans," "Montana citizens," "Montana businesses," and "educational institutions in Montana."

On their face, both the New York and Montana executive orders are not at all narrowly confined to their states' proprietary interests. Instead, they expressly reflect the primary goal of promoting net neutrality regulation as a general policy. Unmistakably, both executive orders are "tantamount to regulation," as they are clearly and specifically intended to reimpose net neutrality regulation – albeit through unusual and nontraditional means.

The Supreme Court's decision in *Gould* is particularly instructive here. Just as the Wisconsin statute's prohibitions against the state contracting with employers subject to repeated NLRB sanctions could be triggered by conduct unrelated to the state as a contracting party, so too the prohibitions on contracting with broadband ISPs that do not agree to adhere to net neutrality rules can and almost surely would be unrelated to New York and Montana as contracting parties. Also, just as the statute's prohibitions in *Gould* applied to all of the state's future contracting decisions and not to one particular contract, the prohibitions on contracting with broadband ISPs that do not agree to adhere to net neutrality rules will apply to all of their states' future contracting decisions.

Moreover, similar to the Court's observations in *Gould* that "on its face the debarment statute serves plainly as a means of enforcing the NLRA," the New York and Montana executive orders plainly, on their faces, serve as a means of enforcing core regulatory requirements of the repealed *Title II Order*. Indeed, concerning the statute's aim of enforcing the National Labor Relations Act, the Court in *Gould* stated: "No other purpose could credibly be ascribed." Surely, no other purpose could be ascribed to the New York and Montana executive orders other than enforcing several of the FCC's repealed net neutrality rules. And whereas the Court in *Gould* concluded that the statute "assumes for the State of Wisconsin a role Congress reserved exclusively for the Board," both states' executive orders assume a role regarding information services that Congress reserved exclusively for the FCC and for the free market. As the Supreme Court observed in *Metropolitan Life Insurance Company v. Massachusetts* (1985), "preemption... precludes state and municipal regulation concerning conduct that Congress intended to be unregulated."

Given the solid preemptive authority behind the *Restoring Internet Freedom Order* and given the clash with federal deregulatory policy for information services such as interstate broadband Internet access services created by the New York and Montana executive orders, the FCC should be in a position to preempt them.

Hypothetically Narrower Net Neutrality Requirements Would Also Be Preempted

Of course, even if a state's governor issued an executive order requiring only that broadband ISPs must agree to adhere to net neutrality restrictions in providing broadband Internet access services directly to state government agencies and their employees, such a restriction would still be highly questionable under the market-participant doctrine. Such a hypothetical state contracting requirement would not be narrowly focused and limited to one particular contract. Making adherence to the FCC's repealed net neutrality regulations a condition of state contracting and procurement of broadband Internet access services would remain decidedly inconsistent with ordinary end user actions in that retail mass market. (As previously stated, larger-size customers of broadband services that want customization and specific quality-of-service guarantees typically negotiate with providers that offer what are known as specialized services, enterprise broadband services, special access, or "business data services.")

Rather, such a requirement would embody a general regulatory policy and thus constitute a state measure that effectively reimposes net neutrality rules in contravention to the *Restoring Internet Freedom Order*'s express preemption proviso. Further, an ostensible proprietary requirement that broadband ISPs agree to adhere to net neutrality restrictions only in providing broadband Internet access services directly to state government agencies and their employees would conflict with the FCC's policy pronouncement that regulatory attempts to distinguish between interstate and intrastate Internet traffic are impossible or impractical and would result in harmfully inconsistent regimes among states and affect interstate broadband Internet access services.

Finally, it should be noted that, aside from the FCC's authority to preempt, there is a whole separate line of authority not discussed here under the Dormant Commerce Clause jurisprudence that, as a constitutional matter, likely would invalidate the state executive orders and similar state actions.

Conclusion

The *Restoring Internet Freedom Order*'s repeal of public utility regulation of broadband Internet services and reclassification of those services as largely unregulated information services established a free market-oriented national framework based on the deregulatory goals of the 1996 Telecommunications Act. The FCC's order, which is backed by congressional policy, agency precedent, and Supreme Court jurisprudence, expressly preempted any measure that effectively would reimpose the repealed rules at the state level. Given the solid preemptive authority behind the *Restoring Internet Freedom Order* and given the clash with federal deregulatory policy for information services like the interstate broadband Internet access services that are the subject of the New York and Montana executive orders, the FCC should be in a position to preempt them.

* Seth L. Cooper is a Senior Fellow of the Free State Foundation, an independent, nonpartisan free market-oriented think tank located in Rockville, Maryland.

Further Readings

Randolph J. May, "Internet Giants Aim to Preserve Their Regulatory Advantage," *FSF Blog* (January 19, 2018).

Theodore R. Bolema, "Paid Prioritization Arrangements Improve Telemedicine Prospects," *FSF Blog* (January 9, 2018).

Randolph J. May and Seth L. Cooper, "Why Consumers Won't Be Left Unprotected," *Perspectives from FSF Scholars*, Vol. 13, No. 2 (January 5, 2018).

Seth L. Cooper, "The FCC's Defining Case for Repealing Internet Regulations," *Perspectives from FSF Scholars*, Vol. 12, No. 48 (December 13, 2017).

Randolph J. May, "The Sunshine Act and Transparency at the FCC," *Perspectives from FSF Scholars*, Vol. 12, No. 47 (December 12, 2017).

Babette E. Boliek, Timothy J. Brennan, *et al.*, "Reactions to the FCC's *Restoring Internet Freedom Order*," *Perspectives from FSF Scholars*, Vol. 12, No. 45 (December 4, 2017).

Daniel A. Lyons, "Revisiting Net Neutrality," *Perspectives from FSF Scholars*, Vol. 12, No. 40 (November 10, 2017).

James E. Prieger, "Net Neutrality Regulation, Investment, and the American Internet Experience," *Perspectives from FSF Scholars*, Vol. 12, No. 36 (October 25, 2017).

Theodore R. Bolema, "The FTC Has the Authority, Expertise, and Capability to Protect Broadband Consumers," *Perspectives from FSF Scholars*, Vol. 12, No. 35 (October 19, 2017).

Theodore R. Bolema, "Recent Claims of Internet 'Throttling' Do Not Justify a Bright-Line Ban," *Perspectives from FSF Scholars*, Vol. 12, No. 32 (September 20, 2017).

Reply Comments of the Free State Foundation – *Restoring Internet Freedom*, WC Docket 17-108 (August 30, 2017).

Joshua D. Wright, "Antitrust Provides a More Reasonable Framework for Net Neutrality Regulation," *Perspectives from FSF Scholars*, Vol. 12, No. 27 (August 16, 2017).

Comments of the Free State Foundation – *Restoring Internet Freedom*, WC Docket 17-108 (July 17, 2017).

Theodore R. Bolema, "Allow Paid Prioritization on the Internet for More, Not Less, Capital Investment," *Perspectives from FSF Scholars*, Vol. 12, No. 16 (May 1, 2017).

About the Authors

Randolph J. May

President, The Free State Foundation

Randolph May is founder and President of the Free State Foundation. Before entering the think tank world, Mr. May practiced communications, administrative, and regulatory law as a partner at major national law firms. He previously served as Associate General Counsel at the FCC. Mr. May has held numerous leadership positions in bar associations, including serving as Chair of the American Bar Association's Section of Administrative Law and Regulatory Practice and a member of the ABA's House of Delegates. He is a Senior Fellow of the Administrative Conference of the United States, and a Fellow at the National Academy of Public Administration. He has published more than two hundred and fifty articles and essays on communications, administrative, and constitutional law topics. Most recently, Mr. May is the co-author, with FSF Senior Fellow Seth Cooper, of *#CommActUpdate: A Communications Law Fit for the Digital Age* and *The Constitutional Foundations of Intellectual Property*. He is the author of *A Call for a Radical New Communications Policy: Proposals for Free Market Reform*, published in 2011, and is editor of two books, *Communications Law and Policy in the Digital Age: The Next Five*

Years, published in 2012, and *New Directions in Communications Policy*, published in 2009. In addition, he is the co-editor of two other books, *Net Neutrality or Net Neutering: Should Broadband Internet Services Be Regulated?* and *Communications Deregulation and FCC Reform*. Mr. May received his B.A. from Duke University and his law degree from Duke Law School.

Seth L. Cooper

Senior Fellow, The Free State Foundation

Seth Cooper is a Senior Fellow at the Free State Foundation. His work on federal communications and technology policy at the Free State Foundation began in 2009. He previously served as Director to the Telecommunications and Information Technology Task Force at the American Legislative Exchange Council (ALEC). Mr. Cooper served as judicial clerk to the Honorable James Johnson at the Washington State Supreme Court. He has worked in law and policy staff positions at the Washington State Senate and at the Discovery Institute. He is a 2009 Lincoln Fellow at the Claremont Institute. Mr. Cooper is the co-author, with FSF President Randolph May, of *#CommActUpdate: A Communications Law Fit for the Digital Age* and *The Constitutional Foundations of Intellectual Property*. Mr. Cooper previously contributed to chapters in *Communications Law and Policy in the Digital Age* (2012). His work has also appeared in such publications as *CommLaw Conspectus*, the *Gonzaga Law Review*, the *San Jose Mercury News*, *Forbes.com*, the *Des Moines Register*, the *Baltimore Sun*, the *Washington Examiner*, the *Washington Times*, and *The Hill*. Mr. Cooper earned his B.A. from Pacific Lutheran University and received his J.D. from Seattle University School of Law.

*   *   *

Members of the Free State Foundation's Staff and Members of Its Board of Academic Advisors Who Contributed to One or More Papers

Theodore R. Bolema

Senior Fellow, The Free State Foundation

Theodore Bolema is a Senior Fellow at the Free State Foundation. He previously served as Director for Policy Research Editing at the Mercatus Center at George Mason University. Previously, Dr. Bolema held positions as a Principal with Anderson Economic Group, LLC, an economics consulting firm; an attorney with the law firm of Weil, Gotshal & Manges, LLP; and a trial attorney with the Antitrust Division of the U.S. Department of Justice. He has taught at Central Michigan University and George Mason University School of Law. Dr. Bolema received his Ph.D. in Economics from Michigan State University and his J.D. from the University of Michigan Law School. He received his B.A. from Hope College. He has been cited on regulatory law and economics topics in numerous publications including *The Washington Post*, *Chicago Tribune*, *The Detroit News*, *Politico*, and the *Los Angeles Business Journal*.

Timothy J. Brennan

Professor of Public Policy and Economics at the University of Maryland, Baltimore County and Senior Fellow, Resources for the Future, and a Member of the Free State Foundation's Board of Academic Advisors

Timothy Brennan is a Professor of Public Policy and Economics at the University of Maryland, Baltimore County and Senior Fellow, Resources for the Future. He has served as a staff economist at the Antitrust Division, senior economist for industrial organization and regulation with the Council of Economic Advisers. In 2006 he held the T.D. MacDonald Chair in Industrial Economics at the Canadian Competition Bureau and in 2014 served as chief economist at the Federal Communications Commission. He has authored numerous publications on antitrust, regulatory economics, energy policy, and telecommunications.

Robert W. Crandall

Nonresident Senior Fellow, Economic Studies, Brookings Institution and Technology Policy Institute, and a Member of the Free State Foundation's Board of Academic Advisors

Robert Crandall is a Nonresident Senior Fellow in the Economic Studies program at the Brookings Institution, as well as at the Technology Policy Institute. He specializes in industrial organization, antitrust policy, and the economics of government regulation. He is the author of numerous books and journal articles on communication policy and regulatory reform. He has taught economics at Northwestern University, MIT, the University of Maryland, and other educational institutions. Prior to joining Brookings, Mr. Crandall served as acting director, deputy director, and assistant director of the Council on Wage and Price Stability.

Michael J. Horney

Research Fellow, The Free State Foundation

Michael Horney is a Research Fellow at the Free State Foundation. He is a recent graduate of George Mason University, where he received a Master of Arts in Economics and was awarded a Mercatus MA Fellowship. He earned his Bachelor of Science with an Economics major and Political Science minor at Towson University. Mr. Horney was an MA Fellow and Research Assistant on policy research at the Mercatus Center at George Mason University, focusing on regulations, technology policy, and education policy, and he served as a Graduate Intern for the Committee on Ways and Means' Subcommittee on Social Security.

Justin (Gus) Hurwitz

Assistant Professor of Law at the University of Nebraska College of Law, and a Member of the Free State Foundation's Board of Academic Advisors

Justin (Gus) Hurwitz is an Assistant Professor of Law at the University of Nebraska College of Law. His work builds on his background in law, technology, and economics to consider the interface between law and technology and the role of regulation in high-tech industries. He has a particular expertise in telecommunications law and technology, including data- and cybersecurity. Professor Hurwitz previously was the inaugural Research Fellow at the University of Pennsylvania Law School's Center for Technology, Innovation and Competition (CTIC). From 2007-2010 he was a Trial Attorney with the U.S. Department of Justice Antitrust Division in the Telecommunications and Media Enforcement Section. Professor Hurwitz received his J.D. from the University of Chicago Law School, an M.A. in Economics from George Mason University, and a B.A. from St. John's College.

Daniel A. Lyons

Associate Professor at Boston College Law School, and a Member of the Free State Foundation's Board of Academic Advisors

Daniel Lyons is an Associate Professor at Boston College Law School. He specializes in the areas of property, telecommunications, and administrative law. Before joining the faculty, Professor Lyons practiced energy, telecommunications, and administrative law at the firm of Munger, Tolles and Olson in Los Angeles. He also clerked for Judge Cynthia Holcomb Hall of the Ninth Circuit Court of Appeals. Professor Lyons has participated in rulemaking proceedings before both the FCC and the California Public Utilities Commission and has represented clients in federal and state litigation involving numerous regulatory issues. He has also spoken at workshops nationwide on the effects of technology convergence on telecommunications regulation. Professor Lyons received his A.B. from Harvard College and J.D. from Harvard Law School.

James E. Prieger

Professor of Economics and Public Policy, Pepperdine University School of Public Policy, and a Member of the Free State Foundation's Board of Academic Advisors

James Prieger is Professor of Economics and Public Policy at the Pepperdine University School of Public Policy. He is an economist specializing in regulatory economics, industrial organization, and applied econometrics. He has written for scholarly journals on the impact of telecommunications regulation on innovation, broadband deployment, and the digital divide. His recent work includes studies of competition in the California market for broadband Internet access and how regulation affects investment in business broadband services in rural areas. Professor Prieger served as a Senior Economist with the Federal Communications Commission.

Dennis O. Weisman

Emeritus Professor of Economics, Kansas State University, and a Member of the Free State Foundation's Board of Academic Advisors

Dennis Weisman is Emeritus Professor of Economics at Kansas State University. Professor Weisman is on the editorial board for the Review of Network Economics, the Journal of Regulatory Economics, and Information Economics and Policy. His primary research interests are in strategic behavior and government regulation, and he is the author of numerous publications in these fields. Professor Weisman's work has been cited by the Supreme Court.

Joshua D. Wright

Professor of Law at George Mason University School of Law, and a Member of the Free State Foundation's Board of Academic Advisors

Joshua Wright is a Professor of Law at George Mason University School of Law. He also is the Executive Director of GMU's Global Antitrust Institute and holds a courtesy appointment in the Department of Economics. From 2013 to 2015, Professor Wright served as a Commissioner of the Federal Trade Commission. He previously served the Commission in the Bureau of Competition as its inaugural Scholar-in-Residence from 2007 to 2008. He rejoined George Mason University School of Law as a full-time member of the faculty in the fall of 2015. Professor Wright is a leading scholar in the antitrust, economics, intellectual property, and consumer protection fields.

About The Free State Foundation

The Free State Foundation is a non-profit, nonpartisan think tank. Its purpose is to promote, through research and educational activities, understanding of free market, limited government, and rule of law principles at the federal level and in Maryland.

The Free State Foundation focuses on eliminating unnecessary and counterproductive regulatory mandates, especially those applicable to the communications and other high-tech industries, and on reducing overly burdensome taxes, protecting individual and economic liberty, including property rights, and making government more effective, efficient, and accountable.

Led by Randolph J. May, FSF's President, the scholars of the Free State Foundation have decades of experience in the public policy arena and academic settings promoting free markets, secure property rights, and individual liberty. Mr. May is a nationally known legal and policy expert in the field of regulation, as well as a widely recognized expert in communications, administrative, and constitutional law. FSF's scholars combine solid academic expertise with professional and practical experience in a way that makes their research especially impactful in influencing both federal and state public policy.

Other Free State Foundation Books of Interest

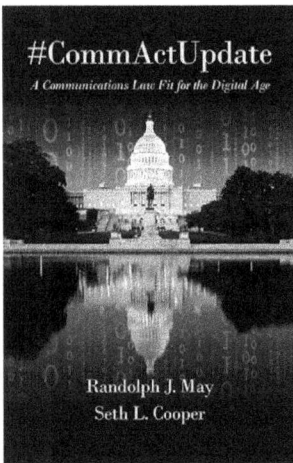

#CommActUpdate - A Communications Law Fit for the Digital Age, by Randolph May and Seth Cooper, is available on Amazon in paperback and as an ebook from multiple online retailers.

The Constitutional Foundations of Intellectual Property, by Randolph J. May and Seth L. Cooper, is available from Amazon and from Carolina Academic Press.

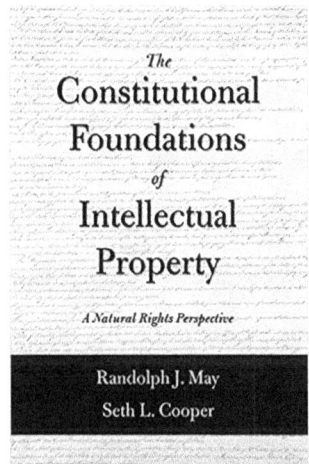

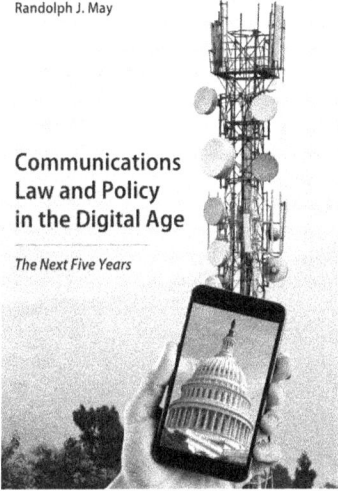

Communications Law and Policy in the Digital Age: The Next Five Years is available from Amazon and Carolina Academic Press.

New Directions in Communications Policy is available from Amazon.

www.ingramcontent.com/pod-product-compliance
Lightning Source LLC
Chambersburg PA
CBHW060335220326
41598CB00023B/2719

* 9 7 8 0 9 9 9 3 6 0 8 1 1 *